MW00534035

CELEBRATING in the ISLANDS

CELEBRATING in the ISLANDS

a novel

Russell Clark

Islandtude
Tropical Adventures

This book is a work of fiction. The names, characters and events in this book are the products of the author's imagination or are used fictitiously. Any similarity to real persons living or dead is coincidental and not intended by the author.

Celebrating in the Islands

Published by Islandtude Tropical Adventures

Copyright © 2022 by Russell Clark
All rights reserved. Neither this book, nor any parts within it may be sold or reproduced in any form or by any electronic or mechanical means, including information storage and retrieval systems, without permission in writing from the author. The only exception is by a reviewer, who may quote short excerpts in a review.

Library of Congress Control Number: 2022934399

ISBN (hardcover): 9781662926891
ISBN (paperback): 9781662926907
eISBN: 9781662926914

ONE

PAUL AND LISA finished their early dinner at home in St. Maarten. They sat back, relaxing, waiting until time for Paul's new assignment. Paul had successfully completed prior missions, sometimes calling on skills developed as a state wrestling champion, in combination with his meek outward appearance, to overcome dangerous predicaments. He liked to think his special brand of help was employed mostly for worthy causes.

His wife Lisa normally asked no questions about his assignments, instead waiting for Paul's return from his outings to hear whatever he was willing to share about them. She was curious as usual. This time she surprised Paul.

"Can you tell me what's going on?"

"Yes, it's not a big deal. Nothing that should take long or be all that exciting."

"Tell me about it."

"I got a request from a new client to pick up a delivery for him tonight. It's supposedly an Arawak artifact of some value. I did a little research, and it looks like the value of rare Arawak artifacts can be as much as six figures. I don't know what I'm to pick up will look like or its value, but with the secrecy surrounding it, I'm guessing it's worth a lot. I only know it's packaged to where I can carry it without anyone knowing what it is, and that it's smaller than a breadbox."

"What are you supposed to do with it once you have it?"

"Once I've got it in hand, I'm to contact the museum curator, and tell him I've received an artifact from someone who wants to remain anonymous. He wants the curator to authenticate the piece, and if it proves to be real, will donate it to the museum."

"If he's going to give it to the museum, why the secrecy? Why doesn't he just give it to the curator himself and take credit for the donation?"

"I'm sure he has his reasons, but he didn't share them with me. I'm just the hired help."

Lisa leaned forward, anxious to hear more.

"Is this a safe trip you're taking tonight? You're not expecting anybody to chase you to try to get it from you, or worse, willing to kill you for it?"

"I'm not aware of anybody who will be after it or me, but I'm not sure. I'm going at night, picking up a rare artifact from a hidden location, and am being paid good money to do it. There must be some element of uncertainty, possibly danger, or I wouldn't be paid a lot for doing this. But I think it's basically safe."

"Well, if it's safe, how would you like company? After I helped capture the Maho robbers, I'd like to do something more exciting than coach people on improving their careers. I love what I do, and it's valuable, but I don't get an adrenalin rush from it like I did that night facing a man pointing a gun at me."

Paul shook his head uncomfortably.

"What I'm doing tonight requires hiking up a mountain. I don't think you'd enjoy that. And like I said, the fact that I'm paid to do this, at dark where no one will see me retrieve the artifact, lets me know there's at least the possibility of danger."

"So you don't think I'm able to hike up the mountain, or you think it's too dangerous for me?"

"No, I'm sure you're capable. It's that it's not glamorous. It's a steep climb, there's scratchy underbrush, and you'll be sweating. In the midst of that underbrush at night, there might be mosquitoes. I don't think you'd like it, and there's nothing there to produce an adrenalin rush, only scratches and bug bites."

Lisa pressed on. "Okay, I understand. Where is it?"

"It's the mountain where Emilio's restaurant is at the bottom. You know it, it's where the Flying Dutchman zip line is."

The Flying Dutchman was featured as the main attraction on the Rockland Estate in Dutch St. Maarten. Billed as the world's steepest zip line, it drops 1,050 feet in elevation over 2,800 feet of cable.

"Oh my gosh, that's a real mountain. How long do you think it will take you to get to the top and back down?"

"I don't know. I looked at the website, and the mountain is over 1,000 feet high. The zip line down is about 3,000 feet, so I'm guessing the trail up is about the same distance as the zip line. It will take 30 minutes up if I can cover 100 feet per minute. There are probably some uneven areas, and with it being dark, I'm guessing it might take me 45 minutes or so to get up there. I'm hoping coming down will be quicker, but I'll double the time and guess I'll be down in an hour and a half. With the drive over, parking a ways from the chairlift trail, and the car ride back, I'm guessing I could be gone about two and a half to three hours."

"Okay, when do we go?"

"Huh, that's a good one. I'm only guessing how long it might take me. I could be way off, but I don't think I'll be quicker than that. However long it takes me, it could take you longer, maybe a lot longer. I don't think you'd like that."

"You're right. I wouldn't like it. I'd love it!"

Lisa looked Paul square in the eye before continuing.

"Hiking a mountain at night, grabbing a valuable, secret item, all while watching my footing to keep from getting hurt. And then coming back here for the added rush of unveiling what I found. This is going to be great!"

Paul sighed. He knew she was serious and arguing at this point was useless.

"If you want to go, let's get changed."

"Really? You're going to let me go with you?"

"If that's what you want, let's do it. I recommend you wear a light-weight shirt and long pants. And, of course, tennis shoes and socks. We can carry a couple of waters with us. We'll need them for the hike up."

"This is great. You won't regret it. I promise I'll stick right with you. When do we leave?"

"Let's head out about six-thirty. We can find an out-of-the-way place to park and begin our way up the mountain. Hopefully we'll be at the top resting between eight and eight-thirty. I hope you're going to like it." He paused. "I must say, it will be nice to have some company."

Paul gave her an encouraging smile before a quick kiss. She took that as her cue to change into her hiking clothes.

"I'll be right back."

She walked into the bedroom and returned dressed in a t-shirt and pair of lightweight sweatpants.

"So, what do you think?"

"That should work," Paul replied after an appraising look.

Dressed in blue jeans and a black t-shirt, Paul had a miniature pen flashlight strapped to a small folding knife in his pocket.

"Are you ready to get us an artifact?"

"Absolutely, I'm feeling a rush already. I'll grab us a couple of waters and we can go."

The two went down to the parking garage and were on their way in their sport utility vehicle. They drove around the traffic circle and past Emilio's, finding a turn off where Paul backed the vehicle out of sight from the road. He would be ready to leave in a hurry if needed. Paul turned to Lisa before stepping out.

"Last chance. You can stay here with the car if you'd like."

"No way. I'm so pumped, you might have a tough time keeping up with me. Let's go."

They hopped out of the SUV, and with no passing traffic, exited from where it would be mostly hidden. Once they made it to the main road, they held hands as if on a night stroll. They began their walk toward Emilio's restaurant. The restaurant was closed, but a few others were out and about on the grounds surrounding the historic restaurant.

The Flying Dutchman closed at 4:00 p.m. Even when closed, it was not unusual for a few tourists to stop there to size up the steep descent in planning a trip or trying to decide if they had the courage needed to jump from the mountaintop.

Lisa and Paul made their way to the chairlift area, and with no one else in view, disappeared into the underbrush. They found a path leading up the mountain. The intermittent clearance they followed was below the chairlift path, where the support poles were maintained under the ride allowing visitors to reach the top of the mountain.

Paul left the penlight in his pocket, relieved that the moon light was enough to illuminate the path. He did not want to have a light track their progress up the mountain.

"Lisa, are you all right? Am I going too fast?"

"I'm fine. This is a good pace. I don't think I can go much faster, though, between my footing being bad on some of the loose rock along with the uneven ground, and not seeing as well as I'd like."

"Okay, we're doing fine. Let me know if you need me to slow down or need to take a break."

Under the illumination of the moon, Lisa looked up the path.

"I can see the platform marking the halfway point not too much further. Let's stop there for a minute so I can have some water."

"Sure, no problem. We should be there in less than ten minutes."

They trudged on, slipping on the slick rocks and tripping in tall grass, but made the halfway mark.

"Let's stand here and sip the water. Try to save some for when we reach the top."

Paul chose not to drink any water on the break. He was fine and wanted to save it if Lisa needed it before they finished their hike.

As they stood, Lisa's legs began to shake slightly from the exertion. She decided not to mention how tired she felt. She concentrated on knowing she was halfway there, would rest at the top, and the trip down would be much easier. She gave herself a silent pep talk, confident she could do this. As if reading her mind, Paul took one of her hands in his.

"You're doing great. Why don't you stay here, I'll go grab the artifact, and be back with you soon?"

"Thanks, but no way. I can do this. I won't forgive myself if I go halfway and not finish. I'm ready. Lead the way."

"All right. If you need to stop any time, let me know." Reaching his hand out, he continued. "I'll carry your water."

She handed him her half full water bottle.

Paul started the climb up again, keeping with the same pace as before. He wanted to make it to the top soon, and was beginning to worry how they would handle it if something went wrong.

A few minutes later, Paul abruptly stopped. He leaned into Lisa, pressing his lips to her ear.

"I want to listen for a minute. No more conversational talking until we reach the top. Okay?"

Lisa nodded her understanding.

"Let's stay alert," whispered Paul. "I thought I might have heard something down the mountain from us. Not much further until we reach a clearing. Let's stop before we come out of hiding. Follow me and watch your step."

Some minimal crackling and swishing from light steps on rock and through underbrush accompanied them as they continued their climb. A few minutes later, Paul stopped just shy of the clearing. He continued to communicate in whispers.

"We're about to step out where there's no more ground cover. Once we go these next few steps, if anyone is around, we'll potentially be visible. How are your legs holding out?"

Lisa's pointer finger and thumb formed a circle giving Paul the okay sign.

"It's about a half minute run from the edge of the clearing to the platform. From there, we'll go up the steps to the top where we'll see the mountain top bar. What we're after should be behind some boxes under the bar. You drink some water while I'm grabbing the artifact. I hate to tell you this, but going down, we'll need to stay in the underbrush instead of following the cleared path back down. I don't think it's too thick, so I think we'll still be down quicker than the walk up."

Lisa merely nodded her acceptance.

"Okay, you need to be completely honest with me. I want to be very quick. I'm going to run. If you're able, you can come on up. If you're not sure, you move about fifteen feet over into thicker brush, and I'll be right back."

"I'm good. I'm ready to run."

Paul gave her an assessing look, then took the few steps to the edge of the clearing. Lisa was by his side.

"Okay, time to run."

The clearing was smooth with a carpeting of wild grass. Hunched over with the continuing incline, they sprinted toward the platform edge. Reaching the wooden steps, Paul placed a finger to his lips, and they stepped quickly but silently up the stairs to the upper most deck.

Paul handed Lisa both bottles of water. She sat on the wooden floor and drank the full bottle as he moved away from her to explore behind the bar.

The bar was an open bar top counter with nothing to prevent access behind it. Boxes of napkins, paper plates and plastic ware were shoved underneath the work surface.

Paul removed the boxes, set them on the floor, and spotted the cotton bag with a pull string drawn tightly closed. He reached for the bag and opened the top only enough to see inside. Looking up at him was a nude male figurine less than ten inches tall. He pulled the string taut before placing the boxes of supplies back exactly where he found them.

Stooping low, he crab-walked back over to Lisa, holding the bag out in one hand, a smile on his face.

"Got it," he said in a low tone. "I want to get out of here."

Lisa smiled in response, holding the remaining half bottle of water out to Paul. He took a sip and handed it back with a nod. Lisa finished it off.

"I want to take a look down the mountain," said Paul, "before we start back."

Staying flat, he worked his way to the edge of the top deck on elbows and knees. He peered through the slats of the wooden safety railing. After twenty seconds he shuffled to the opposite side of the deck and again peered down.

Lisa sat, following his movements with her eyes. Paul crawled to be back beside her.

"You need to be ready. We have three minutes."

"Okay, but why three minutes?"

"We have company and they're not following the chair lift path up. They're on both sides and look like they're fanning out."

TWO

JASON, A NEW partner of DK Gems International in Philipsburg, began his closing ritual at 5:30 p.m. It had been one year since he and his wife were invited by Jeff to join the DK Gems team. Jason gathered the magnificent stock of jewelry from the display cases and locked everything up for the night.

He was eager to get home for the planned dinner with his wife, Lekha. Their roles with the prestigious jewelry store recently expanded to more fully participate in managing the business. Both had been spending long hours selecting inventory to stock the store, as well as establishing themselves as trusted faces for their customers. They quickly created a loyal following of customers expecting a greeting from at least one of them when on their shopping excursions. Jason and Lekha worked long hours and were ready to celebrate another successful month.

Jason drove home, where his beautiful wife greeted him with a kiss as soon as he walked through the door.

"Whew, it's good to be home. It was a busy day today, and I'm ready for a break. I'm looking forward to a relaxing meal at Chesterfields."

Chesterfields was an oceanfront restaurant and bar located in Philipsburg. It overlooked the marina and Great Bay Beach.

"It's good to have you home. I've been reviewing a couple of new lines for the store. I think you'll like them."

"I'm sure I will. I trust your judgment. Give me a minute to freshen up and I'll be ready. Did you make the reservation for seven?"

"It's all set. Our standard table is waiting for us. I'm going to change now and will be ready when you are."

Jason went to shower, and fifteen minutes later was dressed casually for the dinner out. He walked into the living room where Lekha was waiting. She looked stunning in the outfit she chose.

"Wow, you look beautiful."

She wore a black off-the-shoulder mini dress. As she often did, she wore only a minimal amount of her exquisite jewelry.

"Thank you. You look pretty handsome yourself."

Lekha closed the distance to where Jason stood admiring her beauty, melting into him with her hug. With an upturned face, she spoke in a quiet voice.

"I'm looking forward to a great dinner, and then time here with you. I have a few pieces of jewelry laid out to model for you when we're back."

Jason leaned down, his lips searching for hers.

"A perfect date night," he murmured.

His kiss moved from her lips to her neck. She tightened her hold around him and caught her breath.

"If we're going to make our reservation, we should be leaving now," she managed to whisper. "We'll pick up here when we get back."

Jason reluctantly broke his hug. He reached for her hand and led her to their car. Within ten minutes they were seated at their favorite table. The waiter was quickly over.

"Do you need menus tonight?"

"No, I don't think so. I think we'd like to start with a bottle of wine to celebrate such a clear, beautiful night. We can also give you our food order."

They placed their order, and Jason approved of the wine brought to the table. He and Lekha chatted quietly while marveling over yet another great date night. Time moved quickly, and their meals were delivered.

"My New York Strip is cooked perfectly tonight. Lekha, how is your fish?"

"Very good, as usual. I guess we can come here again," she kidded, knowing that Chesterfields was one of their main go-to restaurants.

As they completed their entrees, the attentive waiter returned to their table.

"Any dessert tonight?"

"No, thank you, but everything was wonderful. Just the check."

The check was brought, and Jason quickly paid. He reached for Lekha's hand as they returned to the car.

"Do you mind if we stop for gas on our way back? I'm close to empty."

"No, that's fine. I'll still give you your private jewelry show. It'll just start five minutes later."

Taking his hand, she ran it down the nape of her neck before letting it go.

Jason was on a mission to fill the tank and be home as soon as possible.

THREE

LISA SAT STUNNED when Paul told her they were on a three-minute countdown. Instead of the adrenalin rush she sought, she instead felt the onset of panic.

"What do we do?"

"Get undressed, now," Paul commanded hoarsely. "But keep your shoes and socks on."

"I'm just wearing the t-shirt and sweatpants. You want me to take them off now? And that's going to help?"

Paul was slipping his shirt off.

"Yes and do it quickly."

Paul unzipped his jeans and slid them off. He was left wearing his boxers. He took a shoestring out of one of his shoes before placing them back on his feet.

"But I'm not wearing underwear," Lisa pleaded, not understanding the need to get undressed.

"It doesn't matter, just do it. Here, if this helps, I'll join you," he said and slipped out of his boxers.

She hoisted her t-shirt over her head and lifted her backside slightly from the wooden deck, pushing her sweatpants down and off over her shoes.

She sat nude, other than her socks and shoes, as Paul gathered the items of clothing.

He hurriedly took his boxers and placed them inside of the jeans, as if preparing for someone to slip into both the boxers and jeans at once. Next, he rolled Lisa's t-shirt and placed it inside the boxers, draped across the crotch and extended into the upper portion of the jean legs. Finally, he took her sweatpants and pushed the legs of her sweatpants into the blue jeans, stretching them over the t-shirt, through the boxers, and out the legs of the jeans covering them.

"What are you doing?"

"I'm preparing our escape."

Next, he took the shoestring he had removed and threaded it through the string on the artifact draw bag. He tied the shoestring in a secure knot and slipped it over his head.

"We probably have less than a minute."

Bent at the waist and staying low, Paul scurried to a platform railing, looked down, and hurried back to Lisa. He looked up at the taut cable above, where when open, riders of the Flying Dutchman are secured in harnesses for the steep ride down.

"Are you ready? We're taking the zip line down."

"How? It's not open. There's no contraption for us to ride down."

"We have our ride right here."

Paul held his hand out toward the clothes he had woven together. Not knowing if the friction of the clothes on the metal cable on the way down would wear and possibly burn the clothes, ending their ride prematurely, Paul had fashioned multiple layers. He hoped the jeans would hold, but if not, trusted that the other layers would keep the legs together long enough to ride all the way to the bottom.

"Are you crazy? We can't hurtle down the mountain with that. I have a paralyzing fear of heights."

"Which do you fear more, staying here, being tortured and then killed? Or closing your eyes and hanging on for forty seconds until our feet touch ground near the restaurant?"

"Oh Paul, I don't know if I can do it."

"It's your choice. I'll hit you over the head, knock you unconscious, and try to carry you down. Or you can hold onto me for forty seconds and not wake up with a headache. You have thirty seconds to decide."

"Oh my God! All right, let's do it. I love you, Paul. If I die, you know I love you more than life."

"All right. We're going into the ride stall. I'm going to go up a couple of the footholds to be able to reach the cable, and drape the clothes with a leg on each side of the cable. I'll roll the bottom of the legs around my hands and wrists to give me a more secure grip. Then you're going to hop up, hop on my back, and hang on. You'll put your arms over my shoulders and around my neck, your legs wrapped tightly around my waist. I'll push off the side barrier, and we'll be on our way down. Ready?"

"No, but okay."

"Good, because I'm sure they're in the clearing by now and about to come up the steps. It's time. We can't wait any longer."

They scampered into the launch stall where Paul climbed up several footholds to the cable above. He slipped the makeshift carriage into place, crossing the legs beneath the cable, effectively securing them in a loop. As he rolled the legs around his gripping hands, he saw two men on the steps below and nodded for Lisa to be ready.

She came up behind him and climbed onto his back, burying her mouth into the nape of his neck so as not to scream. Her hands circled his head, where she held onto her arms with a death grip.

"Let's do this," he said, determination in his voice, as he pushed off with his feet with all the strength he could muster.

There was an immediate drop, with Paul clinging to the pant legs and Lisa clinging to Paul. The weight of the duo created great speed, overcoming the slowing friction of the clothes, and within seconds they were hurtling parallel to the ground below at a pace greater than fifty miles per hour.

After ten seconds, and close to a thousand feet into their journey along the cable, Paul exclaimed in a hushed tone, "It's working! We're going to make it!"

However, ten seconds later, and hundreds of feet above ground, Paul began to lose his grip. "Dear God, just a little longer. Give me strength."

The steepness of the cable began to decline. They slowed as the space between them and the ground grew smaller. At the thirty second mark, they were suspended about twenty feet above the path below. Their pace continued to drop rapidly, the friction of the clothing on the cable winning, stopping their descent before their feet touched.

"This is as far as we go. Slide down my body and get to the ground before I drop us both."

With her legs still wrapped around his waist, she removed her hands from around his neck. She grabbed hold around his waist, letting her legs stretch out below, then dropped the remaining distance to touch the earth. She rolled down the hill a few feet as Paul swung his legs forward to try to shorten his fall. Two swings later he let go, landing and immediately stopping in his roll up the incline.

Lisa was up and rushed over to Paul.

"Paul, are you okay?"

He moved into a sitting position, the artifact still dangling around his neck.

"Yes, I think so. Let me try to stand."

He pulled himself up, tested both legs, and was certain he was fine.

"Nothing broken or sprained. I'm good as ever. How are you?"

"I'm okay. I see you still have the artifact," said Lisa, a pleased look on her face as she pointed to the bag around his neck.

Paul lifted the bag from around his neck and pulled his shoestring loose from the tie bag. He kneeled, placed the wrapped statue on the ground, and quickly threaded the shoestring through the eyelets of his tennis shoe.

Lisa was practically dancing about.

"I can't believe it. After five seconds of terror, I absolutely loved it. I can't believe I went from terrified of heights to having the best time of my life. I would do it again, any time. What a rush!"

"Super. It was touch and go when I was afraid I was going to lose my grip, but we did it!"

Paul stood, his arms exhausted, holding the small draw bag by his side. He looked at Lisa, relieved his arms had not given out.

Lisa returned his gaze, her eyes alive with excitement.

"Not only did we do it, I loved it! And you know what else?"

She walked to Paul and wrapped her arms around him.

"I feel like I just ate an entire bag of green M&M's. Seeing as we're both standing here naked, what do you say? Let's join the mile high zip line club here on the ground. Right now."

"I feel it too, but we might have only a ten-minute head start on those guys who were coming up the mountain. Hold on to that thought, but let's get out of here."

Lisa continued her seduction.

"Just really quick. Two minutes, that's all. I promise."

Lisa pressed her body against him, her hands around his neck. She began a trail of kisses from the side of his face to his chest.

"In addition to the short lead we have," Paul began, doing his best to continue, "Do you realize that other than our shoes, all of our clothes are still stuck on that cable above our heads?"

Lisa took a step back and did a little provocative dance for Paul.

"I don't care," she replied, laughing at their clothing predicament. "I've never felt more alive. I could slow walk my way down the busiest street in St. Maarten back to our car and it wouldn't matter to me. I'll sing the whole way back. I'll invite everybody we see to join in. This is the best!"

"You understand we can't hang around? It's not just the ones behind us on the mountain. Others could be coming and be here any time."

"Yes, I hear what you're saying," she responded. "Come on. Let's get back to the car. But once we make it to the car, I'm not waiting any longer!"

Her legs, which had been trembling with exhaustion on the way up the mountain, had plenty of spring left as she grabbed Paul's hand for the walk back to the car.

FOUR

DEBI AND DEAN had been engaged since July of the prior year. After much consideration and planning, it was time to get married.

There had been great debate on where to have their marriage ceremony. Debi liked the idea of a large wedding in Orillia in Ontario, Canada, where she lived before moving to St. Maarten. The ceremony and reception could be held in Orillia at Couchiching Beach Park. She wanted to be surrounded by family and friends when she and Dean exchanged their vows. Although marrying in Orillia would be convenient for Debi's family to attend, it would limit the number of their new friends, as most lived in St. Martin.

Debi also considered the possibility of a destination wedding. A few years back, Vegas would have been a prime consideration. However, with the time Debi had spent with Dean's casino in St. Maarten, the allure of Vegas was no longer as strong.

They considered other places for a destination wedding, but struggled to agree on one that they liked as much as St. Martin. Without confidence of selecting a location comparable to St. Martin for a honeymoon, they also considered honeymooning in St. Martin. But that did not meet their goal of going to a phenomenal new place.

They finally reached their decision. They would have a traditional wedding ceremony in Debi's hometown of Orillia. After celebrating with family and friends, they would board a plane the next day for part two. The couple would have a second wedding on the island of St. Martin surrounded by their many friends living there.

After exchanging their vows a second time, Debi and Dean would embark on their honeymoon. They would board a sailboat and cruise the islands around St. Martin for a few days. When they returned, a stay at a lodging on their favorite beach, Orient, would be the perfect ending.

At 3:00 p.m., on a cloudless day in Orillia, Debi and Dean stood before family and friends in Couchiching Beach Park.

The minister held his hands out, gesturing toward the couple as he spoke.

"Friends and relatives, we have gathered here today at the invitation of Debi and Dean to share in the joy of their wedding. This outward celebration today is an expression of the love and devotion they have toward one another. This marriage is a covenant with God, and Debi and Dean come today desiring to be united in this sacred relationship of marriage."

Debi looked radiant, dressed in an off the shoulder traditional white gown with a short train, giving the appearance of a fairy tale princess marrying her prince. Her glowing smile and moist eyes were focused on Dean, who was dressed in a formal black tuxedo, fulfilling his role of a prince marrying his princess.

"The ceremony of marriage in which you come to be united is one of the first and oldest ceremonies in the entire world, celebrated in the beginning and in the presence of God himself. Marriage is a gift, one in which Debi and Dean give of themselves totally to the other. Marriage is a gift to comfort the sorrows of life and to magnify life's joys."

"Debi and Dean, will you please hold hands?"

Dean reached for Debi's hands, enveloping her hands in his.

"With the clasping of hands, we have the blending of two hearts and the union of two lives into one. Your marriage must stand, not by the authority of governing officials or even the seal on your wedding certificate, but by the strength and power of the faith and love you have in one another."

Dean squeezed Debi's hands, and she smiled as she returned his squeeze.

Dean and Debi took turns affirming their vows, repeating after the minister.

"Debi, I take you to be my wife, to have and to hold from this day forward, for better or worse, for richer or poorer, in sickness and in health, I promise to love, honor and cherish you."

Dean looked Debi squarely in the eyes, beaming with admiration for her.

"Dean, I take you to be my husband, to have and to hold from this day forward, for better or worse, for richer or poorer, in sickness and in health, I promise to love, honor and cherish you."

The minister touched their clasped hands, then turned to their family members and friends.

"The word of God tells us that love is patient, kind and not jealous. Love does not brag and is not arrogant. It does not rejoice in unrighteousness, but rejoices with the truth, for love bears all things, believes all things, hopes all things, and endures all things, but above all, love never fails."

"Dean and Debi have rings to give one another today."

The minister turned his attention back to the couple.

"These rings have great significance. They are made of a precious metal and remind us that love is not cheap or common, but instead is very costly and dear to us. These rings are made in a circle and their design tells us that we must keep love continuous throughout our whole lives even as the circle of the ring is continuous. As you wear these rings, whether you are together or apart for even a moment, may these rings be a constant reminder of the promises you are making to each other today."

Debi and Dean attentively looked at the minister, and repeated after him their next vows.

Dean placed the wedding band on Debi's finger.

"Debi, with this ring, I promise to be your faithful and loving husband, as God as my witness."

As he looked from the ring on her finger to her sparkling eyes, a surge of emotion flooded his senses.

Debi looked lovingly back at Dean before sliding his ring on his finger.

"Dean, with this ring, I promise to be your faithful and loving wife, as God as my witness."

The minister reached out and held Debi's and Dean's hands adorned with their wedding bands.

"Debi and Dean, you have come here today before us and before God and have expressed your desire to become husband and wife. You have shown your love and affection by joining hands, and have sealed these promises by the giving and the receiving of the rings. Therefore, it is my privilege as a minister, I now pronounce you are husband and wife. Dean, you may kiss your bride."

Dean leaned in and gladly followed the minister's direction.

"Ladies and gentlemen, it is my privilege to now introduce to you the newly married couple."

There was an eruption of applause and whistles. Debi and Dean kissed again briefly, before holding their clasped hands above their heads as they faced the onlookers. It was time to mingle. The party began.

FIVE

LEKHA AND JASON were speeding toward the gas station. A quick stop for a few gallons of gas was all that stood between them and Lekha's home jewelry show for Jason, with love making to follow.

Jason pulled into the traffic circle and stopped at the nearest gas pump at the Texaco station. He hopped out to pump the gas as Lekha went inside to present her credit card, as customary on the island, for filling the tank to full.

From inside the store, she nodded the go ahead to Jason to begin filling the tank. She waited inside, and when the handle of the fuel spout was returned to the pump cradle, she turned to the clerk as he processed the purchase. Retrieving her credit card, she opened the store door and took several steps toward their car. Jason was sitting in the driver's seat waiting for her. As she neared their vehicle, she heard someone calling her name.

She stopped, looked around in a full circle, but saw no one.

She took the remaining steps to her car, and as she grabbed the door handle, heard her name again, this time more loudly. She looked, trying to find the source of the voice.

"Over here. Lekha, it's me Lisa. I could use your help."

"Lisa, just a minute."

Lekha opened her car door and looked in at Jason.

"I hear Lisa calling out to me. I think she's just the other side of the traffic circle, but I don't see her. I'm going to walk over. I'll be right back."

Jason gave her a confused look.

"Okay, I'll be right here."

Lekha began walking in the direction of Lisa's voice. She reached the circular road, and when no traffic was coming, crossed to the wooded side.

"Lisa? I'm here, where are you?"

"I'm coming. Everything is fine, so don't be alarmed, but I'm not wearing any clothes." Lisa broke into a bout of laughter.

She walked into a clearing where Lekha could see her.

"Oh my God! What are you doing naked?"

"It's not just her," Paul responded, walking into the clearing beside Lisa. He sported a smile and tennis shoes, but nothing else other than the draw bag in his hand.

"Have you guys lost your minds?"

"No," giggled Lisa, "But we have lost our clothes."

She bent over in laughter, the absurdity of the situation made even more hilarious by the look of shock on Lekha's face.

"Our car is just down the road. I spotted you and Jason getting gas. If you wouldn't mind too terribly, would you ask Jason if he would give two naked hitch hikers a five-minute ride to their car?"

"Both of you, stay here. I'll have Jason come over right away and pick you up."

She turned to cross the road, so rattled she almost stepped out in front of an oncoming vehicle. It passed, and she scampered across the street to her car. She quickly sat, grabbing Jason's right wrist to keep him there while she talked.

"We have an errand to run before we go home. Lisa and Paul are standing on the other side of the road just in the woods. They need a ride to their car which is five minutes away. I don't know what happened, they both seem fine, but neither is wearing any clothes. They don't seem to be upset. In fact, Lisa is laughing about it."

"Do what?"

"Yes, you heard me. That's all I know. Now, will you please pull over through the traffic circle and pick them up? I'll show you where."

Jason followed her instructions, eased the car forward, looked for a large opening in traffic, and pulled into the roundabout. He pulled over onto the shoulder of the road where Lekha pointed and made sure the car doors were unlocked. Lisa appeared, followed by Paul. They took the two steps into the clearing and slid into the back seat.

"We can't thank you enough," Paul began as Jason pulled the car forward. He gave Jason directions to his car. "I owe you an explanation. I'll be happy to tell you all about it."

"Yeah, it'll be full disclosure," giggled Lisa.

That brought a smile to Lekha's face.

"We can't just let you out at your car and let you guys drive around naked. Let us get you some clothes." Jason took off his shirt while driving. "Lisa, take this and put it on. It'll have to do until we get you more."

"Thanks, Jason." She slipped the pullover shirt over her head. "I have an idea, if you guys are willing to let us infringe on your night even longer?"

"Anything. What can we do?" asked Lekha.

"Let us out at our car. Paul can drive us home, and if you will, I'd like you to follow us. This shirt is long enough where I can go through the lobby to our place, slip something on, and Jason, bring your shirt back to you and bring some clothes to Paul. Then you guys can come in for a visit and we'll tell you all about it."

Jason looked to Lekha for her reaction. "Lisa, that's a good plan. Jason and I will follow you over and wait in the car while you get clothes and return."

"Awesome, thank you."

When they reached the area where Paul's SUV was somewhat hidden, Lisa scampered out and into their unlocked vehicle. Paul followed, grabbed a key from the case under the rear bumper, and then pulled out to lead Jason and Lekha to the Cliff. Lisa turned to Paul as soon as they were on the road.

"Since you're driving and we'll have unexpected company, I want you to know I understand my plans for you when we reached the car have to be on hold. I really appreciate their help. But if they stay too long, I may have to signal you for a quick intermission."

She gave him a mischievous grin, placing her left hand on his bare right thigh.

Paul shook his head in response, his demeanor now serious.

"I'm glad you're handling this well. I'm trying to be optimistic. But we've got a lot of unknowns and what could be a major problem. It looked like several people were either following us, or if not, were likely on a mission to get the artifact we have. I don't know if they saw us or could identify us, and don't know if we're in danger. We'll need to think about what we tell Jason and Lekha. By helping us, they could be putting themselves in danger. When we're talking with them, you just follow my lead. I want them to know enough to be careful, but not so much that it puts them in an even worse spot."

"Okay, I will. I won't introduce any new information to them. I'll let you handle that."

She continued to let her hand rest on Paul's thigh, trying to distract him enough to reduce his worry.

They were shortly at the Cliff. Paul pulled into the circle drive and let Lisa out close to the lobby. She pulled the shirt down as far as she could and hopped out. She strode purposefully through the lobby, not making eye contact with anyone, and reached the elevator. She rode alone up to their condo.

Instead of taking a parking place near the lobby, Paul pulled further away to reduce foot traffic past his car. He successfully minimized passersby looking in his car and discovering he was nude. Jason followed and parked next to Paul.

Less than ten minutes later, Lisa appeared smiling broadly. She had thrown on a thin island dress and continued to wear her sneakers. She held Jason's shirt in one hand and a t-shirt and shorts for Paul in the other. Jason stepped out of his car and slipped on his shirt while Lisa climbed in the car with Paul and handed him his clothing. He dressed quickly and hopped out grinning broadly.

"Welcome to the Cliff. Jason and Lekha, so kind of you to drop by."

He led them through the lobby to the elevator and up to their condo.

"Please, come on in."

SIX

SYLVIE AND BRAD were on Brad's sailboat, *Eclipse*, on their way to St. Martin. Their good friends, Terri and Keith, had sailed *Eclipse* from Miami to Jacksonville at their request, so that Brad and Sylvie could join them there. The four vacationed together as they continued their sail to North Carolina. Reaching North Carolina, Terri and Keith disembarked for home and Brad and Sylvie reversed course to sail back to the islands.

They were enjoying their time alone on the boat. Brad loved living on the sailboat and was excited to have Sylvie with him. Sylvie enjoyed being on the sailboat, but primarily was pleased to have Brad far away from Lena, who was competing with Sylvie for Brad's affection.

After stops in several islands along the way, they planned to reach St. Martin Sunday afternoon.

Sylvie sat in the galley after she and Brad finished lunch. Brad was cleaning the dishes.

"Brad, do you think I made the right decision when I turned down Wendall's proposal for us to transport more questionable items? He was offering a lot of money."

"I think you made a good decision. We don't need all the stress that would have come with it. If something less demanding comes along, you can consider it. You're in a good spot without selling out and becoming a slave to what would have been going on for a year or more."

Sylvie's debt from her last project was substantial, but she was able to pay off her note to Gregorio with much more favorable financing arranged through Wealth Management International. With earnings from her company, DEP, and returns on her other investments, she was able to meet the payments on her ten-year loan with a little money left over for living expenses.

"I'm glad you agree with passing on getting involved with Wendall. I would be interested in doing something where we could team up again, but before starting a new venture, I want to have full confidence in whoever I'm working with, or whoever offers the project."

"That sounds smart to me," he agreed. "Are you ready to go topside?"

"You go on up. I'll be there in a minute."

Brad, dressed in long sleeve t-shirt and shorts, walked up to wait for Sylvie. He stared out over the open ocean, enjoying the peace and solidarity on his sailboat. Although a decent size at 53 feet long and 16 feet wide, it was tiny as it made its way across the sea.

Brad breathed in a deep breath of the fresh salt air, letting it out equally as slow. Savoring the moment, he again inhaled deeply, feeling thankful for the life he was living.

"I'm finally here," Sylvie called out cheerfully. "Just like you, I've been getting a lot of sun. I thought I'd stay cool but cover up a bit."

Sylvie wore her tiny red bikini, coupled with her sheer white coverup.

"It's rare to see you so covered, especially out here on the boat. Is everything okay? First you turn down an opportunity to potentially make millions, and now this." Brad grinned, letting her know he was only kidding.

"That's right. You're now sailing with a woman of mystery. Who knows what's going on in my mind and what might be beneath this coverup and bikini?" she teased.

"I don't know what's behind the change, but rest assured, one thing hasn't changed. I'm still crazy about you, and the added mystery is very enticing."

"Brad, if you keep that up, you may be able to convince me to give you a kiss."

Brad stood, looking tenderly at Sylvie, and moved to sit beside her.

"If I may be so forward, I'll take your comment as an invitation, and I accept your offer."

He leaned over and kissed her ever so lightly on the lips.

Sylvie immediately responded to the slight, sensuous brushing of his lips.

"What I'm about to say is not an invitation, but merely a statement. Because of that delicious kiss, if you were to be so forward as to try for second base, I don't know that I have the willpower to stop you."

Brad looked longingly at her and wasted no time with words. They would reduce their sun exposure a different day.

SEVEN

BEFORE STEPPING DOWN from the gazebo where they were pronounced husband and wife, Debi and Dean posed for pictures with Couchiching Beach as the backdrop. The photographer, Chantelle, posed the couple for various photos before inviting friends and family to join in some of the shots. Chantelle set down her camera.

"Okay, that's the last posed picture. I'll mill around and capture candid shots while you two mingle."

Hand in hand, Debi and Dean approached the throng of friends amidst hugs and congratulatory handshakes.

Karen and Rick were first to greet the newlyweds.

Karen reached out and pulled Debi close for a warm hug. It would be Debi's first of many.

"Thank you so much for coming today. It means the world to us. I'm so glad you could make it."

"Absolutely. We wouldn't have missed this," Karen responded. "Selfishly, I'm hoping today could inspire Rick to take the next step," she laughed.

Rick missed her comment as he slapped Dean on the back.

"Congratulations. You two were made for each other. Thanks so much for inviting us."

Rick next hugged Debi. "You're a beautiful bride. A lot of hearts were broken today."

"Oh, Rick, you're so kind. We are so thrilled you could make it. I can't believe what good friends you have become."

"What a beautiful ceremony," gushed Karen. "We needed to be here. We're really enjoying meeting your family and some of your friends. We're going to St. Maarten next and will fly over to the island in the morning."

Debi reached out and grabbed Karen's hand.

"Again, thank you so much. You and the others have been too good to us. We can't believe you'd come to our wedding here, then head to St. Maarten to help our friends have everything ready for our wedding there."

"Oh yeah. If the next one is anything like this one, we can't wait! You guys might start a new trend, where one wedding is just not enough," she laughed. "We'll move along now and let your other friends have a turn with you."

As Karen and Rick stepped away, the procession of friends continued to celebrate with the newlyweds. Debi and Dean remained mostly in place as the flood of well-wishers waited for their opportunity to pass along their congratulations and best wishes.

At dark, a section of the park was cordoned off from the general public where dinner tables were set up. The wedding dinner, seating the ninety-six guests, lasted until 9:00 p.m. when Debi and Dean prepared to make their exit. They left the lead table and stepped back up into the gazebo where they had stood six hours earlier exchanging their vows. Dean addressed the remaining guests.

"Debi and I want to thank you again for being here and making this day so special. We'll be staying only a short time tomorrow but look forward to spending more time with any of you who make the next one. But now, speaking primarily for myself, I'm wearing down and need some rest."

They stepped down, said their goodbyes, and prepared to leave the park. The photographer was the last to leave, having captured in photos and videos the last of the dinner.

"Chantelle, Dean and I thank you for being here and making sure our memories of this day will never fade. We're so fortunate to have been able to book you for the full day and night."

"It was fun. I'll have some proofs ready for you to take a look at within the week. I'll be in touch."

"That sounds perfect. But I have a question for you before you get away."

"All right, how can I help you?"

"Have you ever been to St. Maarten?"

"No, I've heard great things about it, but I've never vacationed there."

"What would you think about doing some photography work and vacationing in St. Maarten?"

"Well, it depends on what you have in mind and my schedule."

"Our second wedding is this coming Saturday. Our friends are working on all the details for us. They have lined up a local photographer, but I'd like you to come over and also work the wedding. The ceremony will be short, but after the wedding, the partying could go on for quite some time. You've hung in with us for over six hours today, and I think you're just the right person to record the party that will follow our next wedding. Would you be available?"

"I do have next weekend free."

"Let's talk about this for a few minutes. Dean, would you mind going to get the car while we talk?"

Dean nodded, grateful to be heading to the comfort of their car.

"I don't have a lot of details, but I will tell you what I know."

Debi shared the limited information she had with Chantelle, and after much coaxing, secured her agreement to record the event. She clapped her hands in delight.

"That is awesome! I know you have some reservations, but I really appreciate you doing this. We'll arrange for you to stay at the Royal Palm in Simpson Bay. All expenses paid."

"Okay, I should have the proofs by then. We can go over all of the details."

"Agreed. We will talk soon," she said with a wave.

Dean was back with the car and stepped out, walking toward Debi as Chantelle headed for the parking lot.

"Okay, Debi, it's really time for us to go."

Debi stepped over to Dean and gave him a quick hug. She whispered seductively in his ear.

"I'm ready. It's been an amazing day. I hope you're not too worn down because I'm planning to make your night equally unforgettable."

Dean grabbed her by the hand, quickly led her to the car, and opened her door.

"Your chariot awaits."

EIGHT

BEN AND LAUREN arrived in St. Maarten and were in their white Corolla from Hertz on their way to Villa Islandtude. They had closed on their real estate purchase of the villa and would be staying in Villa Islandtude for the first time.

"This is so exciting. I know we'll be living most of the time in Miami, but I love that we're going to be in our new island home," she gushed, turning to Ben. "I love you, Ben."

"I love you too. This is going to be a great trip."

"I'm so glad Debi and Dean will be getting married at our villa. What a great reason to see all of our island friends again!"

"Yes, I'm glad Debi talked to you about it. I'm also relieved we're only providing the venue, and that Debi's other friends are in charge of making all the arrangements. I can fill my role as interested bystander without stressing over any of the details."

They pulled into the driveway at the villa and were greeted by Nico. In addition to being a good friend to Ben, Nico had agreed to Ben's request to maintain the villa. He was a knowledgeable contractor on the island with no job beyond his abilities. Having spent much time in the Bahamas, he had become accomplished in all areas, including plumbing and electrical. Ben was confident that Nico would make sure the villa was always ready when they wanted to stay there.

"Here are your keys. Come on up and let me show you around. I'll show you how to work the TVs, air conditioning, pool and pool heater, and can answer any questions you might have."

Nico received big hugs from Ben and Lauren before leading them up the stairs.

They did a quick tour of the property. At the top of the stairs, they were greeted by the view that made the villa special. Walking alongside the oversize pool, they continued to the large sun deck beyond the spa where Debi and Dean's marriage ceremony would be performed. The deck provided a magnificent view of Simpson Bay, the open ocean to the west, and the virgin deep green mountains to the immediate north.

"This is breathtaking. Ben, it's amazing to be back. We're back where Gregorio and Michele filmed their initial promotional materials for his beach hats and other beach essentials. Remember what a fun day it was with the other girls here?"

"I do. It's the day you went from accomplished attorney to aspiring model," Ben teased. "Not only did all of us guys enjoy the photo shoot, but of course, it will always be special to me. That's when we got engaged."

"Maybe the best reason this villa is so special," cooed Lauren, giving Ben a hug.

"Okay, lovebirds," interrupted Nico. "Now that you're here, I will be heading on and let you get settled in."

"Thanks for everything. If you don't have any plans for tonight, would you and Jenny be able to have dinner with Lauren and me? Maybe we could go to the Greenhouse restaurant in Simpson Bay."

"That sounds good. I'll check with Jenny, but I'm sure that will be fine."

Dinner was set for 7:00 p.m. Nico left Ben and Lauren to unpack their few items.

"Thinking of dinner, I'm hungry and thirsty and we don't have anything here," sighed Lauren. "Should we run across the street to the Divico and get some stuff for the next week or two?"

"We probably should. We don't even have any drinking water. I should have asked Nico to pick up a few things for us. Do you want to stay here, or do you want to come with me?"

Lauren looked out over the beautiful view of the mountains and ocean, then looked at the pool calling to her. She was reluctant to leave, but wanted to help.

"I should probably go with you. We're not going to be gone long, are we?"

"No. Three minutes to the store, fifteen minutes of shopping, and three minutes back. Add in a few minutes for me to bring everything in, and we'll be done in less than thirty minutes."

"Good, let's get going. It's three-thirty now, at four o'clock I plan to be in our pool."

They drove to the front of the neighborhood where just across the street was the Divico grocery store. They picked out essential items including snacks and water, and the needed ingredients for making rum punch.

"I think we've got everything we need for now. We can come here again later in the week. If we leave now, I'll have time to make up some rum punch and still be in the pool by four."

"I'm good, let's go."

They checked out and loaded down the small Corolla trunk with their purchases. Ben drove them back up the side of the mountain to their villa.

"I'll grab a few things and get the door for you. Paradise is waiting for us just up these stairs."

Ben made several trips with the groceries, then mixed up some rum punch while Lauren found the reggae station on the Bose music box and grabbed two towels. Five minutes later they were in the pool sipping rum punch made with the award-winning Topper's Rhum.

"Lauren, this is what I call the start of a great vacation."

"Yes, we are so lucky. It's hard to believe this is real. I love our villa."

Lauren wrapped her arms around Ben's neck. Ben, reacting to the hug, looked deeply into her eyes.

"Yes, this is amazing. It's just you and me in paradise. No people and no clothes. It doesn't get any better."

The vacation was off to a great start.

NINE

....

LEKHA AND JASON followed Lisa inside the condo that she and Paul owned at the Cliff.

"Come on through. Let's sit out on the balcony."

Lisa slipped off her shoes and directed Lekha and Jason to a couple of chairs overlooking Cupecoy Beach. "Can we get you something to drink?"

"I'm fine," answered Jason. "Lekha, anything for you?"

"Lisa, are you having anything?"

"I'll have a glass of red wine. Would you have one with me?"

"Sure, that sounds good."

"And I'm sure Paul will have a Coors Light. Jason, let me bring you something. A glass of wine, or a beer like Paul?"

"Okay, I'll join Paul in a Coors Light. Thank you very much."

Lisa brought some bowls of assorted nuts and small pretzel snacks and sat across from Lekha and Jason as Paul poured the two glasses of wine. He delivered the wine, then returned with the two beers.

"What a beautiful view you have from your balcony. This is a real treat."

Eager to hear an explanation on why Lisa and Paul were in such a compromising position, Jason moved the conversation beyond the initial pleasantries.

"I'm glad Lisa was able to get Lekha's attention tonight at the gas station."

Paul took a seat at the table beside Lisa across from Lekha and Jason. Seeing their curious faces, he began to tell about the evening to answer their questions.

"Okay, we owe you an explanation. First, thank you very much for coming to our rescue. Getting back to our car without wearing clothes would have been a lot more to deal with if you guys hadn't stopped for gas when you did."

Lekha and Jason responded with smiles, but neither spoke.

"So here goes. We consider you guys as friends, and you certainly proved to be tonight. You've always shown yourselves as stable and conservative, and because of that, I feel more comfortable than I otherwise would with telling you more about tonight. I recommend that what happened not go further than this balcony."

"Oh no," Lekha spoke up. "We would never tell anyone about your embarrassing situation."

"Thanks," continued Paul. "It's not so much that if others heard about it that we would be embarrassed, although probably we should be. In fact, Lisa actually found it to be quite funny, and while I'm being totally candid, we both found it sort of sexy. Especially Lisa, who found it to be a rush, a total turn-on."

Paul looked at Lisa. Instead of being mad at his characterization, she responded by holding her hands out as she shrugged her shoulders.

"I can't deny it. I told Paul I felt like I had just eaten an entire bag of green M&M's," she snickered. "If you know what that means."

Lekha visibly colored at Lisa's blunt admission. Lisa loved Lekha's reaction, and in a spirit of fun, could not stop herself from continuing.

"When we found ourselves naked and no way to get our clothes, I was ready to do Paul right there. He talked me into holding that thought, but I told him, once we got back to our car, I wasn't waiting any longer."

She continued to watch for Lekha's reaction and grinned broadly as Lekha's mouth fell open in disbelief as Lisa openly shared those thoughts.

"It's okay, though. I've gotten it under control, but I am planning to make sure that Paul and I both sleep great tonight."

Lisa nodded to Lekha, indicating she had finished sharing on the topic.

Lekha recovered from her shock, saw the humor in what she had just heard, and began giggling, setting off a giggling jag from Lisa as well.

Paul tried to get the conversation back on point.

"So, the purpose of all that, if there was a point, was that we, and especially Lisa, would not be embarrassed if a few people at some time were to hear about the story. The unfortunate reason for asking that neither of you mention any of what's happened, is that it could be dangerous."

"Oh my," uttered Lekha. "You can be assured that we won't mention this to anyone."

"Okay, here goes. I got a call from a client wanting me to do some work for him. The work included me going up the mountain where the big zip line is, the Flying Dutchman. I was telling Lisa about what I was going to do, and she wanted to come along with me. So, anyway, we parked where you saw our vehicle, and walked from there. I see the looks on your faces and you're wondering why I didn't just park in the lot at Emilio's restaurant at the foot of the mountain. The answer to that is although I thought it would be safe, I wanted to take the extra precaution of not parking where I would be seen. You guys with me?"

Jason had not spoken since Paul began his story. He nodded to Paul.

"This is fascinating. Please, continue with your story."

"So, we get to the base of the mountain and start working our way up. Again, I think it's okay, but I'm not doing anything to call attention to us. We are walking up the mountain following the path of the chair lift above us. We make it to the top, but I thought I had heard some noise down the mountain a ways as we got close to the top. Once we were there, I looked out from the platform at the top, and saw some people walking up the mountain. Just like it was unusual for us to be walking up the mountain, I didn't know why others would be doing it. Maybe it was just a lark, and it's no big deal, but I wasn't sure. I didn't want to take any undue chances."

Lekha was mesmerized with the story.

"So, what did you do?"

"That's when we got naked. I took all of our clothes and fashioned a sling out of the clothes for us to hold on to for riding the zip line down to the bottom of the mountain. We rode down, but when our ride ended, our clothes were still bound around the zip line. I couldn't get them down, so we had to leave without them. We were working our way back to the car when Lisa spotted you two at the gas station. And as they say, the rest is history."

"Oh my! That's a lot to process. You don't need to tell us anything more, but I'd certainly be interested in knowing what was at the top and why you think those other people were also walking up the mountain."

Jason looked at Lekha, and she was nodding her agreement with him.

"Well, I don't know for sure, but I'm guessing the people walking up the mountain were either going up there to get the same thing I was after, or they were after me, or both. I've been thinking about it some more, and I don't know why there would be more than one or two people going up to get what I was after. It makes me think they were either just going up unrelated to why Lisa and I were there, or they believed it possible I would be there with the item, and there were more than just a couple of them so that they could subdue me and take what I found."

Paul paused, took a sip of beer, then continued.

"I didn't want to stick around to find out. If they were after me, and with Lisa with me, I decided the best way out was to go down the zip line. I'm glad it worked."

Lisa sat quietly with Jason and Lekha, letting Paul continue the story without interruption. She checked the reactions on the faces of their guests, then focused back on Paul.

"Are you going to tell them what you got up there? I haven't seen it myself."

"I wasn't going to tell them or show them. Not that I don't trust them, but if someone comes around asking, it would be better to not know."

Lisa looked questioningly at Paul.

"Well, if someone comes around asking, aren't they going to say what they're asking about? If anyone approaches Lekha and Jason about this, won't they tell them when they do what they're after?"

"Probably."

"Well, I know this isn't my area, and it would be better if I sat back quietly and let you handle the debriefing, but I think you should go ahead and tell them. If someone comes up to them and asks about it, they can pretend to know nothing about what you got, as well as pretend they never saw us."

"Okay, Lekha and Jason, do you want to see what I brought down from the mountaintop?"

"I guess so, sure," replied Jason. "Lekha, what do you think?"

"I'm curious, but I don't know. This makes me nervous. Paul, do you think someone is going to approach us?"

"I hope not. When we zipped down from the top, I'm not sure anyone saw us, or if they did, would be able to identify us. The question I have is if anyone saw two naked people once we were down, and if they did, even if they didn't recognize us, did they see us getting into your car? If someone saw two naked people getting into your car, and found clothes for two people tied on the zip line, they may not know who we are, but they could come after you to find that out."

"This is so unbelievable and confusing. I guess, since we're already involved to some extent, I'm okay with seeing what all the excitement is about."

"I'll go get it."

Paul walked over to where he had set the draw bag down containing the artifact and brought it out to the balcony.

"Okay, here it is."

Paul opened the bag, reached in, and pulled out the diminutive artifact.

Lekha gasped and again colored.

"Is that a fertility relic of some type? It looks like a little naked man, and he's ready to make babies."

"So that's why I was feeling aroused," snickered Lisa. "It's a sex voodoo doll and the thing cast a spell on me. Paul, I don't know how much longer I can wait," she laughed. "I thought it was the combination of thinking I was about to die, facing my fear of heights, our naked hug flying through the air, and exhilaration flying and landing. On top of that, a sex spell was cast on me."

That put a smile on Jason's face.

"Okay, I'll bite. What makes that little man worth so much trouble that you climbed up a mountain at night to get it, and others may have been coming after it and you?"

"That's a good question. There's a lot I don't know. What I was told, however, is that this is a genuine Arawak artifact. It's believed that the Arawaks were the first inhabitants of St. Martin. A group of Arawaks, the Ciboney Indians, probably first settled on the island 3,500 years ago. Then some 2,000 years later, another group of Arawaks came here from South America's Orinico Basin. They were drawn here because of the big salt pond near Philipsburg and had a farming and fishing society. They were very smart and lived in straw-roofed buildings that were strong enough to resist hurricanes. They were, as a group, spiritual and very artistic. They were skilled carvers and made objects and figurines from bone, wood, shell and stone, in addition to clay like this one."

Paul paused and finished his beer.

"I think I'll have one more Coors Light. Can we freshen up your drinks?"

"We're going to need to leave soon, but I'll join you in one more quick beer."

Lisa hopped up.

"I'll get you guys cold beers and pour a fresh glass of wine for Lekha and me. I'll be right back. I don't want to miss the rest of the story."

They sat quietly, and when everyone had fresh drinks, Paul continued his story.

"Historians believe the Arawaks lived peaceful lives until the Carib Indians arrived. The Caribs were also from the Orinico Basin area of South America. This group, also called Caniba but better known as Caribs, were a warring group and likely practiced cannibalism. They were enemies of the Arawaks and killed the Arawak men and made slaves of the Arawak women. Early Spanish explorers used the term Arawaks for groups they considered friendly and Caribs for indigenous groups that were hostile. When Europeans began exploring the Caribbean, the Caribs had greatly replaced the Arawaks in St. Martin. The Carib name was given to the Caribbean Sea, and its Arawakan equivalent is the origin of the word cannibal in English."

"So, what makes this Arawak artifact worth pursuing?"

"I'm guessing that this particular artifact was found in St. Maarten. The simple answer could be its value to collectors. Some of these artifacts are worth hundreds of thousands of dollars."

"Paul, thank you for sharing all this information, and thank you both for your hospitality. Lekha and I should be on our way, but before we go, what should we do? Any suggestions?"

"This night never happened. You haven't seen us in some time now, and hopefully no one ever approaches you. I've got this artifact and I'm going to need to do something with it, so there will be new developments. If anything happens that could have an impact on you guys, I'll be sure to let you know. My best recommendation is to pretend this never happened and carry on your lives like normal."

Lekha piped up. "That's what we'll do. We were on our way home. We had a great meal at Chesterfields and a quick stop for gas. If anyone saw us there, it's true we stopped for gas, but we went straight home after filling up at the gas station. Once we got home, well, I don't need to get into that, as I normally wouldn't," she grinned.

Lekha tipped back her glass, finishing off her wine. Jason slugged back the rest of his beer. The snacks were mostly uneaten.

"Jason and I really had a great time, and I'm glad we were getting gas tonight when we did. Your secret is safe, and I would have hated to miss out on this night. Let me help you put stuff away."

Lekha placed her empty glass on the kitchen counter and Paul threw the beer cans in the recycle bin. Lisa put away the food while finishing the last of her wine.

"Paul, don't forget the artifact on the balcony."

Paul retrieved the statue and placed it in Lisa's outstretched hand.

"Here you go baby. This started the whole night."

Lisa looked intently over the statue.

"Lekha, here you go. You need to hold this too. I can tell, it's got enough power to cast a sex spell on you too."

Lekha giggled as she accepted the offer to hold the statue. She ran her fingers along the statue before handing it back to Lisa. She leaned into Lisa.

"If truth be told, on this night of surprising confessions, I was going to be seducing Jason as soon as we got home. The statue is at a minimum a reminder to me of that," she smiled mischievously.

"Good for you," snickered Lisa.

The four exchanged hugs goodbye. Paul opened the door for Jason and Lekha.

Seeing the look of surprise on Jason's face caused Paul to look back at Lisa. She stood there naked clutching the statue, having thrown her dress to the floor.

"Lekha and Jason, please forgive us for not walking you back to your car. I'm not waiting any longer. Paul, I'm taking this horny Arawak to the bedroom with us tonight. Lekha, I'll call you tomorrow if I'm not in the hospital. In fact, if I'm in the hospital, I'll still call you and tell you all about it. You two have fun."

They walked laughing to their car while Paul was rushed into the bedroom.

TEN

THE GROUP OF men ascended the steps to the platform at the top of the mountain. They began scurrying around, taking apart the bar and removing all contents under it. Finding nothing, one of them made a call to report their failure to locate anything of value.

"This is Antonio. We're at the top of the mountain and have looked all around. We've not found what we were sent to find."

"Antonio, how can that be?"

"I'm not sure, but as we were just about to get here, I heard some noise when I was under the platform about to take the steps up. I don't know, because of it being dark, but looking back down the mountain, either one or maybe two people were riding down the zip line."

"What are you talking about? It's closed."

"Yes sir, the ride is totally shut down. But that didn't stop somebody. I don't know how it was done, but I'm certain at least one person was here and took the zip line down. He must have gotten what we're looking for."

"Well go down the zip line after him. What are you waiting for?"

"I can't go down the zip line. It's closed. I have nothing to be able to ride the zip line down."

"You just assured me that somebody rode down it while you watched. Do whatever that person did and get down there."

"That's the problem, sir. I don't know what that person did. The only way I know to get back down is to hike it."

"Well stop wasting time. Get back down the mountain now and find him. Call me when you have it."

"Yes sir. We'll go down now."

As Antonio instructed his men to hustle back down the mountain, Antonio's boss placed a call to Gregorio, the wealthiest and most powerful man on the island.

"Gregorio, I'm sorry for calling you after hours tonight."

"Nonsense. You know I don't observe anything such as standard work hours. How can I help you?"

"I'm working on a business deal and could use some help on the ground. Does Baldo still work for you?"

"Yes, he does."

"Would you be able to loan him out to me? I have something I'd like checked out right now as we speak, and my regulars are on a wild-goose chase. Could I call him now for some emergency help?"

"Sure. He's a solid and loyal worker. He's not the brightest I've ever had, you already employ Antonio, who's more talented than Baldo. But Baldo will give you everything he's got. And loyalty goes a long way."

"Great. I need him now."

"I'll call him and tell him to expect your urgent call. You and I will work out the compensation for this, as I trust you to pay your bills," affirmed Gregorio. "We have history. Give me two minutes to encourage his participation in your plan and I am certain he will drop whatever he is doing and begin work for you right away."

"Thank you, Gregorio. I owe you."

Of course you do thought Gregorio as he disconnected the call.

Gregorio called Baldo, who immediately answered when he saw it was his employer. Eager to please Gregorio, Baldo agreed to help and waited for his next call.

"Good evening, Baldo. Did you just talk with Gregorio?"

"Yes sir. How can I help you?"

"I have a situation over at Emilio's Restaurant. I believe someone is making away with something that belongs to me. I can't describe it to you, but it's likely in a small box or container of some sort, and the box could be as small as 12 inches by 18 inches. Would you ride over to the area around Emilio's and keep your eyes open for a bit, maybe for an hour or so? You may see Antonio and a few others in the area."

"Yes sir. I'll drive over now. I can be there in ten minutes."

"Excellent Baldo. Gregorio highly recommended you. Thank you for not letting me down. You will be rewarded."

The call was ended and Baldo hopped in his car and raced to Emilio's. He parked in the nearly empty lot and started walking around the area, looking for anyone carrying a small package. He assumed if it was stolen, the person would not be walking around with it as if finishing a shopping trip. He would call in an hour to give a report, or sooner if he spotted what might be the package.

ELEVEN

ANTONIO SIZED UP the four muscular men who had walked with him to the mountaintop. They looked as if their regular workout routines emphasized lifting heavy weights. The audible breathing of the four reflected less attention to their cardiovascular fitness.

"All right, we've been instructed to get back down now. Someone is leaving with what we came for."

A collective groan was heard. One of them piped up.

"We just got here. How about we help ourselves to something at the bar first?"

"We need to be down in ten minutes," replied Antonio. "Let's get going."

"There's no way we can get all the way down in ten minutes. No need to hurry when we know we can't do it."

"I'm going down now," Antonio growled. "Stay here if you want. You'll have to answer to the boss why you didn't get down there when told."

"This is shit man. I'm not breaking no leg running down the mountain in the dark. I'm coming, but if you can be down in ten, don't wait for me. I'll be there as soon as I can without serious injury."

Antonio chose not to respond, and instead started down along the path under the chairlift line. The others followed him as he knew they would. The path, although somewhat cleared, was uneven terrain with patches of rock and tall grass interrupting the cleared ground. Coupled with the steep decline, it was impossible to move at a pace much beyond a fast walk. Almost twenty minutes passed before Antonio was standing at the bottom of the chairlift path. He looked over to the zip line cable and saw something wrapped around the line. His men reached him a minute later.

"Come on, let's go to the zip line. We need to check it out," he said, pointing to whatever was hanging from the line.

They walked over to the end of the zip line cable. Dangling above, fifty feet from the end, appeared to be a pair of men's pants.

"What the hell?"

The men stared up at the clothes.

"Let's get them," barked Antonio.

"How do you think we're going to do that?"

"Just watch me." He gave the men instructions. "Boost me up."

The four men circled Antonio, two stooping down, with Antonio placing his feet on one man's shoulders and his hands on the shoulders of another. As the two men stood, the other two men held on to Antonio for him to retain his balance. With one of them firmly gripping his ankles, Antonio stood wobbly on the shoulders supporting him. The men grabbed his ankles, and as if an acrobat, pushed his feet above their heads. Before tumbling forward, he was launched another foot, where he successfully grabbed the cable above. He pulled himself hand over hand to the clothes, untied the bundle, and it fell to the ground. He dropped from the cable and was caught by two of his men.

"Let's see what we've got here."

Antonio held the pair of men's pants up for the others to see. He reached inside the pants and pulled out the other clothes that had formed layers for Paul and Lisa's ride down.

"Look what we have here. Pants, boxers, sweatpants and two t-shirts. It looks like whoever rode that cable down might have been left without any clothes. One of these t-shirts is smaller, and it looks like this is a woman's sweatpants. My guess is we've got us a naked man out there. We have a woman in underwear, or if she wasn't wearing underwear the way I like my women, we've got us a naked woman with him. This is going to make our search a whole lot easier. Fan out, you two go in that direction, you two over that other way. Let me know if you see anything. In about forty-five minutes, meet me at the front of Emilio's restaurant."

The men took off in opposite directions, looking for two naked people trying to remain concealed along the foliage.

Antonio walked to the front of Emilio's restaurant, pleased with his finding. He would take a break and let his men do the work for a bit. After a few minutes, he was bored and walked to the main road to assist in the search. He was surprised but pleased when he saw his good friend Baldo.

"Hey man, what you doing here tonight? Your boss Harrington sent you here to wish me a good night?"

"Yeah, in a way. He called me and said there's a new assignment, that I need to help your boss. I figured it was because you couldn't get the job done and needed my help," he kidded. "You look like shit."

"Yeah, you asshole. Next time you go running up and down that damn mountain and see how you're doing. I'm glad to see you. How long you been here?"

"I got here about ten minutes ago. I looked around, but I haven't seen anything worth reporting. I'm going to walk around for a while, and when I don't see nothing for another thirty minutes, I'm going to call your boss and tell I got nothing. Maybe after that we can go get a beer?"

Antonio quickly dismissed the thought of sharing with Baldo that the search was for a naked man and woman. He liked Baldo, but business was business. He wanted to show his boss that he was still the man and did not need help from Baldo or anyone else.

"I don't know, man. I got to deal with some numbskulls out here tonight," he said, waving his arms toward the edge of the trees. "It ain't easy being management."

"All right. Let me know when you done managing. You might need to call your secretary to check your calendar. If you got an opening, let me know."

"I'll do just that," he responded, allowing Baldo to have his joke. "Find me before you leave. I'll be in front of Emilio's. We'll talk then."

Baldo left Antonio to continue looking for anything that might be worth reporting along the main road. Thirty minutes later, still seeing nothing worthy of reporting, he called to give an update.

"Sorry, but nothing here. No one carrying anything that looked like it might be what you wanted."

"All right, keep looking a while longer. If you see anything, let me know. Otherwise, call me tomorrow morning. Have you seen Antonio?"

"Yeah, he's out looking. He said he had some others looking too. I beat him here by at least ten minutes. I'm guessing if I didn't see nothing, he won't neither."

"Okay, thanks Baldo for getting there right away. I'll let you know what more I need tomorrow morning."

The call ended and Baldo walked to the front of Emilio's as requested to meet Antonio.

"I just called in. I'm to look around another thirty minutes, then I'm ready for that beer. Are you ready?"

"No, but I should be by then. My guys will be here in fifteen minutes. We'll talk, then I'll see if there's anything more for tonight. Why don't you go over to Rembrandt's Bar when you're done and save me a place? I'll be there when I'm done."

Café Rembrandt, a whiskey, wine and rum bar, catered primarily to locals. The authentic Dutch pub run by Marjan, Ben and Marcella was nearby in Madame Estate.

Baldo left for his final look around while Antonio waited for his troops to return. Fifteen minutes later, Antonio was getting the report from his men.

"We saw nothing. Nobody naked was walking around or spotted hiding out. We didn't see anybody carrying a package. What do you want us to do?"

"Go on home. I'll call you if I need you."

The men were glad their night had ended and merrily left from Emilio's restaurant. Antonio called in to give his report.

"We've not spotted anything, so I just sent the men home. I have some ideas about how to find what you're looking for. Let me think on it some more tonight, and I'll keep looking. It might take me a few days, but I'm optimistic I'm going to find what you want."

"Okay, let's keep in touch. Call me tomorrow."

The call was disconnected, and Antonio walked to his car. He would think more on how to track the man who had escaped with the prize. But tonight, it was time to have a few beers with his friend Baldo.

TWELVE

LISA WOKE UP at 7:00 a.m. It had been a night that she would always remember. The crazy excursion she had invited herself on with Paul had been more than either she or Paul had anticipated. After Jason and Lekha came to their rescue and their visit ended, Lisa whisked Paul into the bedroom. She was exhausted but exhilarated when she awoke. She looked over at Paul, who was still sleeping soundly. She would let him recover for several more hours before waking him.

She walked into the living room and turned on the television. Although tempted to call Lekha, she instead sent her a text message inviting her to call when convenient. With daylight, Lisa felt some embarrassment about all that had been revealed to Lekha and Jason the prior night. Despite the embarrassment, she liked having a female friend with whom she could openly share her innermost thoughts, and believed Lekha was becoming that friend. She hoped Lekha would soon call her and feel that same way.

Lisa sat mindlessly looking out over the ocean at Cupecoy Beach. Her phone vibrated with an incoming text message. Hopeful it was from Lekha, she was nonetheless pleased to see it was from Karen asking her to call.

Lisa immediately called Karen.

"Good morning, Lisa, I'm glad you're up."

"Good morning, Karen. I'm happy to hear from you this morning. Does this mean you're back in St. Maarten?"

"Yes, Rick and I are back. I'd like to get together with you sometime today if you're available. I'm thinking it would be good for a few of us to get together, talk about ideas for having the wedding the way Debi will want, and then we can give her our ideas. She and Dean should be back late tonight."

"Okay, I'm available any time today. Do you have anyone else in mind?"

"Yes, Debi's good friend Jodi, who was on island when Debi met Dean, and Terri, who spent a lot of time with Debi during that same time, are both here. Maybe we could all meet today, and then meet again with Debi tomorrow. Is that good for you?"

"Yes, just let me know when and where. I'll be available and will wait to hear back from you."

"Thanks. I'll check with Jodi and Terri now and will call you back in a few."

The girls ended the call. Karen placed calls to Jodi and Terri, who agreed to meet at 10:00 a.m. They would meet at the beach, the best place on the island for fun as well as a common place to discuss business.

Karen called Lisa back.

"Jodi and Terri will meet us today at ten. Is that okay with you?"

"Sure, where are we meeting?"

"I suggested we meet at the beach. I know you and I consider Cupecoy as our favorite beach, but Jodi and Terri are more Orient Beach people. I hope you don't mind, but I set the beach at the Perch as our meeting spot."

"That's great with me. I do love Cupecoy, and it's very convenient for me, but I also love Orient. I'll be happy to meet at ten."

They ended their second phone call of the day.

Lisa prepared a beach bag and waited for Paul to wake up before leaving. At 9:00 a.m. she heard him stirring.

"Good morning, sweetie," she whispered as she walked into the bedroom and sat on the edge of the bed.

"Good morning yourself. You look refreshed this morning."

Lisa smiled broadly. "I am. That was quite a night, and I'm not referring to the trip down the mountain."

"Yes, it was," agreed Paul. "But I think I'm ready to face the day now."

"Yes, it's a beautiful morning. I just got off the phone with Karen and she wants to meet about Debi's wedding. I agreed to meet her, Jodi and Terri at Orient at ten. It will probably be late afternoon before I'm back."

"That's fine, I'm sure you'll have a great time with them. I don't think I need to say this, but you know not to mention anything about last night, right?"

"Oh yes, I definitely know to mention nothing from last night to anybody. If asked, I'll just share we had dinner in."

"That's good. I need to do some thinking on what to do next. I may alter the plan to take the artifact to the museum curator. I'm not sure what's best, but I want to take some steps this morning in case whoever we saw on the mountain last night finds out we were there."

"Okay, I'll have my phone with me as always. If there's anything you think I should do, or if you think I need to come home early, just call me. Otherwise, I will be partying a bit with the girls."

"Have fun. And no matter how tempting, as the partying is underway, remember, nothing about last night."

"I've got it."

She leaned over and kissed Paul on the cheek before standing.

"I'm heading out now. See you late this afternoon."

THIRTEEN

PAUL PULLED HIMSELF out of bed as Lisa drove to Orient Beach. After the wild night at the Flying Dutchman, Paul had concerns. He called his new client, Augustus, to try to better understand what had happened.

"Paul, I've been waiting to hear from you. Have you gotten the artifact?"

"Augustus, I made the trip up the mountain. We can talk about the artifact in a bit, but I have some questions for you that I need answers to before we begin discussing your mission again."

Augustus could tell from Paul's tone that there was a problem.

"Okay, what's wrong?"

"Are you where no one can overhear you?"

"Yes, sure. I'm by myself, no one's around. I can talk freely without being heard."

"Here's what's happened. I went up to the mountaintop as you requested. On my way up, I saw I was not alone. I can't be certain as to how many there were, but it looked like there were five men following me up the mountain. How do you explain that?"

"I don't know anything about that. That makes no sense to me."

"Well, who have you been talking to? It sure seems someone besides me was expecting to find something of value. Either that, or they were hoping I would find something of value and follow me to get it. What have you been saying and who have you been talking to?"

"I promise I've told no one about our conversations."

"But did you tell anyone about an artifact? That you found an artifact?"

"Not exactly."

"What does that mean?"

"I promise I've said nothing to tie you to helping me. I did say to a couple of buddies that I thought I may have found some valuable relics and that I might be cashing in soon. You know, just general stuff where alcohol may have had me bragging a little. But I never said anything about you. I never mentioned your name."

"Okay, I believe you. I need to know who is interested in your find and how they knew to go up that mountain."

"That I don't know."

Paul pressed on, knowing there was more to the story.

"Well, you give it some thought. You said alcohol was involved. Were you in a bar when you were talking about what you found?"

"I was in Rembrandt's. I was talking to a couple of close buddies. I know them like brothers, they wouldn't do anything like you've described. I'm certain of that."

"When was this?"

"A few nights ago."

"Who else was at the bar?"

"I don't know. The usual group, I guess. There's always some businessmen there, but I didn't mention anything to any of them. It was just shop talk with my buddies. We got off work, went to Rembrandt's and had some beers. We do that sometimes, you know. It's what we do."

"How close were the others to your group?"

"Not that close."

"All right. Here's what I think. I think you went to Rembrandt's, had some beers, were blowing off steam, and shared with your buddies that you were going to cash in on some valuable stuff you found. Maybe you even gave a timeline as to when and where it would be retrieved. You thought you were just talking to your buddies, but maybe the beer had you talking a little louder than you remember, and one of those suits at the bar heard you, or heard enough to fill in the pieces. I think he had a lookout at the Flying Dutchman, and could have seen me going up the mountain. It wouldn't be too much of a jump in logic to think I was going up the mountain to retrieve what you were bragging about. Why else would I be going up the mountain at night when the attraction was closed? Do you think that's possible?"

"I guess it's possible, but I don't think that happened."

"You could be right. It might not have happened that way. You've not told me your plan. I know there must be more to it than I take the artifact to the museum curator, and if it is determined to be genuine, you'll donate it to the museum. I've been thinking about that and why you would do that. There are more artifacts where you found that one, aren't there?"

"Why do you say that?"

"So, there are more. If you want my help, now is the time to tell me everything. Otherwise, I put the artifact back where I found it and you can hire someone else to help you."

"Okay, here's the deal. You're right, I did find more artifacts. In fact, a lot of artifacts. I want to get all of them, but I can't because of where they are and I won't be able to remove them without being seen. I need someone else to help me with that. But before I do that, I need to know they're real. If the museum says they're real, then I can get the rest of the goods and sell them at a high price to a collector. That's my whole plan, I promise. I need you to keep me as anonymous, have the museum say the statue is real, then I plan to remove the rest of the items found and sell them for a lot of money. So now that I've told you everything, are you going to help me?"

"Maybe. I could be wrong on my first guess on what happened last night. If I'm wrong, my next guess is you said more to your buddies than you told me. In addition to telling of finding something of value, you may have said where you hid it for someone. Maybe said something like you couldn't be seen with it and that you arranged for someone to get it. Maybe even said a night it would happen. If you want me to help you, you've got to remember now. If I think you're lying to me, I put the artifact back."

There was a long pause.

"Okay, here's the deal. I told my buddies that I found what I thought was valuable antique stuff. You know, one buddy bragging to another. But they didn't believe me. They said they've heard crap like that before and laughed at me."

"That made me mad. I told them that they'd see and because they were giving me a hard time, I might not share any of my newfound wealth. They continued to laugh. That's when I may have told them to keep their ears open, they'd hear for themselves soon enough, that I had someone going to retrieve it from the mountaintop last night."

Paul was not surprised with the story he finally was able to pull out of Augustus.

"That explains why there were people there. One of the businessmen in the bar must have heard you and arranged for an expedition of his own up the mountain last night. Knowing someone else was also planning to get it, he sent more than one or two in case they were second to arrive, and could take the item from whoever beat them to it. It all makes sense now."

"So will you still help me?"

"I'll help you, but I might need to change the plan a little bit. Let me think about it."

Augustus was not pleased with Paul's response.

"Look, I just came clean with you. I'm sorry. I didn't give your name like I said all along. I need to know if you're going to help me."

"I said I would, but there might be a change of plans. If that's not good enough, I'll put the thing back where I found it, I'll tell no one, and you're free to do whatever you want."

"Okay, okay, let me know if you change the plan. But I need to get this done quickly. If someone does know what's going on, they might be coming after me soon."

"That's right, so I might need to change the plan. Let me think about it some more. I'll be in touch soon."

Paul disconnected the call. He did a little research and found that reproductions of Arawak artifacts began being displayed in Anguilla in 2021. The artifacts were hand sculpted by an Anguillian artist. A collection of the items that were made would also be available for purchase by the public at a cost of $1,500 per item.

Paul placed a call to the museum to inquire about the possible production of an artifact not on display. He was referred to a sculptor, Marcus Richards. Paul sent several photos of the artifact uncovered by Augustus to Marcus, who negotiated a price to have a clay replica created within two days. Paul would make the quick trip to Anguilla to pick up the reproduction when it was ready.

Paul placed another call, this one to Nico.

"Nico, I have an urgent project. Would you be able to help me later today?"

"Jenny and I are meeting Ben and Lauren at the beach this morning. We'll finish up with them and can be available sometime beginning around three o'clock. Is that too late?"

"No, that works fine. Will your boat be ready for a quick trip to Anguilla?"

"It's always fueled and ready."

"Great, I need you to take a friend to Anguilla this afternoon. I'll call you back with the details.

Paul disconnected with Nico and placed another call to Augustus.

"Augustus, here's the new plan. You're leaving the island this afternoon. I'll arrange for you to take a quick trip to Anguilla. I have a place you can stay there, and you'll need to be there for a few days. I'll let you know when it's safe for you to return."

"I can't go to Anguilla today. I'm due back at work in the morning. If I don't show up, it will be proof that something's going on."

"The people who matter already know something is going on. You can call from Anguilla if you want to say you're sick and can't come in. That's up to you. But if you go in, you could end up worse than sick."

"All right, tell me how it's going to happen."

Paul went through the details with Augustus of his boat trip to Anguilla before sharing the next part of his plan.

"You need to tell me exactly where the rest of the artifacts are."

"What are you going to do with that information if I give it to you?"

"You want to get rich off your find, don't you? Well, the more details you tell me, the better chance you'll be rich."

Paul continued asking questions until he was satisfied that he had all the information he was going to get. After ending the call with Augustus, he called Nico back with instructions where to pick up Augustus and where to drop him in Anguilla.

With that part of the plan final, it was time to give more thought to keeping Lisa safe while getting the artifacts out of their hiding place.

FOURTEEN

BEN AND LAUREN had a delightful dinner with Nico and Jenny, and all agreed to meet the next day at Orient Beach.

Before 8:00 a.m. the next morning Ben woke Lauren with a kiss. They prepared for the beach, packing towels, books and a small cooler of rum punch, and dressed in t-shirts and shorts for a breakfast stop on the way.

Their favorite breakfast restaurant was the Croissant Royal in the Marigot Marina Royale. Marigot was a short seven-minute drive from their villa.

"Ben, it's great to be back at the Croissanterie," she said as they walked to the restaurant.

"Yes, it's like home here."

The owner, who would also be their waitress, saw them walk into the open-air area of the restaurant and select a table. Less than five minutes later she delivered their standard breakfast of chocolate croissants and raisin bread.

"I love that in addition to remembering us, she also remembers our breakfast order. Not only is the food the best, she makes me feel so welcomed here. This has been a real prize that I'm not sure many tourists would spot here in the marina."

Ben nodded his agreement as he took a bite of his croissant.

"And of course, when we finish eating, I'd like to start the shopping part of my trip with my first visit to Boutique Ananas next door. You know I can always use an extra island sarong or two."

"Of course, I definitely know that," Ben responded lovingly. "I like playing with the owner's bichon in addition to seeing you so happy shopping. And, as convenient as it is, it minimizes shopping time we would spend elsewhere, which will add to time available for the beach."

"I'm glad you like it too," Lauren responded, choosing not to acknowledge Ben's primary reason of agreeing, which was to minimize time spent shopping.

They enjoyed looking out over the marina as they finished their breakfast. As had also become their custom with encouragement from Ben, Lauren delivered their payment and tip to the service counter without waiting for the bill to be delivered. The owner grinned and waved to Ben, and he followed Lauren to her favorite shop.

Lauren was immediately drawn to a rack of pareos.

"What do you think about this one?" Lauren held the colorful wrap up for Ben's assessment.

"I think it's great."

"It is. You may not have noticed, but it's the right size. It's a little larger than average which will make it easier to make into a dress."

"Oh sure, I can see that," he teasingly agreed. "Why do you think I told you so quickly that it's great?"

"I'm sure it had nothing to do with you wanting to get to the beach," she replied, playfully returning the banter. "Don't worry, I'm almost ready. I'm also eager to get to the beach."

After a few more minutes of shopping, Lauren carried her purchases of two pareos and several bars of scented soap to their car. Ben drove them along the waterfront in Marigot and through Grand Case to reach their destination.

Orient Beach, a beautiful crescent of white sand over a mile long, is the most famous of beaches in French Saint Martin. Its clothing optional status invites seasoned naturists as well as curiosity seekers to sun and swim in the crystal-clear water. The wide assortment of casual restaurants and bars offering exceptional quality at reasonable prices helps beachgoers stay on Orient Beach as their destination for the full day.

Ben parked in the dirt lot at the entrance to the Perch Restaurant. Its food and drinks served to those who wished to not dress for the day was largely responsible for the greater number of sunbathers in that area of the beach.

"It's great to be back at my favorite beach. I'm looking forward to spending a little time with Jenny and Nico today. We didn't see them much on our last trip."

"Yes, it's great to be back. If you'll carry our towels, I can get the cooler and beach bag."

Lauren led Ben to the chairs she wanted that were set up on the beach. She tossed a towel on a chair for Ben and tucked hers in the slats of her lounger.

"This is the life. Now, time for the sun."

Lauren undressed to her bikini, putting her t-shirt and shorts in the beach bag. She then removed her swimsuit and placed it in the bag as well.

"I'm putting the bag on the chairs next to us to save them for Jenny and Nico."

Ben undressed and handed his shorts and t-shirt to Lauren. She placed them in the bag with her clothes.

They blended in with the great majority of beachgoers taking full advantage of the clothing-optional status of the beach.

Reclining in their chairs, they basked lazily in the warm Caribbean sun.

"Ben, this is the best. Our first full day on the island, and what a beautiful one it is. Light breeze, warm sun and beautiful water."

"Do you want to dip in?"

"I think I'll let the sun bake me for a while first. Sand gravity has taken control of my body."

Lauren held her hand out and looked admiringly at her engagement ring, mesmerized by the exceptional sparkle emitted in the sunlight.

"But if you'd like to take a short walk, I can stop staring at my ring and go with you."

"No, I'm content to hang here. I'm glad you like it. We've got plenty of time for a walk later."

"Yep, I'm good sitting back and enjoying the view for a while. It's everything I want. Do you want me to grab your book for you?"

"No, I'm good. I'm just going to lay back and be part of the beach scene. I may not spend the energy to read today."

They sunned blissfully for the next hour when Ben saw Nico and Jenny walking on the beach toward them.

"Hey guys, we finally made it," Jenny called out. "It looks like you saved us chairs."

"Glad you're here," Lauren responded. She moved her beach bag for Jenny and Nico to place their towels. "It's great to see you this morning."

The four greeted with hugs, with Jenny and Nico taking their chairs, Jenny next to Lauren.

"Jenny, thank you again for everything you and Nico did to get the villa ready for us."

"Yes, thank you both very much," added Ben. "We'll try to keep it looking fairly nice for Debi's wedding. Thanks for volunteering to help get it ready for Debi and Dean's big day on the island."

"I'm planning to come over to help clean Friday afternoon to make sure everything will be ready," responded Jenny.

"Great. We'll do anything we can to help, also. We're just glad we're not in charge," added Lauren.

"Debi and Dean are flying back into St. Maarten. I don't know what's expected or proper, but once Karen has finalized the plans with Debi, I'll be around to help as needed," offered Jenny.

"I'm sure they'll appreciate that. Just treat the villa as yours and come over any time and do whatever you need to do. Ben and I will stay out of the way."

"Ben, listening to all that wedding talk has made me thirsty," laughed Nico. "Do you have any rum punch in that cooler?"

"Yes, Nico, I do. Come on over. It's time we break it out."

Ben poured a cup of rum punch for Nico, then encouraged Lauren and Jenny to join in. The four of them enjoyed rum punch at their chairs until they would walk to a local restaurant for lunch.

"It's after noon and I'm hungry. Is anybody else ready for lunch?" asked Lauren.

Jenny looked at Nico, saw he was ready, and stood.

"We're ready. Where do you guys want to eat?"

"What about Orange Fever? I'd like a pizza. Is that good with everybody?"

"Pizza it is. Sounds good to me," agreed Nico.

They dressed in swimsuits for the short walk and entered the open-air restaurant with the orange umbrellas and chairs with orange cushions on its beachfront. The waiter gave them their choice of tables and handed them menus. Fifteen minutes later they were devouring their pizza.

"Ben, this has been a great outing for me. It's been too long since we got together." Nico leaned forward in his chair, taking hold of Jenny's hand.

"Yes, and I'm enjoying spending some time again with you Lauren," added Jenny.

"As much fun as we're having, I'm going to need to be leaving early today. I have a special work project this afternoon at three o'clock for a mutual friend. I received his last-minute call this morning. But I'll be helping Jenny get the villa ready for the wedding. Hopefully, Jenny and I can get with you guys again soon."

"That would be great," responded Ben. "When we get back to the chairs, I hope you'll have time for another rum punch before you go."

"Absolutely."

The early lunch ended, and they walked back to their chairs. Ben poured another round of rum punch for the group, and they toasted to another beautiful day in St. Maarten. Nico and Jenny left the beach within the hour, with Nico to go to Anguilla for Paul, leaving Ben and Lauren to enjoy the afternoon sun without them.

FIFTEEN

LISA ARRIVED AT Orient Beach. She was fifteen minutes early, but the friends she was meeting were already there. She walked over to the empty beach lounger they were holding for her.

"Good morning, everyone. It's great to see everybody."

Lisa's friends hopped up and greeted her with hugs.

She set her beach towel on her chair, undressed as had her friends, and placed her clothes in her beach bag.

The girls formed a small huddle, with Karen moving to sit on the foot of Lisa's chair and Jodi perching on the end of Terri's chair.

"I'm really excited that you guys could be here this morning. Debi is scheduled to fly in tonight. Of course, we want to do whatever Debi wants for her wedding. She planned her entire wedding in Orillia, which was amazingly beautiful, by the way, but she told me she wants this to be a surprise from her friends. When we finish planning today, we can decide how much to share and what to keep a secret. If you're all available tomorrow, I'd like us to meet here again but include Debi to get her reaction. If she wants to know more, we'll tell her more. But I really think she wants this as a gift, and she wants to be surprised." She paused for a deep breath. "So, our assignment is to plan a special ceremony celebrating our friendship and love for Debi and Dean. Outsiders might think that our handling the details instead of Debi and Dean is downright crazy. But that's what they want, to be surprised. It's unbelievable, but when you know them, it's really not. As beautiful and special as their wedding was in Orillia, we need to make this one just as special, her island wedding. And we all know, it's going to be a lot different from the formal wedding she just had."

They all laughed, hoping to fulfill their undertaking by having the most special, yet the most different, wedding ceremony ever held on the island.

"I talked with Debi, and the only request she had was for the photographer. She wants to use the same photographer that she used for her Orillia wedding. I know we have someone we talked to about it, but if she has someone coming, I'm thinking we can just go with her photographer. What do you think?"

They readily agreed only one photographer was needed.

"I'll call the photographer here and work it out with him. There was no commitment, but I'll pay him for the time he would have been working, so all should be fine."

"What about music? I'm not familiar with any bands other than Island Dreamers," shared Terri.

"Yes, that's who Debi and Dean had perform for the grand opening of Deb's Royal Flush. I thought we should arrange for a band. Does everybody agree?"

They all agreed that Island Dreamers was a good choice.

"I talked to Kerry and Dave of Island Dreamers a while back. They agreed to perform if we wanted them to. I think we should call them now to confirm. We can call them again later today or tomorrow to let them know how long we'll need them."

Karen called and was pleased when Kerry answered. He confirmed that he and Dave would be there. They would plan to play for several hours, but were open to stay for as long as requested. Karen promised to call him later that night to confirm all details.

"How many people do you expect to attend the wedding?" asked Jodi.

"Debi provided her list of people she wants invited. Unfortunately, everybody won't be able to make it, but we'll still probably have about seventy to seventy-five total."

"That's a great turn out. What should we do to feed all those people?" asked Lisa.

The group tossed out different types of food and different names of potential caterers. After an hour of discussion, a decision was made to take a lunch break. Lisa stood up first.

"All this talk of food has made me hungry. I suggest we go up to the Perch for a quick bite. I'm also thirsty. I can't believe it's after one o'clock and we haven't had anything yet to drink."

"Lisa, good idea," replied Terri. "We can take a break from wedding talk during lunch and give our brains a rest."

They walked over to the Perch. On their way, they saw Nico and Jenny, then noticed Ben and Lauren.

"Hey guys," called Karen. "I didn't know you were on Orient today. How long have you been here?"

"We were here early," responded Lauren. "I saw you guys all huddled together a little before ten, but everyone looked really serious. We decided not to interrupt you and walked to Orange Fever for an early lunch with Jenny and Nico."

Terri laughed. "It was a very serious discussion. We're talking about using your villa and planning the details for Debi and Dean's wedding. Instead of throwing a shower, we're throwing a wedding. Nobody's ever heard of such a thing, that's part of why it will be so special. And yes, we know we don't have much time, so that's why we were so absorbed in what we were doing. We plan to have everything decided by the end of the day today. We have the music lined up and are close to a final decision on food. We know how many to plan for, so after our lunch we'll finish picking out food and go over seating arrangement, position of the band, and that kind of stuff. We should have everything planned and calls made to start putting it in place no later than tonight."

"Sounds good. We're glad to help after you've made everything final. Any time you want to come over to the villa, or have others that need to be there, just do it. You know where the key is."

"Thanks," responded Karen. "After lunch, we'll finish our planning. But before the day ends, how about coming over and joining us for a drink?"

"We'll be there," answered Ben. "Enjoy your lunch break and we'll see you guys later this afternoon."

The four wedding planners sat at a picnic table in front of the Perch building. They began with a glass of white wine while they decided on their lunch. When the wine was brought, each ordered fish and a salad.

"Looks like we're dieting to go to a wedding," kidded Karen. "Cheers to great St. Martin friends."

Clinking their glasses, they toasted, and not long after, their food arrived. Thirty minutes later, they were on their way back to their chairs carrying to-go cups of wine.

"All right," began Karen. "Let's get this planning finished."

They discussed at length, and after two hours of thrashing out all the ideas, they agreed they were done. They were excited about what was expected to be Debi's second incredibly memorable wedding.

"It's time to celebrate," announced Karen. She looked over to where Lauren and Ben were reclining. "I'm going to invite them to come join us. I'll be right back."

Ben saw Karen as she approached.

"Hey, does your coming this way mean you're done?" called Ben.

"It sure does. We'd love for you two to join us as we celebrate. Where are Nico and Jenny?"

"They had to go, but we're ready to come over."

Lauren and Ben hopped out of their chairs and walked with Karen to the group.

"I understand congratulations are in order, that the planning is complete. Give me your drink order and I'll get everyone a round. Lauren, will you help me carry the drinks?"

"Sure, what's everybody drinking?"

"We've been drinking white wine," answered Terri. "I'll stick with that."

The others decided to continue with wine as well. Ben placed the order for five cups of wine and a pina colada for himself. The group cheered when he and Lauren were back and handed out the drinks.

"All right, have a seat. Let us tell you all about what we have planned," offered Karen.

"We're all ears, aren't we Ben?"

Ben nodded, also interested to hear, but not as enthusiastically as Lauren.

"That's good, because the plans include you and Lauren. And there will be some special entertainment that we think Debi will love."

Karen continued as the primary speaker for the group, and with a few additional comments from the others, shared all the wedding plans.

"You guys have been listening very intently. What do you think?"

"That's a great question," responded Ben. "I need to think about this. While I'm thinking, I have a question for you." He paused, assessing each of their faces. "How much did you have to drink when you finalized these plans?" he smiled.

"What do you mean by that?" asked Terri. "Don't you think Debi will love everything? I sure hope so!"

"Yes, I hope so too. Are you planning to go through all of it with her like you did for Lauren and me?"

"No. We'll ask her, but she already told us that she doesn't want to know everything," responded Karen. "She wants to be surprised. I'm guessing Dean feels the same way, but if he doesn't, I'm sure Debi will let him know that he does, if you know what I mean?"

"Yes," Ben laughed. "Debi can be very persuasive, especially with Dean. Lauren, what do you think?"

"I think they've done a great job planning. It will be an honor for me to participate, and I'm sure Debi will have an amazing time. And she should, it's her wedding, and all of her special friends will be here."

The drinks were polished off quickly and Lauren sent Ben to the bar for another round. Instead of joining in, his participation for the remainder of the day would be serving drinks to the others.

"I'll help you bring them back this time," offered Jodi, as she stood up and stretched. "Lauren, take my chair. I'll take good care of your fiancé. We'll be right back."

Jodi and Ben were back quickly. A few toasts later, all the cups were again empty.

Terri held up her cup.

"I'll have another. I'm staying right here on the beach at La Playa. If anybody wants to stay the night with me, you're welcome to, so keep me company with another if you will."

The drinks were consumed and refreshed in quick succession.

"In addition to Terri's offer, I'll be happy to drive anybody back," offered Ben. "I'm done drinking for the day, so I'll be good to drive. So, drink up if you like, I'll be your personal Uber."

The planning committee plus Lauren had one more cup of wine before ending the day. With that, their day of celebrating on Orient Beach came to an end.

SIXTEEN

WHEN LEKHA NOTICED Lisa's text message she was already in DK Gems helping set out the jewelry for the day. Although eager to talk to Lisa, she knew she could not speak as freely as she would like with the others around. She sent a text message explaining her situation and that she looked forward to calling her tonight.

While Lekha was setting up the store for the day, Antonio was out trying to get a lead on the naked people who got away with the artifact. He called Wendall Thomas to tell him he was still working on the job.

"I'm back in the area of the Flying Dutchman. I'll be checking the area for any signs of whoever got away last night."

"I'm glad you're working on it, but what have you got planned?"

Antonio chose not to share that he found clothes bundled on the zip line.

"I'll look around, most likely whoever took it is long gone, but I'll check for a while just in case. Then I'll check with some of the nearby stores. Some might have cameras, too. See if they have the same people working as last night, see what they saw. If there are different people working, I'll find out when last night's workers will be back, probably tonight, and check again."

"That's good. Keep me posted. Do you want me to send some people out to help you?"

"It would be good to have some help, but I don't think so. This is a delicate matter. I can't just go in and ask if they saw somebody running away with stolen goods. I got to use some sense on getting the information. I don't think the guys you had out here with me last night will be good for this work. I recommend you save them for when I find where the package disappeared to. They might be the muscle you want to get it back. But first, let me find where it is. Once I find it, if I need help getting it, I'll let you know."

"Okay, stay in touch. Let me know when you have something for me. I need this quickly, and when you get it for me, there will be an extra reward for you."

"Yes sir, you can count on me."

The call ended and Antonio was pleased. He would find the artifact, get bonus money, and firmly establish that he was invaluable to his employer.

Antonio began searching the area, along the foliage and into the woods, on the off chance that the package was ditched to be picked up later. After several hours of looking, he was fully convinced that whoever took the artifact was no longer around, and neither was the package. Antonio began canvassing the local businesses. Certainly, somebody saw two naked people last night.

By early afternoon, he was satisfied that he had covered most of the businesses that might be of help. Several of the businesses had a different shift of employees working instead of those on duty the prior night. He would return to those businesses later after the night-shift employees were back at work.

SEVENTEEN

PLEASED WITH THE call he received from Antonio, Wendall Thomas was nevertheless eager to do more to find the artifact. He called Baldo.

"Baldo, I trust you slept well last night and are ready to resume the search for the missing package."

"Yes sir, I'm ready, just tell me what you want me to do."

"I appreciate you going right away last night when I called. I described the size of what we're looking for, but I didn't tell you what was in the package. This is top secret, and you must tell no one. Do you agree to do that?"

"That's not a problem. If I told secrets, Mr. Harrington would not have me as his top man. Tell me more."

"Very well. The object is an artifact, a very old statue. Even I have not seen it. I have merely heard it described. It is a primitive looking statue made out of clay. It is a strange looking naked man. That's the best description I can give you."

"Okay."

"Have you heard anyone talking about something like this? Something that is old and could be something one might see in a history museum?"

"No, I'm sure I haven't talked to anyone or heard anybody talking about history or a museum."

"All right," responded Wendall, frustrated with Baldo's response. "I didn't think you would hear anything about a history museum, but I want to know if you've heard anyone talking about a figurine, or a statue, or some kind of art or carving, that they thought was old and valuable."

"No sir, I haven't heard any of those things."

Wendall hesitated, not sure if he should continue along this line in his search for the missing artifact. Knowing Baldo was of limited intelligence, and that he might unwittingly say something to complicate matters, he still moved forward, as his desire to find the artifact outweighed his concerns about Baldo.

"Here's what you can do for me. Do you know any of the guys who work at the Flying Dutchman?"

"Yes, sure."

"Do you ever talk with them, have a beer with them, that sort of thing?"

"Sometimes."

"What I'd like you to do is call one or two of them, see if you can meet them for lunch. Ask them how work is going, you know, shoot the breeze. Maybe they'll volunteer something about what went missing."

"Okay, I can do that. Do you want me to ask them if they know about this missing statue?"

"No, whatever you do, don't do that. If they know something about it, they'll likely bring it up. It would be big to them and most likely they'll share without you mentioning it. If they do mention it, don't ask any questions, just listen to what they say and then call me. They may know where it is."

"Okay, I can do that. So, all you want me to do is go to lunch, listen to what they say, then call you and tell you about it?"

"That's right."

"All right, I'll call you later."

Wendall ended the less than satisfying call. He knew it was a longshot, but he wanted to do all he could without delay to locate the missing artifact.

Wendall knew he had made several mistakes. He listened to the bar conversation at Rembrandt's, heard about the artifact, and believed that it was to be retrieved from the mountaintop bar at the Flying Dutchman. His first mistake was being late in getting the relic. It had taken too long to organize the group charged with bringing it down for him. His second mistake was not finding out the name of the man bragging about his plan to get rich. He would try to remedy that himself. He would go back to Rembrandt's for a drink early evening and inquire of the bartender. Perhaps he was a regular that Wendall had not taken note of before, and if so, the chances the bartender could identify him were greatly improved.

EIGHTEEN

SYLVIE AND BRAD'S trip on his sailboat was coming to a close as they pulled into the protected water off of Orient Beach in late afternoon.

"It's so good to be back. Brad, did you have enough sailing to be content back on land for a while?"

"Yes, I'm glad to be back, too. I did enjoy our time away though, and when you're ready, you know I'll sail you away from here again."

"I know, and I love your willingness to do what pleases me. You're the best."

"Why don't we celebrate tonight? We can get dressed up and take the boat over to Big Fish for dinner."

"That sounds perfect. Should we call some of our friends to see if any of them can meet us there? I know it's last minute, but probably a couple of them could make it."

"We could do that if you'd like. I'm thinking, though, of a romantic dinner for the two of us, unless all this time on the boat has you wanting to see some friends."

"No, I love your idea. We have plenty of time for friends. I'm sure we'll see some of them on the beach tomorrow. Before we go, I want to call in to Paul. I think everything is going okay, but I have a payment on my debt that's about to come due. I'll be able to relax and enjoy the meal more if Paul tells me I have plenty of money to make the payment," she grinned.

"You've turned into a worrier, but I like that you're keeping track and have taken more interest in the running of your business. Give him a call, then we'll get ready to go."

Sylvie called Paul, but instead of answering, he sent a message that he was on the phone and would call her right back. Sylvie was showering when he returned her call.

"Hey Paul, it's Brad. Sylvie will be out of the shower in just a minute, but I can tell you why she called."

"Sure, I hope everything is okay with you two."

"Oh yes, we're well. In fact, we're planning to have a little celebration tonight, celebrating that we've just made it back to St. Martin, and celebrating life in general. How are you and Lisa?"

"We're doing well, thanks. Now that you guys are back, we'll have to get together soon."

"For sure. Let me tell you why Sylvie called. She thinks a debt payment is about to come due. She wants to know how she's doing financially and making sure she'll be able to make the payment."

"Yes, everything is under control. I can give her an update on how she's doing."

"Great. Sylvie's stepping out of the shower now. Hold on and I'll get her."

"Sylvie, it's Paul." He handed Sylvie her phone as she walked towards him toweling herself dry.

"Hey, Paul. Thanks for calling me back. We just made it to St. Martin thirty minutes ago and I wanted to check in with you."

"Yes," Paul interrupted. "Brad was just telling me that. You're right, a payment is about to be due, and everything is set for it. You have plenty of money for it, but I would like to get with you sometime soon to go over the business. Maybe we could have Ben join us for an update from his investment firm, too, to give you a complete picture."

"That would be great, thanks."

"Okay, I'll set something up. I'm glad you called. I was thinking about trying to reach you anyway."

"Really? Okay, that's intriguing. What's going on that you would call me?"

"I have a small business opportunity for you. It's not worth millions, but it could still be substantial. Are you interested in hearing more?"

"You know I am. I had an opportunity from Wendall that he promised could be worth several million dollars, but I still don't completely trust him. And besides, I think it was going to be a long, drawn-out project. That scared me, too much time for something to go wrong."

"Well, this one will be quick. Why don't you and Brad go and enjoy your dinner, and then you call me back. It will give me a little more time to get my plan organized."

"I definitely will. This gives us something else to celebrate at dinner. Thanks Paul, I'll call you later tonight."

Sylvie ended the call and looked at Brad.

"Paul has a business opportunity he wants to discuss. What do you think?"

"I know nothing about whatever he has cooked up, but you and I totally trust Paul. If it's something he recommends, I'm guessing it's a go."

"That's what I'm thinking. One more reason to celebrate tonight."

Sylvie approached Brad, giving him a big hug while letting her towel drop to the floor.

"I'm all clean from my shower. Why don't I help you with yours?"

Their dinner plans and a call back to Paul were happily delayed.

NINETEEN

IT WAS A busy day at DK Gems International. Five cruise ships were in port, and a steady stream of new and repeat customers were shopping for jewelry. At 4:30 p.m. the traffic in the store quieted down.

Lekha, finally getting a minute to breathe, smiled over at Jason.

"It's been a busy day. I think I'll go home now. I'm thinking of resting a bit, then I'll fix dinner."

"That sounds good. I think the rush is over. I'll be home right after I help close up."

"Great, I'll be looking for you. Dinner will be ready when you get home."

Lekha stepped out to her car and was home within a few minutes. She changed out of her work clothes and remembered to call Lisa. When Lisa did not answer, she left a message that she was home and could talk.

She sat back in her recliner with her feet propped up after a long day of standing. She thought back over the encounter with naked Lisa and Paul and a smile involuntarily filled her face. Not only had it been a crazy night, but she had also immensely enjoyed her time with

Lisa and hearing the far-fetched tale from Paul. With her head back, she closed her eyes and dozed off.

She was awakened by the sound of Lisa's incoming call.

"Hey Lisa, thanks for calling me back. How's your day been?"

"It's been an amazing day. One of my good friends, Debi, was recently married, but is having an island wedding on Saturday. But you already know that, you're invited to the wedding. But anyway, a few of us are in charge of planning it, and we met on Orient Beach today. We got it planned and had a blast while we were there. There was a lot of drinking while we were having fun, and I'm just getting in. How was your day?"

"It was another busy day in town. With five cruise ships in port, we were slammed all day. It was a great day, and some of my favorite customers who have become friends were in visiting. It was fun but I'm tired. I haven't had anything to drink today, but think I will have a glass of wine while I'm preparing dinner."

"Sounds like you could use a drink. I've had plenty but I am still tempted to have another. I must not have had too much, though, since I'm using discretion to not have any more for a while," she laughed.

"Wish I had been with you on Orient today. I'm sure you had a great time. Maybe we could plan a beach trip sometime."

"That sounds phenomenal. I'd love it. I'm glad my antics last night didn't scare you off to where you'd be afraid to be around me anymore."

"No, absolutely not. In fact, that's why I'm glad you sent me a text message this morning. I was afraid that my reaction might have scared *you* off. I'm so glad it didn't."

"No, I know that with everything that went down, some of it was over the top. Some way over the top, like when I pulled my dress off and was naked again before you guys were even out the door."

"I loved it. I won't lie, I was a little embarrassed and not sure how to react, but at the same time, I admire that you were able to do it. That's so foreign to me, I couldn't have pulled it off, so to speak," she snickered. "I think it would be good for me to spend more time around you. You're a successful businesswoman, but still can have what I'd call uninhibited fun."

"You don't know how relieved I am to hear that. I was thinking how much I enjoyed having someone to confide in. I have a lot of friends who are also uninhibited as you put it, and I have a great time with them. But last night I wasn't just having fun, I was speaking from the heart. I don't know if I can explain it any other way. My other friends are great, I wouldn't trade them for anything, but I just felt a connection last night, and I hadn't been drinking."

"Same here. I'm glad we're in agreement. Now, for the other part about last night, I thought you and Paul would like knowing that nothing unusual happened today. Nobody came around asking any questions, not that I thought they would."

"Good. Nothing came up with me today, either, and I'm guessing the same with Paul, or he would have let me know. We'll keep being cautious, and hopefully nothing will ever come up about last night. That will be a relief."

"Well, Jason will be home soon, and I promised him I'd have dinner ready when he got here. I should probably go, fix my glass of wine, and start dinner."

"Okay, I don't want our new friendship to create any problems," she said cheerfully. "Let's get together soon, and if anything comes up, I'll let you know right away."

"Same here. Give my best to Paul. I'm assuming he got your best last night," she kidded.

"You better believe it," Lisa agreed laughing. "I slept in a bit this morning and Paul was still zonked out. It was a great night. I might be wrong, but the gleam in your eye made me think you were planning a good night too."

Lekha colored and was glad Lisa could not see her reaction.

"I don't know that the intensity of my night matched yours, but I'm not complaining," she giggled. "Let's talk soon."

The girls ended the call, Lekha to begin preparing dinner, and Lisa to catch up on the day with Paul.

TWENTY

ANTONIO WAS READY to resume his search for information to identify the naked couple. It was 5:00 p.m. when he parked at Emilio's Restaurant. He decided to walk south, expanding his area to canvas, but stopped less than a mile from Emilio's to begin his night search. Although he had largely eliminated the businesses that closed before the relic was taken, he still stopped at a couple of those stores on the off chance someone had been working late.

He began at a restaurant, The Fresh Shawarma Man. When he walked in, he could tell by the arrangement of the restaurant that it was highly unlikely any of the employees would have seen anything. There was a better chance that one of the diners when leaving could have information, but he knew he could not begin hunting down customers. He talked to several of the employees, and satisfied that the restaurant was a dead end, moved on.

Antonio walked north, reaching the Shop-4-Less that would close at 6:00 p.m. Although expecting nothing helpful, he stopped for several minutes to chat with the owner. He made up a story of some dangerous motorcycle activity that night, and asked the owner if he had seen anything. The owner closed at 6:00 p.m. and was not there to see anything much after he closed. Satisfied that there was nothing to gain from any further discussion, Antonio continued northward toward Emilio's. Checking with the businesses was already becoming a tiresome process.

As Antonio left the Shop-4-Less, Wendall was pulling into the parking lot of Café Rembrandt. He took a seat at the bar and ordered a beer on tap. The bartender recognized him and called him by name.

"Wendall, what brings you back out again today? Twice in one week, what a nice surprise."

"Thanks, Marcella, you know you're my favorite bartender in my favorite bar, but I've just not been able to be out and about much lately. I'm trying to make up for lost visits," he responded with a nod. "Looks like you're here every time I come in."

"That's probably true. I'm almost always here. If someone needs an ear or a shoulder, it's likely I'll be here to listen."

"That's what I thought. You must get to know about everybody who comes in."

"Yeah, if someone comes in more than once or twice, we end up talking a little. There aren't many people who come in here who I don't know. Kind of like that old sitcom, *Cheers*."

"That's one of the reasons this is my favorite. It always feels like home. I can sit here and talk freely, and have a good time where everyone here becomes a friend, then head on home."

"Wendall, I've been tending bar for a long time. You don't really need to keep plowing a story for me. Why don't you just spit it out. Just tell me straight out what you want, and if I can help you, I will."

"Okay, fair enough. You're right, I am wanting some information. The reason I'm looking…"

"I just said, no need for any more background," the bartender interrupted. "What would you like to know?"

"A name."

"Okay, I've got lots of them. Help me give you the right one. Which knockout broad are you trying to track down?"

"I'll save that for another visit. This time I'm looking for one of your male customers, but I assure you, as a friend, no romantic interest."

That brought a hearty laugh from Marcella.

"Okay, give me a description of the handsome man you're after."

Wendall described the man and where he was sitting.

"The one who was bragging to his friends that he was about to come into great wealth?"

Wendall was ecstatic but kept a poker face. "Yes, that's the one."

"Of all the people you could ask about, you'd have to ask about him. I told you I know nearly everybody. You probably shouldn't buy a lottery ticket with this luck, though, because I don't know him."

"Shit. You really had my hopes up. I just knew you were going to give me his name."

"Sorry buddy." Marcella paused. "Because you've been pranked."

She doubled over laughing.

"You should have seen your face. Man, that made my day. Sorry for doing that to you. You were just so eager, and it was too easy not to do it. The guy comes in here pretty regular. His name is Augustus. I can even tell you about where he lives."

The two talked more and before Wendall left Rembrandt's, he had the man's full name and looked up his address.

"Thanks, my friend. I'll be in again soon."

"No, thank you. I'll be reliving that one for a few days," she said as she began laughing again. "Don't be a stranger."

As Wendall walked out of Rembrandt's, Antonio continued his search in the vicinity of Emilio's, walking into the fine dining restaurant, Mark's Place. They were open and the same wait staff was working as worked during the relic getaway time.

Antonio knew one of the waiters and began with him.

"No, sorry bro. I didn't see anything or hear about anything out of the ordinary. If somebody else working here did, I'd be surprised because I would have heard about it."

"Okay, thanks. I thought it was a longshot, but worth a try. Good seeing you man. If you do hear anything, how about letting me know. It could even be worth a little cash to you."

They bumped fists and Antonio stepped out of the restaurant. Feeling hungry from visiting the restaurants, he decided to stop at the Texaco station for a sandwich and beer. He took a couple of bites before continuing his quest.

"How are you tonight?" he asked the attendant.

"Fine," was the concise response.

"Good. This is a good sandwich and I really appreciate the beer."

The attendant merely nodded.

"I heard something really funny. I don't believe it, though. Somebody told me they saw two naked people last night around here, in public walking around. Is that not the craziest thing you ever heard?"

"Yes, it is. Not only did I hear it, I also saw it."

"No way. I have a bet that it didn't happen."

"Well, you're gonna lose your bet. I saw them. It was a man and a woman and they were right out there."

He pointed across the roundabout.

"Do you know them?"

"No, I don't know them, but they came out of the woods and hopped in a car."

"You're kidding. I don't want to lose my bet without proof. Did you see what kind of car it was?"

"Sure did."

"Well, I'll be. Tell me. I guess I'm losing this one."

"Yep, you sure are. Not only did I see the car, I know the people who picked them up."

Antonio tried to contain his excitement, keeping his voice calm.

"You know, if you're mistaken on that, I can still win my bet if it's checked out and they say it's not true."

"Oh, it's true all right. The person I saw walking over to talk to them before they got in the car is quite a looker. Her name is Lekha, lots of people would recognize her. She works at DK Gems Jewelry."

"Well, I'm feeling mighty generous. I've already lost this bet, thanks to you. But to show there's no hard feelings, let me buy you a beer. You pick it and I'm paying."

"I'll do that."

The two talked for a few more minutes before Antonio stepped out to place his call.

"Mr. Thomas, I have good news for you. I don't have the statue yet, but I know who can tell me who has it and then I'll bring it to you."

"Great job, Antonio. I have good news, too. I just found out the name and address of the person who found the artifact. Before you follow your lead, I want you to make a surprise visit tonight to the man's house. Make him tell you who has it and force him to give it to you."

Antonio agreed to the directive and Wendall gave him Augustus's description and address.

"Call me when you see him."

Wendall ended the call with Antonio. He could not believe his good fortune. In one night, he had found out who orchestrated the disappearance of the artifact, and Antonio had the name of someone else who also could identify the artifact thief. Excited about what looked to be a certainty in grabbing the artifact with the help of the bartender's information, Wendall asked for no details from Antonio. He turned his car around, parked, and went back inside.

"You're back," said the surprised bartender.

"Yes, I was just thinking, what the hell, I haven't been in here much lately. So, what's the hurry. I might as well make a night of it at Rembrandt's."

TWENTY-ONE

PAUL FINISHED HIS call with Sylvie and needed to make one more call. He called Nico and asked him for an update.

"I picked up Augustus and took him to Anguilla as planned. I didn't see anyone watching us when we boarded the boat, and no boats followed us. I think he's been delivered without anyone knowing where he is."

"Good. He could be in some danger, and if he's found, he might lead the wrong people to me. Do you think he understood the importance of staying out of sight for a couple of days?"

"I think so. The question will be more meaningful after he's had nothing go wrong, if he decides he's bored and thinks there's no harm in venturing out."

"Would you be able to check on him tomorrow? Make an unannounced stop to see what's happening and if he's staying out of sight?"

"Sure, I'll check on him mid-morning tomorrow. I'll remind him of what he needs to do."

"Thanks Nico. You're the best."

Paul heard Lisa coming in from her day at the beach while on his call to Nico. Finishing his call, he walked into the living room, saw Lisa was on her phone, waved and walked back into his office to wait for her call to end. After only a few minutes, she waltzed into his office.

"I had a wonderful day at the beach," she said, swaying slightly. "How was your day?"

"Everything is going well. I've been working on some loose ends to get rid of that statue as soon as possible. Once it's gone, our lives can resume with no worries."

Lisa walked over to Paul and gave him a hug.

"Why don't we go in the living room? Come on out of your office, enough work for today."

She led him by the hand to the living room couch. Paul sat and she snuggled up against him.

"I just got off the phone with Lekha. You'll be pleased to know her day was completely normal. Nothing about last night came up today."

"That's good to hear."

"And by the way, nothing came up at the beach either. Nobody asked about last night, and I didn't mention anything. I did good."

"I had complete confidence in you. You've never divulged anything that was not to be shared, even though you've had plenty of opportunities."

"But what I did talk about was Debi and Dean's wedding for Saturday. We've got it all planned out. We're meeting again tomorrow, this time with Debi. We'll only tell her as much as she wants to know, which won't be much, since she wants to be surprised."

"That sounds good. I'm sure you'll all have a great time welcoming Debi back."

"Is there anything I should know about what you've been working on with that relic?"

"I made some calls, and I found out what was intended as the complete plan. I'm making some changes though because now I'm sure those people coming up the mountain behind us wasn't just some random event."

"Okay, I don't want to know any details that I don't need to know."

Paul's smile communicated his appreciation for her understanding and her faith in him to go along without additional details.

"Why don't we step out to dinner? I'd like to go to Mama's if that's good with you?"

Mama Restaurant, a great Italian eatery, was nearby in Porto Cupecoy.

"That sounds perfect," agreed Lisa. "I can be ready in less than thirty minutes."

"All right, Mama's it is. When we're back, I'm expecting a return call from Sylvie. She and Brad are back. I called her and dangled a request for her participation in my project. She and Brad were going to dinner, and she's going to call me back about helping with the project after they're done."

Lisa accepted the information without asking any questions.

"Okay, I'll get ready now. I'm looking forward to our dinner."

Lisa peeled off her cover-up she had worn home from the beach. She stood wearing only a grin.

"After your call, we can continue where we left off last night," she cooed, looking back over her shoulder on her way to shower.

He watched with delight as she walked away.

"I'll keep the call brief."

TWENTY-TWO

DEBI AND DEAN were back in St. Maarten late Sunday night. They were both tired from the trip following the full day and night of entertaining friends and family members. They were home, waiting to officially start their honeymoon following the coming Saturday's ceremony.

"Are you going to the casino in the morning? I know you want to check on everything there after being away."

"I probably should. I don't want to make a full day of it, but I can spend a few hours there while you go meet your friends. I know they're excited and want to welcome you back."

"Yes, they've sent several messages that they want to meet in the morning. If you don't mind, I'll go meet them for a short while."

"Sounds good. I know you guys don't start rolling until around eleven. Why don't I plan to take care of stuff at the casino in the morning, then meet you for a late lunch on the beach, let's say one or one-thirty?"

"I would like that. I think the girls will want to see you, and I know I will."

She gave him a light kiss.

"It's late, but not too late," she whispered. "If you're not too tired."

Debi's phone began to ring.

"I'll ignore that."

"You don't need to do that. Just make it quick."

"Okay, hold that thought. I see it's Karen. This won't take long, I promise."

With her phone in hand, she continued to walk to the bedroom, undressing as she answered.

"Hey Karen, it's good to hear from you. Thank you again for going all the way to Orillia to see us get married."

"I wouldn't have missed it. It was one of the most romantic weddings and setting that I've ever seen. I loved being there."

"Thanks. I'm guessing you're calling about tomorrow morning. We just got in about five minutes ago, but we've already discussed it. Dean is going in for a few hours to handle some things at the casino, and I will be on Orient Beach bright and early. We're not thinking of it as our honeymoon yet, but Dean will be coming to the beach for a late lunch. I'll let all you girls look him over as an unavailable married man, then we might have a lunch, just the two of us."

"That sounds perfect. We're eager to see you and Dean, too. We want to make sure we give you one more chance to share any requests for Saturday. Mainly though, we just want to celebrate that our good friend is now married."

"All right, I'll see you in the morning. I don't mean to rush you off the phone, but I'm sitting here naked on the bed and I'm trying to entice Dean to pounce, but it's hard to do while I'm holding my phone."

Karen laughed. "Say no more. Have a good night, I know you will, and I'll see you tomorrow."

They ended the call.

"How was that for keeping the call quick?"

"You did good, real good. I was impressed how you could talk on the phone and undress at the same time. You have real talents."

"And that was just the beginning."

TWENTY-THREE

SYLVIE AND BRAD were back from dinner. Sylvie called Paul, who was back from Mama Restaurant in Cupecoy and eagerly waiting for her call.

"Okay, Paul. We just had a great dinner, but I must say, I was at least a little distracted wondering what you might have for me."

"Thanks for calling me back. As I mentioned, I have an unexpected opportunity that's come up. I could use your help, as well as some others you've worked with before."

"Who else are you thinking of?"

"You'd vouch for Rick and Gary who helped you on a prior project?"

"Without question, yes."

"Here's what's going on. I had an assignment that did not go well, and I'm working through what went wrong and how my plans are changing. I'm still working through the details, so I don't have much specific to tell you yet. What I can tell you is I am going to try to retrieve some valuable items. I will need to work in secret. Your role will be to help me by providing a distraction. With your help, I can get to the items without being seen. I can't promise there's no risk involved, but I think any risk to you will be minimal. If you're unsuccessful, however, I will be thwarted in getting the valuable items. You've handled yourself well in some tricky situations, and I have confidence in you."

"I can help you. When you work out your plan, tell me what you need and I'll do it."

"That's what I was hoping to hear. Once my plan is final, I'll share the details before you decide if you want to commit."

"I've signed over authority to you for millions of dollars to run my business. You've literally saved my life! I have complete confidence in you, Paul. Count me in. Now tell me about the roles for Gary and Rick."

"I want help with some physical work. That's where Gary and Rick come in, to help me retrieve the items I'm after. Nothing against Brad, but if anybody who knows you and Brad are a couple were to see the three of us, and Brad disappears with me leaving you behind, they will be on alert and the plan won't work."

"I understand."

"I'd like you to talk to Gary and Rick to see if they're interested in doing another deal. If not, I'll try to handle the physical side on my own."

"Do you want me to call them? I can call them now, they won't care, especially once they hear there's a new project for them."

"Yes, let them know there's a new project. Here's something for you that you can share; it involves the Flying Dutchman. If there's initial interest, I'll finish the plan to include them and have the details for all of you soon."

"I'm sure they'll be interested. I'll call them now and call you right back."

Paul's phone rang in less than ten minutes. "They're in."

"That's great. Expect a call tomorrow with details. If everyone is still in, we'll need to move quickly."

TWENTY-FOUR

LAUREN AND BEN had decided to have a shopping day on Monday. Ben awoke early, and at 6:30 a.m. rolled out of bed, letting Lauren sleep a bit longer. He grabbed a towel and padded out to the pool. The clear morning sky welcomed him to the new day. He slipped into the pool, the water temperature comfortable despite the early hour, and leisurely swam several laps before pausing to embrace the view of the deep green mountain vista. It was another day for celebrating life in St. Maarten.

At 7:00 a.m. hunger propelled Ben out of the pool. He quickly dried, stepped inside, and dropped his towel on the tile floor. He turned on the 70's music channel and walked back in the bedroom where Lauren was beginning to stir.

"Good morning, sleepyhead."

Lauren rubbed her eyes and reached over to check the time on her phone. Her focus shifted to Ben.

"Good morning. I see you're up early," she smiled. "Is it me or the thought of shopping in Philipsburg?"

"You know how much I love shopping," he joked, slipping back into bed, no longer thinking of breakfast.

Later that morning, showered and dressed for a day off the beach, Lauren and Ben set out for breakfast. They stopped at Croissant Royal and selected a table looking out over the marina. They watched as a Yachtline 400 puttered from a sailboat in the harbor. The couple pulled their rigid inflatable boat to the dock and tied it to two open cleats. Hopping out barefoot, they sat at a nearby table for their morning meal, bringing the total number of customers dining to ten.

Lauren looked dreamily, from the sailboat to the young couple seated nearby.

"I just love the feel of this place. We have a great life, but just look at them," she whispered. "Living on a sailboat, breakfasting barefoot in the marina, there's still more to dream about."

"I can help you achieve half your dream. Take your flip flops off and tuck them in your bag. You can take mine, too, but the sidewalks in Philipsburg might be hot."

"Ha-ha, very funny. You know what I mean."

"I do, and I see the romance and adventure they're living. It's always good to have something to aspire for. Maybe we can do a vacation sometime, get a few other couples, and rent a sailboat for a week. We can be, at a minimum, barefoot the whole time."

"If you're serious, I would like to try that sometime."

"We'll do it. After Debi and Dean finish the sailing portion of their honeymoon, we can check with them for ideas and plan a short vacation for later this year."

The Croissant Royal's owner brought them their standard breakfast and Ben and Lauren gobbled down the food in silence.

"I was famished," said Ben contentedly. "This is starting as a great day. Ready to pay and head on to Philipsburg?"

"Oh yes. I'd like to shop for a couple of hours, have some lunch on the boardwalk, then finish up at Rima's and drop in on our new friends at DK Gems. Are you sure you're okay with a day of shopping? It's a beautiful day and you might want to wait until the weather is more sketchy to be off the beach."

"No, I'm good for shopping today. When we finish, we get to go home and can spend an hour or two in our pool. I'm being serious, I think it will be great. And I do like watching you when you're in shopping mode."

"Thanks, I *knew* when I saw you first thing this morning you were thinking about shopping," she joked.

Ben smiled while nodding in mock agreement.

"Okay, let's go."

They walked to their white Corolla and Ben drove them to Philipsburg. They parked in the most eastward paved lot and hopped out.

"Ben, is there anything you want to shop for this morning?"

"No, despite any outward appearances to the contrary, I'm along for the ride. Where do you want to start?"

"I'd like to do a little clothes shopping. I don't have anything in particular I'm looking for. I just like the thought of looking around."

For the next two hours, they looked in several clothing stores, ranging from formal wear to modest t-shirt shops. They walked out of what seemed to be the hundredth store to Ben. Lauren looked appreciatively at him.

"I think I've satisfied my appetite for looking at clothes," Lauren remarked, taking pity. "Are you ready for some lunch?"

"Whenever you say is good with me. I guess I can take a short break for lunch."

They stopped at Dutch Blonde Beach Bar on the boardwalk for hamburgers and French fries. The food was good and the view was excellent.

Sitting across the table from Ben, Lauren reached over and grabbed his hand.

"All kidding aside, you've done great shopping today," commended Lauren. "Now, a stop in Rima's and then DK Gems. I really like Lekha and Jason and want to do some business with them. Then, I'll be ready to go back to our pool."

"Sounds good to me. It's time for Rima's," agreed Ben.

They started walking toward Rima Beach World, the largest resort-wear and souvenir factory outlet in St. Maarten, and one of the largest beachwear manufacturers and traders in the Caribbean. Lauren led Ben inside.

"This is where I found some cute dresses on our last trip. I'm going to look over here for a bit. Feel free to look around at some other stuff. I'll find you."

Taking the hint that Lauren did not want to feel rushed, Ben wandered away, but kept an eye on her from elsewhere in the store. He looked at souvenirs he thought friends might like. When it looked as if Lauren was winding down her dress shopping, he wandered back toward her. She had some clothing draped over one arm.

"How's it going?"

"I'm going to buy these three. Buy two, get one free. I'm happy with these."

They looked around the store a few more minutes before checking out.

"All right, last stop coming up. I'm ready for DK Gems. It brings back wonderful memories of jewelry shopping with you in St. Maarten, with the first piece of jewelry you bought me, my necklace, and of course my engagement ring."

Lauren stopped on the sidewalk and gave Ben a kiss. Holding up her left hand as emphasis, the sunlight caught the brilliance of her diamond. With that, she tucked her arm in his and began walking toward DK Gems International.

TWENTY-FIVE

WENDALL RETURNED HOME from a night of drinking at Rembrandt's. Having not heard back from Antonio, Wendall called him.

"Antonio, what's going on? Any sign of Augustus?"

"No, he's not come home yet. I'm still waiting."

"Don't wait any longer for him to come home. But before you leave, make sure he's not in there."

Antonio had hoped to greet Augustus when he returned to have a persuasive conversation with him to determine the whereabouts of the artifact. Instead, he would confirm he was not yet home.

Walking to the back of Augustus's house, Antonio took his heavy boot and rammed it through the back door, sending its hinges flying before quickly passing through the small house.

Antonio immediately called Wendall.

"I just searched the house and he's not here."

Wendall sighed. He tried to contain expressing his disappointment with the update.

"Okay, Baldo is meeting a couple of Augustus's coworkers for lunch. But you said you could get the artifact for me without the info on Augustus. How are you going to do that?"

"When searching around the Flying Dutchman, I found someone who saw the person leave by hopping in a car. The person even identified the car owner. I'll follow up and will get the name of who has the statue. I'll then pay him a visit."

"Okay, call me later today when you have more."

Wendall ended the call and dialed Baldo.

"Do you have your lunch meeting set?"

"Yes sir. I'll call you as soon as it's over."

Wendall ended the call to wait for positive information from at least one of them.

At noon, Baldo met with two of his acquaintances who worked at the Flying Dutchman. He followed Wendall's orders and never mentioned anything about the artifact. The lunch ended and he had no useful information he could share with Wendall. Baldo called him to give his disappointing update.

"Okay, Baldo, I knew it was a longshot, but it was worth a try. I have Antonio working this from another angle. I'll call you if there's something new for you."

Wendall ended the call. He accepted that Baldo had done all he could without moving him closer to finding the artifact. Despite the setback, he remained optimistic that Antonio would bring him the relic later in the day.

TWENTY-SIX

DEBI WOKE EARLY on Monday morning. She slipped out from under the bed covers and padded into the kitchen. She returned with a breakfast tray for Dean, setting it on the nightstand before sliding back into the bed.

"Good morning, baby."

She edged over to Dean and kissed him on his forehead.

"It's going to be another beautiful day in paradise."

Dean stirred, smelling the aroma of his breakfast and coffee sitting on his tray.

"Good morning. You've been busy."

Debi snuggled up against him. He responded, the warmth of her body contrasting with the cool sheets.

"What a great way to start the day."

She kissed him lightly on the lips.

"Eat your breakfast while it's still hot. I'll be right here to keep you company. If you spill any food, I'll help you retrieve it."

Dean immediately transitioned from sleepy to fully awake and pulled the tray to him. He finished his breakfast in record time, putting the tray back on the nightstand. His mind was now on something else.

"Food check," he said turning to Debi and lifting the covers from his body. Much to his delight, Debi did a very thorough search.

Eventually, the tray and dirty dishes ended up back in the kitchen. Once showered and dressed, they each had plans for the day. Dean drove to the casino while Debi loaded her beach bag, cooler and towel in her car ready for a day with her friends at Orient Beach.

She arrived before 9:00 a.m. and set up lounge chairs while she waited for her friends. She undressed, put her clothes in her beach bag, and reclined on her towel clipped to her chair. The early morning sun was already warm as it penetrated her skin. After a few days without sunning in Orillia, she relished the opportunity to again work on her full body tan.

The early morning walkers who traversed the full beach were finishing their daily walks. Debi waved and spoke to many of them as they passed, opting to join another solitary walker for a short distance before returning to her beach chair. She flipped over, face down on her lounge to even her tan while she waited. Thirty minutes later, she heard the animated chatter of her friends as they approached. She rose quickly and excitedly ran to greet them. Lisa, Jodi, Terri and Karen strode to meet her.

Jodi was the fastest of the group and the first to reach her. She enveloped her in a big hug.

"It's so good to see you again. Congratulations. I'm so excited to be part of your island ceremony."

The others joined in with hugs as they worked their way to the chairs.

"Okay," began Karen, "the main reason we wanted to meet is to see you. The secondary reason is to discuss the plans for your island wedding."

"Yes, we think it will be beautiful and special," added Terri. "We will only share as much information as you'd like to hear so stop us at any time. Or if you want us to simply handle everything and be surprised, we can start celebrating now and skip everything about the wedding."

Debi laughed. "You guys are my best friends. I trust you one hundred percent. Dean is ready to have the wedding and he's very smart. He knows if I'm happy he's happy, so he doesn't need any details since I'm happy."

"Okay, I'm thinking we can skip all this, other than one question that we have," responded Karen. "You have a photographer handling the wedding. Do you want us to coordinate directly with her?"

"That would be great. I'll forward her contact information to you and let her know you'll reach out to her."

"Super. Is she prepared to stay after the ceremony? For food and mingling?"

"Oh yes. Not only is she a great photographer, she was awesome to work with when she was with us in Orillia. She stayed until the very end, for a total of about six hours. I told her we'd want a lot more than just the short ceremony recorded, and she was good with that."

"That's great. Send me her contact info and I'll get in touch with her tonight."

Debi reached in her bag and grabbed her phone. She clicked keys for a minute.

"Done. I sent you her contact information, and sent the photographer, Chantelle, a message that you will be in touch. Her company is KG Photography."

"All right. Sounds like we are done! Let's party," responded Jodi.

The girls undressed for their day on the beach. They settled back in their chairs as Debi moved to her cooler.

"It's way before eleven o'clock, but I think we can begin the champagne brunch now." Without pausing, she continued. "Hearing no objections, grab a cup and let the pouring begin."

The girls began celebrating their close island friendship. After two cups of champagne each, the party moved into the protected cove of Orient Beach where they all congregated in the waist-deep water.

"So, tell us all about Orillia," requested Lisa. "We know Karen was there, but the rest of us would love to hear all about it."

Debi recounted everything from the emotional ceremony to the last of the guests leaving Couchiching Beach Park. Debi also shared her history with the photographer, making them feel as if they already knew her.

They walked back to their chairs before noon, and Lisa and Terri volunteered to make the trek to the Perch bar for white wine. After their return, they sipped their wine and enjoyed the sun drying their skin.

"Are we going to see Dean today?" asked Jodi.

"Yes, he'll be here around one-thirty. I want all of you to give him a warm welcome back. But then, he and I will leave you guys for a lunch on our own. I'd like to get together again before the day is out, but a little mid-day flirting from me with Dean will be fun. After all," she giggled, "we are newlyweds."

"Well, we don't have long with you. We better make sure we make the most of it until he gets here. I'm going to dip in, but when I get out, I'll get us each one more wine to carry us until he's here," offered Lisa.

The five dipped again in the refreshing sea, before returning to their chairs and drinking more wine. Dean arrived at 1:15 p.m.

They watched as Debi stood to greet him. Seeing that, Jodi looked at the group, nodded, and they all jumped up and hustled to beat Debi in greeting Dean. Jodi was first, wrapping her arms around him with a naked hug.

"Dean, it's so good to see you again. You know, there's something about a married man that's *really* attractive. Maybe it's the concept of forbidden fruit."

Still being squeezed by Jodi, the other girls joined in to make it a group hug, Karen and Terri on each side, and Lisa standing back snapping pictures with her phone.

Debi howled laughing, mainly at the look on Dean's face.

"Now that's what I call a great welcome back. Dean, after that, do you think you'll be content with just me for lunch?"

"Wow. I'm overwhelmed. Thank you all for the amazing reception. Lisa, I'm glad you recorded it. If I wasn't a married man, I don't think I could do it, but I'm going to try to break away for a romantic lunch with my beautiful wife."

"Ah, you guys are so cute," responded Jodi. "Girls, I guess we better release him to his bride. You guys have a great lunch and come back to see us before you leave today."

The girls released him from the hug and smiling broadly, Dean stepped over to Debi and hugged her. She slipped into her coverup and the two of them began walking down the beach for lunch.

"We'll be here waiting," called Terri. "Have fun."

After they left, the girls gathered their towels to sit on for lunch at the Perch. They watched Debi and Dean walk down the beach toward the Aloha Restaurant.

"This is our first meal as a married couple on Orient Beach," said Debi dreamily. "What do you think?" she asked, sliding her foot under the table, running it along the bottom of his leg.

"I think it's going to be a superb lunch." He reached across the table and placed his hand on hers. "Let's savor it."

The romantic encounter at Aloha continued until late afternoon.

"Your friends may think we've forgotten them. We probably shouldn't keep them waiting any longer."

"To make up for being gone so long, let's take them drinks," suggested Debi. "With my friends, a free drink is the best way to soothe any hurt feelings," she laughed.

Debi and Dean walked back carrying drinks for the group. Finishing that final drink, the beach goers packed up for the day, exchanging goodbyes and words of excitement about the upcoming island wedding.

TWENTY-SEVEN

AFTER NICO BOATED to Anguilla, he called Paul.

"I've met with Augustus. He is tucked safely away. I emphasized the need for him to stay out of sight. I'm not sure, but I think he understands."

"Okay. Let's emphasize to him how he needs to cooperate. I don't know that anyone is searching for him, but I think they probably are. I'd like you to hang out a few hours, then pay him another visit. That will do two things. One, we'll get another chance to see him when he's not expecting visitors, and two, he might wonder when the next unscheduled visit comes. When you see him, tell him someone is definitely looking for him, even though I don't know that. Also, tell him if he hangs in for just a while longer, this will be over. He can come out of hiding soon, but he has to wait until I give him the okay."

"All right, I'll call you after I see him again. I'll let you know what's happening."

"Thanks Nico. I'm not sure yet, but I might need a boat ride to Anguilla tonight. If I work out what I need there, would you be willing to take me over?"

"Sure, no problem. Just let me know what you need."

"Thanks, I will. I'll make a call now and call you back."

Paul ended the call with Nico before placing a call to Marcus Richards for a progress report on the clay replica he was making.

Marcus, seeing it was Paul calling, immediately answered.

"Marcus, I'm checking to see how you're coming along on that statue."

"I'm getting there, everything so far is going fine."

"That's great to hear. I have a question for you. Is there any way you could finish up for me tonight instead of tomorrow?"

"Sure, there's a way, but I don't know if you'll like it. The photos you sent have a lot of detail that I'm making in my model. I can finish quicker if you don't need so much detail. I could sort of smooth the statue some, skip some stuff, and have it for you in an hour."

"I don't need it that quick. Here's what I'd like. Put in as much detail as you can and still be done by eight o'clock tonight. I'd like to come over there then to get it."

"I can do that. It won't look exactly like the pictures you sent me, so as long as you're okay with that, it will be ready."

Sensing Marcus did not want the change order to result in him getting paid less, Paul assured that he would be fine with the final product and would pay him the full agreed upon amount.

"Okay, I'll get off the phone now and do what I can. I'll have something for you tonight at eight."

"See you at eight," replied Paul before ending the connection.

He called Nico again, who was waiting on his call back. They planned for Nico to bring Paul to Anguilla to meet his contact at eight o'clock.

TWENTY-EIGHT

ANTONIO DROVE TO Philipsburg on a mission to find out who had the missing artifact. After eating a late lunch, he began walking toward DK Gems. He glanced inside as he passed the storefront. He looked to spot Lekha, believing he could more easily extract the names of the people who entered their car Sunday night from her than from Jason. He did not see her, but saw only Jason and two other co-workers, busy assisting customers.

Waiting a few minutes, he passed by again from the other direction. He wanted to be certain he could see everywhere in the main room of the jewelry store. He paused as he passed, giving a more lingering glance before continuing, satisfied that she was not there. He decided to walk further down the street, keeping the storefront in sight. He planned to walk by again in thirty minutes. He decided to walk several more store fronts, watching for her if she returned. His patience paid off.

Walking briskly on the sidewalk, Lekha appeared several storefronts away. She continued purposefully and opened the door, stepping inside the jewelry store. He waited several minutes to allow time for her to settle into her routine of helping customers.

Ten minutes later, Antonio casually walked into DK Gems International.

One of Lekha's partners nodded his recognition of a potential customer as Antonio stepped inside.

"Good afternoon. Welcome to DK Gems. Is there something I can help you with today?"

Antonio looked in the co-worker's direction, nodded and smiled. Seeing Lekha also available to assist, he quickly turned his attention to her.

"Good afternoon," Antonio responded, his greeting primarily directed toward Lekha.

He continued further inside, stopping at the display counter directly in front of Lekha. He glanced down at the items in the showcase as if interested before looking up with a smile.

"I'd like to purchase a small trinket for my girlfriend. Something nice but inexpensive. You look like you might be able to give me some good suggestions."

"Certainly," she responded. "I'd love to help you. Earrings are always a well-received gift. Does your friend have pierced ears?"

"That's a great question. We've just begun seeing each other, and I really haven't noticed." He chuckled as if from embarrassment. "I'd like to make a good impression with a surprise for our second date. I don't think she will be expecting a gift of jewelry, but she may be the one. I'd like to surprise her, but nothing too much, as that may have an unintended effect of scaring her away."

Lekha responded with a sweet, understanding smile.

"Let me show you a couple of very casual items. Here's a palm tree pendant that can be worn on a thin chain. It's great for every day, a fun piece of jewelry."

She laid the delicate necklace on a foam pad for him to inspect it, then lifted it to eye level.

"I'll put it on, give you an idea of how it might look on her."

She clasped the necklace around her neck, stepped back, and stood tall for him to size it up for possible purchase.

"You're very good at what you do. I think what you've picked out looks perfect. How much is that?"

Removing the necklace and placing it before him once again, she punched a few buttons on the calculator before turning it around for him to see.

"I'll take it. I was hoping to find something for under $500 as my top amount, but I didn't really want to go that high, you know, I don't want to appear desperate on just a second date. I'm pleased this is well below what I think is the scare-her-off level."

"I'll put it in a jewelry pouch for you. This says you're interested, but not desperate," she smiled. "She should be pleased."

Antonio reached into his pocket and pulled out cash to complete the purchase.

"Thank you so much for all your help today. Who knows, maybe in a few months, I'll be back shopping for an engagement ring."

"Thank you and good luck with that. I'll be here to help you when you're ready."

"Thanks so much."

Antonio turned, preparing to step out of the store. As if something just occurred to him, he stopped and turned back.

"Quick question. Are you Lekha?"

"Yes, my husband Jason and I are usually here, or at least one of us is."

"Well, this has nothing to do with how helpful you were today, but I heard a funny story earlier."

"Oh? What's that?"

"Well, someone told me something very unusual. That there were two naked people out and about a couple of nights ago, walking around near the Texaco station not far from here. Is that not the craziest thing?"

Lekha flushed, looking at the customer before averting her eyes.

"I was told you helped them out, and they jumped into your car. Is there any truth to that?"

Still blushing, Lekha began to stammer.

"That's quite a story. If I had seen such a thing, I'm not sure how I would have responded."

"You've been so kind and helpful to me today, I'm guessing if you knew them, you were helpful, and offered the safety of your car for them, so they wouldn't be wandering about naked," he laughed.

"Oh yes, but no, I'm not sure how you heard such a thing, but it wasn't me. I try to be helpful, but I haven't helped naked strangers into my car," she laughed, trying to regain her composure.

"Okay, well, it's a funny story. No one has mentioned this to you? If I heard the story, I'm guessing a lot of people have heard it. As a compliment, you're quite attractive and recognizable here in St. Maarten. You might want to be prepared for others questioning you on it."

He turned to leave. Laughing, he called back to her.

"You must admit, that's a pretty unusual and funny story. You have a great day, and thanks again for your help."

He stepped out of DK Gems and down the street away from the storefront. As Antonio disappeared down the street, Lekha stepped outside to try to calm down. She stood, thinking about her strange encounter with the customer. Her thoughts were interrupted by a familiar voice.

"Good afternoon, Lekha," greeted Lauren as she and Ben approached the jewelry store for the last stop of their shopping day. "We were just coming to see you. You know, one can never have too much jewelry."

Ben and Lauren, in addition to becoming loyal customers, were also friends of Lekha and Jason.

"Hey guys," Lekha responded. "It's good to see you."

Ben noticed Lekha did not seem to be herself despite the cheerful greeting. She seemed somewhat distracted.

"Are you okay?"

"Yes, I'm fine. I'm going to let Jason know I'm stepping away for a break. Give me a second, and if this is a social visit instead of business, you can keep me company."

"That's great," responded Ben quickly, before Lauren could insist on going inside to shop. "We'd love to visit with you on your break."

Lekha stepped back inside. Seeing Jason with a customer, she merely waved and mouthed she would be back in about fifteen minutes.

"All set. Let's step over to Juggie's."

Juggie's Place was close by on Front Street and offered food and drinks in what was billed as the smallest bar in the world. The fun atmosphere of the outside bar with several hundred women's brassieres hanging overhead created an atmosphere not unlike that found in Key West.

Juggie motioned for them to sit in three available chairs, brought Ben a beer, and chatted with them for a minute before returning his attention to his other customers.

Lauren followed up on Ben's earlier observation.

"Okay, now that we're sitting here away from others, what's wrong?"

"Oh, nothing's wrong. Everything is fine. I just had an unusual meeting with a customer."

"Were you threatened?" asked Ben immediately.

"Oh no. It's fine."

"Lekha, would you please tell us what's going on? Ben and I are going to worry if you don't tell us more than 'everything is fine.'"

"Well, at first it seemed normal. A man wanted a present for his girlfriend, I helped him pick something out, he was pleased and made the purchase. As he was leaving, he asked me about something from a couple of nights ago."

"What happened that has you so shook up?"

"Well, I shouldn't say anything more."

She paused, saw that neither Ben nor Lauren was willing to let it drop, and decided she could trust them to tell more of the story.

"He asked me about Saturday night. He said someone saw me in my car that night, letting a couple into the car."

"What's so strange about that?"

"They were naked. I'm not prepared to tell any more, it was strange, sort of funny, nothing happened that was bad. But I didn't think anybody saw anything and it has me a little shook up."

"I don't understand, but we won't press you to tell us more. If I can help you, I'm here. Let's sit a few more minutes. If you want to tell us more, we're good listeners. Otherwise, in a few minutes, we'll go back with you to the store and let Lauren do some shopping."

"Okay, thanks for listening. It's possible something bad could come out of what was our attempt to help a couple of people in need. I denied the story to the customer."

"Well, based on your reaction and how you still looked when we saw you, whoever you told would not believe you. I'm sure your reaction was too apparent for him to believe your denial."

"I know, and that's part of why I'm so worried."

"Do you think you're in danger? Should we file a report with the police?"

"No, it's nothing for the police to be involved in."

"Well, I'm willing to help, but I'm not sure what I can do. Maybe you should talk to Paul. He seems to have experience in some of those things that don't involve the police but maybe should."

"That's not necessary. He already knows. He and Lisa were the naked couple, and Paul warned me to deny anything about the night. I did, but the problem is, I knew I wasn't believable. I did the best I could, but I was taken off guard after he made his purchase, and I might as well have told him the truth for all the good my denial was."

They sat for a few more minutes as Ben finished his beer.

"Okay," said Lekha, "I'm ready to head back. Come with me. It might help me get back to normal if you guys want to look around in the store."

"Sounds good to me," responded Lauren. "Your store was on my shopping list today anyway!"

As the three walked into the store, Ben and Lauren greeted Jason. The store was now filled with new customers, so Ben and Lauren waved their goodbyes as a customer asked Lekha for her assistance. They drifted off to another display counter away from earshot of others.

"Ben, I'm worried about Lekha. Is there anything you think we should do?"

"I don't think we know enough to help. I suggested she call Paul, and I'm sure she'll update him, and didn't need my suggestion to do it. Lekha is clearly worried, and if what happened was supposed to be a secret, that cat is out of the bag."

TWENTY-NINE

ANTONIO WATCHED AT a distance as Ben, Lauren and Lekha walked to Juggie's Place. He phoned his friend Samuel, a bartender at the Red Piano.

"I have an assignment for you. I've identified someone who has information I need. I'd like you to do what you do best. Get that info for me."

"Sure. It's been some time since I did work for Mr. Vaughn. I haven't had much work along those lines since he disappeared."

"Sam, if you get this right, there'll be plenty more business for you. Are you working at the Red Piano tonight?"

"I was. For the right price, I can let them know something's come up, that I need to take the night off."

"It's a simple request."

Antonio discussed what he wanted of Samuel.

"Do you think you can take care of that for me? I have $2,000 waiting for you when you give me the name."

"I'm on it. You'll have what you want soon."

The men ended the call. Antonio decided it was time to call Wendall with an update. Wendall immediately answered when he saw that it was Antonio calling.

"I found the person who gave the thief a ride. She's denying it, but clearly lying. She's tucked away at work, but when she leaves, she'll be convinced to give up the name. I'll have what you're looking for soon."

"Good. I'll be expecting your call. Once you get the artifact, bring it to me immediately."

Wendall ended the call.

Antonio was pleased, confident that Samuel would extract the name he needed. No one would connect him to what would come next.

THIRTY

PAUL WAS KEEPING Nico busy. After delivering Augustus to a hideaway in Anguilla Sunday afternoon, Nico boated to Anguilla again the next day. Back from the short boat ride to the neighboring island, Nico once more was on board his boat. It was 7:15 p.m. and he waited for Paul.

Paul was early and pleased to see Nico waiting for him.

"Good evening, Nico. Thanks so much for all you're doing for me. I have a meeting set with an artist tonight and I'm eager to see what he has for me. I thought you'd be here early."

Paul boarded the boat. They were in Anguilla in twenty minutes, leaving a short walk for Paul to meet Marcus.

Nico walked with Paul down the dock before stopping.

"I'll be here with the boat when you're done."

"Thanks, I shouldn't be more than thirty minutes. It's been a long day for both of us. I'll be back soon."

Paul walked to the house as instructed. He knocked and the door opened right away.

"Good night. Are you Paul?"

"Yes, Marcus Richards?"

"In the flesh. Come on in."

Paul followed Marcus inside.

"Right this way to the back. I've converted the back of my house to a studio. That's where I do all of my work."

Marcus led Paul to his studio where Paul saw many sculptures in various stages of completion.

"Excuse the mess. I have what you're looking for right over here."

He stepped behind a counter and lifted up a small figurine for Paul's inspection.

"Here's what I've done. It's a good representation from the pictures you provided. I was not able to include all the detail that I had planned had I more time to work on it."

With no specific expertise or knowledge of the artifact in question, Paul was pleased with the statue he was handed. Although beautifully made, Paul believed the statue would be readily seen by an expert as not an authentic Arawak artifact. That was not a concern.

Paul had decided on a plan different from that concocted by Augustus. He was no longer interested in the museum curator authenticating the relic as genuine. Paul instead wanted the assessment to be quick and definitive that the relic he possessed had no value as a genuine article. The quicker the better.

"So, what do you think?" Marcus appeared hesitant.

"Marcus, you've done a great job. It's just as I wanted. Thank you so much for the quick production. This is perfect."

Relieved, Marcus now waited for payment from Paul.

"You've earned your money. Now, would you like to earn an extra $5,000?"

Marcus raised his eyebrows at the prospect.

"That's very enticing. What would you like, another similar statue?"

"No, this is an easy request. Over the next few weeks, you'll likely hear how an Arawak relic was presented to the St. Martin Museum curator, and that the curator quickly determined it was not an artifact of any historical significance. In fact, it will be seen for what it is, a beautiful reproduction, but not one created hundreds of years ago by the Arawaks. For you to earn the additional $5,000, I ask that you simply not provide any information, including my request and your production. It is not intended to fool anyone into thinking it is authentic, but it will simply be seen as a beautiful reproduction. There will be no malice, but simply our secret where no one is harmed."

Paul pulled out an envelope containing the additional $5,000 and handed it to Marcus.

"Do we have a deal?"

Marcus reached out to Paul to shake his hand.

"It was a pleasure doing business with you. Should you need anything from me in the future, please do not hesitate to reach out. Our secret goes no further."

"Thank you, Marcus. You've done beautiful work and I believe you. I'll be sure to keep you in mind for any future projects requiring your skill."

Marcus brought out a box for Paul to place the replica inside.

"I bid you goodnight. Safe travels."

Paul placed the carving gently inside the box, shook hands again with Marcus, and fifteen minutes after entering his home, walked back to the boat. Nico was aboard the boat when he returned.

"Everything go all right?"

"Perfect, Nico, perfect. Now, let's get out of here. I'm ready to get home."

THIRTY-ONE

LEKHA WORKED THE rest of the afternoon in the jewelry store, not mentioning her concerns to Jason until they were alone and closing for the day.

It was close to 7:00 p.m. when they finished securing all the valuable jewelry to be placed back on display the next morning. Jason leaned against a counter, admiring his wife.

"Lekha, it's been a full day. Thanks for staying late with me. Are you ready to head home?"

"Yes, but before we leave, I want to tell you about something that happened earlier today."

"Why don't you tell me on the walk to our cars? We can pick up a bite on the way home."

"I need to tell you about it before we leave, just in case."

Her ominous words held Jason's full attention.

"Just in case? Just in case of what?"

"Well, what happened earlier might be dangerous for us, and I want you to be prepared before we step out."

"Wow, I'm definitely listening. Let's step in the back and talk."

She told Jason how her customer was very nice and purchased an inexpensive piece of jewelry for his girlfriend. She felt comfortable with him, but as he was leaving, he asked about them opening their car to a naked couple.

"He wasn't threatening at all. In fact, he acted as if he thought it funny. I denied it, but I'm sure he could tell I wasn't being truthful. He let it drop, but he commented that others also knew the story of us giving a ride to a naked couple. Maybe it's nothing to worry about, but I was hoping it would just go away."

"All right. I don't see anything said today as an immediate threat. Let's just be careful, aware of what's going on around us."

"Do you think I should call Lisa and let her know?"

"Probably. If somebody saw us and recognized us, it's possible someone also recognized Lisa and Paul. To be on the safe side, we should let them know."

Lekha pulled out her phone and dialed Lisa. She answered on the first ring.

"Hey, it's good to hear from you."

"Thanks. I hope you'll still feel that way after you hear why I'm calling. I had a customer today who said someone saw me let a naked couple in my car. It's not the kind of thing that somebody would make up. You and Paul may have been recognized."

"That's not good news. What did you say?"

"I denied it, but I'm afraid I'm not a good liar. I think he could tell I wasn't being truthful when I said it didn't happen. He said other people have also heard the story."

"Okay, thanks for letting me know. We had cautioned you and Jason not to say anything about that night, but if someone asks about it, I think you should go ahead and say it's true. But of course, don't say anything about the artifact. Maybe you could just say you saw us, assumed we had too much to drink, and gave us a ride to our car. You went home, and inspired by seeing us naked, had the best sex of your life that night," she laughed, trying to lighten the mood.

Lekha allowed herself a small chuckle.

"That wouldn't be too far from the truth. I don't know what it was about that night. The adventure, the statue, or the whole experience; I don't want to give you and Paul all the credit, but it was amazing when we got home."

Lekha colored as soon as the words left her mouth.

Listening to their conversation, Jason looked quizzically at Lekha, surprised the serious topic had taken a dramatic turn, with Lekha's completely out of character comment of enjoying a great night of sex. A knowing smile crept onto his face remembering that night.

"Well then, that's settled. Paul is out, but I'll let him know. You did great and we've been warned. You and Jason need to be careful, but if asked again, don't deny that you gave a ride to a crazy naked couple. You can even tell our names. It now seems likely someone could have identified us. I don't think you'll hear about it from your customer again, but if you do, why don't you try to clear the air? Just say you denied it earlier because you were embarrassed about the whole thing."

Relieved, and reassured by Lisa's humor, Lekha ended the call after the two promised to get together soon. She turned to Jason.

"The call went well. I'm glad I've let them know. They needed to be warned. And I'm also glad we can tell the truth if asked again. Only leave out the part about the statue."

"That's right. What statue?" said Jason, emphasizing their plan to never mention it, even if asked.

Lekha nodded in agreement. Then she broke into a sly smile.

"But just between you and me, we don't have to erase our memory of the statue. You know, the one you looked like most of the night, starting with the ride home. It was an amazing night, one that I think we should duplicate tonight," she said flirtatiously as she leaned into him.

"It's a date. But first, I want to make one quick call."

THIRTY-TWO

SAMUEL STOOD ON Front Street, keeping a low profile, and blending in with the foot traffic. After the phone call with Antonio, he drove to downtown Philipsburg and parked at the Salt Pond. His plan was to wait for Lekha to exit the jewelry store. Arriving at 5:00 p.m. before closing, he watched as the final customer exited the store an hour later.

Shortly before 7:00 p.m., he had concern that Lekha may have slipped out unseen, so he walked past DK Gems. He saw the closed sign, but lights were still on inside, and he glimpsed Lekha and Jason still there. He moved further away from the store and resumed his watch.

At 7:15 p.m. Samuel received a call from Antonio.

"I'm still waiting to hear a name. What's taking so long?"

"I'm in position. I got here at five, but they had customers until six, and still haven't left the store. I'm watching. She's got to come out sometime tonight. When she does, I'll get your name for you."

"All right. Wait them out. I want that name tonight. Do whatever you got to do."

"Not to worry. I've got this. I'll call you soon."

At 7:25 p.m. Samuel saw two burley guys walk up to DK Gems. He watched as they stood outside, wondering if he had competition to get the drop on Lekha. He was about to call Antonio to ask who else might be planning to kidnap her when he saw Jason open the door. Jason waved the men inside.

"Thanks for coming over so quickly. Lekha didn't think it necessary, but when I told her I knew an off-duty policeman, she was relieved when you and your buddy could be here so soon."

"We're happy to help. What can we do?"

"I don't think it's anything, but because we had a strange customer earlier today, and we're here later than normal, our fears probably got the better of us. Now I'm a little embarrassed that I called."

"Nonsense. Better safe than sorry."

"Thanks. If you don't mind, we'd be grateful if you walk with us to our cars and keep an eye out for anything unusual. I'm sure it's nothing. We'll resume normal life and feel good about everything, I'm sure, once the sun has come up again."

Minutes later, the men escorted Lekha and Jason to their cars.

"All looks clear. You two have a good night."

"Thanks again. We really appreciate you guys coming out here tonight. Jason, I'll see you at home."

The four parted ways as Lekha and Jason pulled into the road to return home.

Samuel called Antonio.

"Bad news. They had two guys who looked like bodyguards show up and walked them to their cars. They're gone. I wasn't able to get to Lekha."

"Shit. I need that name."

"I know, and I'm going to get it. I'll watch their house. I haven't figured out what exactly I'll do now, but I'll get that name. You can count on me."

THIRTY-THREE

LISA GREETED PAUL with a big hug and a Coor's Light when he returned home from Anguilla.

"Is that box for me?"

"Indirectly, yes." Paul pulled the replica of the Arawak artifact from the box and held it out for her to see.

"It looks a lot like what we brought home from the mountain top."

"Yes, it does. We'll keep this here and I'll put the one we found in a safe place. I just picked it up from an artist in Anguilla."

"Let's have a seat in the den. I want to tell you about a call I received from Lekha."

They sat on the den couch while Lisa summarized the call. When she finished, she waited for Paul to respond.

"You did good telling her to not deny what happened if asked again. We'll need to be more careful in case the wrong people are aware of us being the passengers in Jason and Lekha's car. Certainly, someone found our clothes when the zip line opened, if not before. It's not much of a stretch to tie us as the naked couple responsible for the relic removal from the mountaintop. Someone could be coming for our artifact."

Lisa moved over on the couch to snuggle close to Paul, resting her head on his chest. They sat for several minutes, neither speaking. Paul kissed her lightly on the forehead before making motions to stand.

"I need to make a couple of calls. With the news from Lekha, it's even more important that we move quickly."

Paul stood and gave Lisa a reassuring look as she remained on the couch.

"I won't be long. Let me work through a few details and I'll tell you all about it once I know what we'll do next."

He walked into his office to make the calls. His first call was to Sylvie.

"Are you ready for a fun day at the Flying Dutchman tomorrow?"

"I can be ready. What do you have in mind?"

"I'd like to meet you, Rick and Gary there when they open tomorrow. They open at ten o'clock. Maybe we could all meet there around nine-thirty. Does that work for you?"

"Sure."

"I'll send messages to Rick and Gary now. I'd like to set up a zoom call, let's say in thirty minutes, with everyone to go over tomorrow's plan."

"All right, I'll talk to you again in thirty minutes."

Paul sent the meeting invitations and Gary and Rick accepted. Thirty minutes later, the four began their zoom call.

"Thank you all for joining in on this late-night call. Big picture, I had an assignment that began when I thought it was low risk and relatively low reward. I was to make a small one-time fee for retrieving an artifact from the bar at the top of the mountain made popular by the Flying Dutchman zip line. That plan has changed by necessity. The person who found the artifact is in hiding, and I'm expecting us to have a much larger payday. With the bigger project, I need more help. I'm offering you all equal shares of whatever we get."

"I'm in," sang out Rick and Gary in unison.

"Thanks for the enthusiasm, but first, let me tell you what's in store. The attraction opens at ten in the morning. I'd like us to meet at Emilio's at nine-thirty and purchase tickets for the attraction. We'll be part of the first group to go up. The chairlift goes about halfway up the mountain, where it stops and everyone has an opportunity to do something that's like a toboggan ride down the mountain, as well as four small zip lines. Not far from the halfway point, several hundred yards away from the marked trail under the zip line, is a series of caves. That's where my client says there are many more artifacts in a shallow cave. Some are near the mouth of the cave, and others a little further back where we'll need lighting, but a heavy-duty flashlight will do. I want to do an exploratory trip tomorrow morning. There are two things I need to find out. One, of course, is if he's telling me the truth, that there are caves and valuable artifacts inside. The second is I want to see if our small group can get back to the caves without being spotted. Sylvie, that's where you come in."

"What do you want me to do?"

"I want you to do what you do best. I want you to be a visual distraction to the guys working there. If you do your job successfully, they will be so busy looking at you, they won't have a chance to notice Rick, Gary and me as we stray off the standard path to look in the caves."

Sylvie laughed. "I don't know if I should be flattered or insulted that you've called me out as a tease."

"I promise, it was intended as a compliment."

"Well, I have an idea. If I can be a model distraction, what about adding to the distraction? With Rick and Gary involved, Karen and Erica will know what's going on. Why don't they go too? In case you haven't noticed, they can have a lot of power over men with their looks."

"I've noticed, and that's a great idea. Rick and Gary, what do you think? Would you be okay with asking them to help out?"

"Let's ask now."

"I'm in," shouted Erica. "Not that I was eavesdropping or anything. If you want me, I'll give my seductive best!"

"Same here," agreed Karen, who was also listening in. "And Paul, thank you for the compliment. I think you're very attractive also."

"All right, the plan has taken a turn for the better. We'll take the chairlift to the halfway point. The tricky part will be for Gary, Rick and me to be forgotten, as if almost invisible. It's important for me to have them there, though, because if what my client has told me is true, I'll need help gathering the artifacts and carrying them out. If tomorrow morning works, I want us all to do a repeat performance tomorrow afternoon. The park closes at four o'clock. We could be there around three. If you girls are successful, we go in the caves while there is still some daylight, gather all the artifacts, then bring them down the mountain after dark."

"We're in," offered Rick. "It will be fun, and I enjoy an adventure."

"Yes, I'm good with it too," agreed Gary.

"All right. I've described everything and how I hope it will happen. There is risk. Lisa and I may have already been spotted and could have someone following us. There is some danger, and if these things are really as valuable as I think they are, someone will want them very badly. The night Lisa and I retrieved the artifact, a group of men was coming up the mountain when we barely got away. I don't know what might happen tomorrow. We could have some very bad people after us in those caves. It could be more people go in the caves than come out. I hope not, especially for the three of us going in. But just know, it's possible, and if I have to make a choice, I won't hesitate. If we're followed and anyone gets left behind in the caves, I'm prepared to do whatever it takes to make sure the three of us get out."

The mood on the zoom call turned very serious.

"Sylvie has shared that she has complete trust in all of you," Paul continued. "I do as well. If anyone fails to do their part, it won't bode well for any of us."

"I understand. I'm still in," said Gary.

"Same here," added Rick. "We'll be careful and alert to what's going on around us. I'll be doing this with my eyes wide open."

"Okay, the last piece that you all should want to know, is how much are we going to make. That's still to be determined. If they really exist as described, the artifacts might be worth as much as $10 million."

"Wow. Now I'm really interested," said Sylvie. There were several gasps and looks of surprise at the large amount.

"I'm going to propose to my client a fifty-fifty split. Under the circumstances, I don't think he can refuse. With our four groups, Rick and Karen, Sylvie and Brad, Erica and Gary, and Lisa and me, that's about $1.25 million each. Sylvie, for you and Brad, instead of Brad's participation in removing the artifacts, he can do his share by stowing everything we bring down the mountain in his boat. Talk with Brad and let me know if he's willing to do that for us."

"I already talked to him. I thought that might be something you wanted, and he's already agreed."

"Okay, then, the last part of the plan is for you girls to decide what you'll be wearing and how you'll act to be the distraction we need."

"Paul, if you trust us to do what we do best, the three of us can talk about that off-line," responded Sylvie.

"I definitely trust you. You all have a lot to lose if this turns bad."

"Okay, when this call ends, I'll have a three-way call with Karen and Erica. I promise you won't be disappointed."

"All right, if there are no questions, let's end this call. I'll see you all at Emilio's in the morning."

THIRTY-FOUR

LISA HAD A restless night of sleep. She was up early, revising her latest training materials. She had several work appointments scheduled for the next week, and unable to sleep, finished her preparation for the upcoming meetings.

Paul was surprised to wake alone at 7:00 a.m. He climbed out of bed and found Lisa bent over her desk.

"Good morning. Are you okay?"

"Good morning. Yes, I'm fine. I finished some work I'd been putting off. Too much time having fun planning Debi's wedding, as well as all the fun you and I have been having."

"You look wide awake. How long have you been up?"

"I'm not sure. I had trouble sleeping, so instead of tossing and turning and disturbing your sleep, I was up much of the night. Instead of wasting the time, I decided I might as well be productive if I was going to be awake anyway."

"Do you want to talk about it?"

"I think I just had too much on my mind."

"All this about the artifact will be over soon. Today's a big day. Come tonight, if everything goes as planned, all the treasure should be stowed safely away on Brad's boat."

"It will be good for this assignment to be finished. I won't lie, it was a factor in my poor night's sleep. But it was more than that," she continued, trying to convince Paul not to worry about her. "With work piling up and spending time on planning Debi's wedding when I probably should have been working, I just needed to address my work backlog. I've handled more without losing sleep before, and I'm feeling good this morning, especially since I finished the work I needed to do."

Paul gave her a comforting hug.

"Not long now," he reassured before turning to get ready for the day.

"Paul, before you leave, I have a question. Debi's friends that she spent time with in the Bahamas, Kris, Carol and Shelly, flew in yesterday in advance of the wedding. Do you think it would be safe for me to meet them at the beach today? You know, talk about the wedding, and have some fun?"

"That should be fine. We don't know for certain that anyone is after us. Just be careful, but you should be fine on a populated beach."

"Great. That's what I thought, but I don't want to do anything to take too much risk."

"I'll be tied up all day. Just stay with your friends."

"Got it. That won't be a problem."

Lisa's mood lightened considerably. Paul turned again to go shower.

"While you're showering, I'll fix us some breakfast. This should be a good day for both of us."

Lisa left for the kitchen and prepared a breakfast of sausage and pancakes. Freshly showered, Paul walked into the kitchen and took a seat next to Lisa at the counter.

"This looks fantastic, Lisa."

Paul ate heartily, looking appreciatively at Lisa for how supportive she remained throughout all his assignments.

"I probably won't have lunch today. This was perfect. I'll be ready for a celebration dinner tonight, but as usual, I don't know when I'll be back. It could be late."

"I understand. I won't call, I know it could be the worst of timing if I did. I'll wait to hear from you."

They cleared the breakfast dishes, and each finished getting ready for the day. Lisa knew the risk Paul faced and walked over to him. She gave him a tight hug and long kiss before she walked out the door for the beach, knowing Paul would be leaving shortly.

"You be careful. I'll be here when you finish tonight."

Lisa arrived early for her 9:00 a.m. meeting with Kris, Carol and Shelly. There were plenty of others on the beach, including the usual parade of early morning walkers. She was comforted by so many beachgoers nearby.

She found a grouping of four beach lounges, spread her towel on one, and undressed for a day of full body sunning. She placed her beach bag on the adjacent chair and tied her coverup on the other two to save them for her friends.

At 9:00 a.m. Kris, Carol and Shelly saw her at the agreed upon area of the beach near the Perch Bar and Restaurant.

"Good morning," Lisa shouted as they approached. She hopped up for the customary greetings of hugs.

"It's great to see you," exclaimed Kris. "Tell us all about the wedding plans for Saturday."

The three girls undressed and took chairs around Lisa. She laid out the plans and they all agreed that it would be an amazing island wedding. The early morning passed with the girls alternating between dipping in the clear, calm water, and basking in their chairs.

THIRTY-FIVE

SAMUEL ENDED HIS call with Antonio and followed at a safe distance on foot as Lekha and Jason walked to their cars escorted by the two men. He made note of the vehicles and hurried back to his Tahoe. Pulling out onto the main road from the Salt Pond, he drove in the direction he believed they would be travelling. Fortunately for him, two cars were stopped in the road where the drivers, travelling in opposite directions and impervious to the backup they were creating, chatted out their car windows about the day's events and plans for the next day. Samuel saw that Lekha and Jason were trapped behind the two-car roadblock, and for once, was thankful for that common practice among St. Maarten drivers.

After a couple of horn taps from other drivers, the impromptu car meeting broke up and traffic resumed. Now Samuel was within easy following distance and watched as his targets pulled into their hillside home. He continued to drive on past their house. As they stepped inside their house, Samuel resigned himself to the fact that he could not intercept them. He decided to return home and get some sleep before returning in the morning wearing one of his favorite disguises.

Early the next day, he sat in his vehicle not far from their house and waited. His dark hair was now covered with a blond wig, his eyebrows were lightened with fast acting cream bleach, and a prosthetic Jimmy Durante nose sat securely in place. Adding padding around his waist under his shirt, his transformation was complete.

Jason was first out the door to leave for work. Samuel watched as he opened the house door to leave, kissed Lekha goodbye, and hopped in his car.

Although somewhat angered by the wait until morning, Samuel was pleased that his mission had taken a promising turn. He waited a few minutes after Jason drove out of sight and stepped out of his Tahoe. He lifted the hood of his car.

Lekha stepped out of the house, dressed for work. He caught her attention and waved. Curious, Lekha walked toward Samuel.

"Good morning, are you having car trouble?"

"Yes, my car stalled, and I can't get it started. I'm trying to figure out what's wrong with it."

Lekha responded with a sympathetic smile.

"Sorry I can't help you with that. Mechanically inclined I am not. If you were looking for jewelry, I could much better be of assistance."

"I was in a rush this morning and left my phone. Could you call a repair shop and ask them to send somebody out?"

"Sure, do you have anybody in mind?"

"No, not really. If there's anybody you do business with, that would be fine. Otherwise, would you check on-line and see if there is someone close by?"

"Not a problem," she replied, looking at her cell phone. "I see a repair shop listed. I'll call now."

Lekha placed the call, talked for a minute, and called out to Samuel.

"They can have someone here in thirty minutes to look at it. If they can't fix it quickly, they'll give you a tow. Is that okay? Do you want me to ask them to come on out?"

"That would be great, thanks."

Lekha passed along Samuel's request that the repair shop send someone out and ended the call.

"Someone should be here within thirty minutes. Sorry for your problem this morning."

She moved closer to Samuel as she spoke.

"Thanks so much for your help. I'm Bart, pleased to meet you."

Samuel stuck out his hand to shake. Lekha continued over, smiled and shook his hand.

"Hi, I'm Lekha. Glad I could help."

Samuel gave her a disarming smile.

"You mentioned you could help me if I was looking for jewelry." He paused. "I thought I recognized you. Aren't you one of the owners at DK Gems? You've been so kind, when this is over, I'll bring my wife to your store to do some shopping."

"I'd be happy to help both of you."

"You know, it's the funniest thing. I just heard a story yesterday about you helping out a naked couple a few nights ago. And now you're out here helping me. You are one kind soul."

"Oh, well, I'm glad I could help."

"So, tell me, what did you think when you saw those naked people. Were they hurt?"

"No, they were fine. I think they'd had too much to drink. How else could you lose your clothes and be wandering around at night." Lekha's internal alarm began to go off.

"You were lucky. There are crazy people out there, especially at night. As kind as you are, I don't think you're crazy. You must know them to let two naked people in your car at night."

Lekha suddenly felt very uncomfortable with the turn the conversation had taken. Unsure of what to say, she paused and thought back to her discussion with Lisa.

"Well, yes, they're friends of mine. I know they're embarrassed about it."

Samuel held his head back and laughed.

"That's a good one. Sounds like you've got some fun friends. So, tell me, who are they? I'd love to meet them sometime. They sound like my kind of people."

"Oh, I don't know if they'd want their names mentioned. Like I said, they were really embarrassed."

"They sound like fun people. Anybody walking around naked at night, I don't think they'd care if their names were known. They clearly don't have anything to hide," he said, again laughing. "Make my day, maybe you could introduce me to them."

"Yes, maybe one day we'll all have to get together."

"Oh, come on, you've piqued my curiosity. I don't want to leave here without knowing their names. It will be my secret, I promise." He again laughed.

Lekha was becoming increasingly uncomfortable and wanted to get away. She started backing away from Samuel. Not knowing if he was a threat, she recalled Lisa telling her to share their names if asked.

"Oh, okay," she said, still backing away, having put a more comfortable distance between them. She shared their names.

"Well, I'm Bart. When I bring my wife in to shop, we'll give you our contact information. Maybe you could pass it along to Paul and Lisa for us. We won't contact them but will wait for them to contact us if they're interested."

Samuel winked at Lekha.

"My wife and I are in the lifestyle. Swingers. I'm not sure you understood that. I don't mean any offense, and it looks like you might not be interested. But if Paul and Lisa would like to meet, would you mind making the introduction? I think a couple walking around naked at night would be worth taking a chance on."

Lekha smiled but still kept her distance.

"Sure, I'm pretty sure they don't do that, but if you and your wife come into the shop, I'll pass it along."

"Okay, thank you, Lekha. I appreciate your help this morning and won't take up any more of your time. You have a great day."

Lekha turned and hurried to her car, leaving the stranded motorist, and drove to the jewelry store. Samuel waited at his vehicle for ten more minutes until the repair person arrived. When he was able to crank his Tahoe, he thanked the man, gave him fifty dollars for his trouble, and drove off. Now, armed with the names, he was ready for the next step.

THIRTY-SIX

PAUL PULLED INTO the furthest open parking place that was still within the lot for the Flying Dutchman. He stepped out, stood beside his car, and as the others arrived, signaled them into the neighboring spots. He had three backpacks, each holding extra-large dark green laundry bags made of premium nylon blended polyester fabric. Durable, long-lasting and tear resistant, they were each rated to easily hold one hundred pounds without tearing, more than enough to carry out the expected treasure. He slipped on his backpack, which also contained his powerful search light, and handed the remaining two backpacks to Gary and Rick. The three men, now wearing backpacks, walked with the girls to the ticket counter. They waited for the park to open, standing first in line to purchase their tickets.

After buying the passes, they walked toward the chairlift, with Paul giving final instructions.

"We'll split up here into groups. Sylvie, you, Karen and Erica should ride the chairlift together. We'll follow you up, but we'll let another group get in line in front of us, where we'll be two chairs behind you. Rick, Gary and I are counting on you being your distracting best."

The girls were wearing shorts that allowed the curve of their cheeks to peek out from the legs. Their upper bodies looked more conservative, covered by blue and gray t-shirts.

"You girls look enticing with your shorts selection, but your t-shirts don't really draw a lot of attention. Do you plan to make up for that with a lot of attitude?"

"Don't worry about that," answered Sylvie. "What you see is just to get us on the chairlift without any questions, and without getting us arrested. We'll do our job, just don't let us do it so well that we distract the three of you, too."

Paul smiled. "I guess you're one step ahead of me again. Looking good and keep it shaking."

The girls strutted to the chairlift with an exaggerated show of swaying hips.

"Don't you worry, we've got this. It didn't take more than a minute or two to practice our act. You haven't begun to see the real shaking, but the ride workers will be blind if they don't notice us."

The guys were spellbound. The girls hopped into the chair and waved merrily back at the guys. Paul, Rick and Gary stood back, waited for another group of four to pass them, before jumping into the next chair.

The three girls reached the platform at the halfway point up the mountain. Sliding off the chair, they had a choice of beginning the four small zip lines, taking the schooner ride back to the bottom, which was a fast ride along a track similar to the Olympics bobsled but on inner tubes, or continue to the next chairlift to ride the rest of the way to the top. Two couples ahead of them opted for the schooner ride. They decided to create a temporary backlog by standing in line for that ride as well. They watched the next group of four arrive on the platform and they moved to begin the short zip lines. The guys arrived in the next chair a minute later.

It was time to begin operation diversion.

It was the girls' turn to ride the specially designed dry inner tubes down the winding hollowed out path. There was one attendant at the start of the schooner ride. Sylvie checked for other attendants, and the only other one nearby was busy harnessing a customer for the zip line ride.

"Okay girls, you're next. Who's first?"

"I'm first," volunteered Sylvie. "Would you mind taking a short video of us as we ride down?"

"Why don't you girls film each other and I'll give your tube a shove to get you started. We're set up to help you with the initial push, but don't typically take pictures."

"I understand," Sylvie said with a pout.

She lifted her t-shirt over her head, revealing the white, open-weave top hugging her torso. Nothing was left to the imagination.

"I couldn't very well come in the park dressed like this, but I think it will make for some great pictures. Here, hold my shirt. I'll be right back up."

The young park attendant, flabbergasted at the sight, held her shirt as directed. As she sat in the inner tube, she saw the group following them had gone over to the zip lines. Both attendants were now busy, with the schooner ride attendant happily so. Sylvie squealed with delight as she hurtled to the end of the ride.

Erica was next. She did as Sylvie had done, and removed her t-shirt. She wore a see-through orange bikini top and sat in the next inner tube, her hands covering her breasts. When she was certain she had the attendant's full attention, she turned toward him and shrugged her shoulders before lifting her hands high over her head. The attendant's stare followed her ride to the end.

Finally, it was Karen's turn. She looked at the happy attendant and smiled.

"So, I guess you want to do the same? What have you got on beneath *your* t-shirt?"

Karen whipped off her shirt and held it in front of her.

"Hope you're not disappointed, but I forgot to put on an extra layer. These will have to do," she said, moving her balled-up shirt to her side, revealing her breasts for his visual consumption. "I better keep my shirt with me to put on at the bottom of the ride. I don't want to get in trouble, so I probably shouldn't come back to the platform topless. Since you won't be holding my shirt, can I talk you into please filming me on the ride down? Here, let me show you."

She moved next to him and handed over her phone. The young attendant, never taking his eyes off her bare chest, took the camera. Karen leaned in, her breasts brushing against his arm, as she adjusted the setting for taking the video.

"Thanks," she smiled, backing away toward the inner tube, allowing him to continue with his unobstructed view

She sat back, and he gave her inner tube a shove with one hand while filming with the other, panning in on her jiggling breasts. When the girls were back at the platform, Paul, Gary and Rick were at the entrance of the caves undetected.

Sylvie continued to be the spokesperson for the girls.

"That was fun! You rock. I'm wondering, would it be possible to do something a little more daring later today? Maybe near closing, when there aren't so many people around?"

"That would be highly irregular. I shouldn't have gone along with what you've done already. If anybody found out about what you girls did, I could be fired."

"Do you really think any of us, who just rode down the mountain half naked, look like somebody who would tell? Girls, we may be losing our touch."

"Oh, come on," begged Karen. Looking at his nametag, she continued. "David, you should know we just want to have fun."

As if on cue, Erica began singing the Cyndi Lauper song.

"That's all they really want, is some fun. When the working day is done, oh girls, they wanna have fun. Oh girls just wanna have fun."

David laughed and the girls knew they were in control. They would provide a great second act for the final and most important diversion.

"We'll be back here around three o'clock," said Karen, taking the next turn to talk. "I know the park closes at four, so we'll be done before then and let you and your buddies go home on time."

"My buddies?"

"Sure." Erica was back in command. "We entertained you, but I noticed there are two more hard-working guys manning the zip lines. If you want to invite them? We can give you a fitting show to end the day, ride the schooner inner tubes to the bottom, and streak out of the park. Did I say streak? I hope that wasn't too much of a hint."

"I'll look for you around three. I probably won't have any trouble convincing my friends to bend the rules a little, just this once," he smiled conspiratorially. "I'm going to invite them, don't make me look bad by not showing up or chickening out."

Erica turned her back to him, and in one motion slid her shorts and thong bikini bottom to her knees, and mooned him for a full five seconds. She pulled her shorts back up, turned around and smiled.

"We'll be here, and we *won't* chicken out."

She led the girls to the chair lift to ride to the summit for the ride down the steepest zip line in the world. As they rode to the top, Erica smiled at Sylvie and Karen.

"I'd say that went well."

They all burst into laughter, ready for more fun at the top, relishing their all-star performance the whole ride up.

THIRTY-SEVEN

PAUL WAS THE first to step inside the cave.

"I don't think anyone will be able to hear us talking, but let's keep our voices down just in case. I'm going to spend a few minutes filming. At first glance, this does not look like the original site, but looks like they were unearthed elsewhere and brought here. To be on the safe side, and to document the conditions before our removal, I'm going to record everything in case it later becomes important."

Gary and Rick hung back at the entrance of the cave as Paul filmed. After a few minutes, Paul waved them in. They walked over to a large mound of dirt. Small bits of several carvings could be seen above the heaped soil.

"It looks like these may have been hurriedly covered. Maybe he was surprised by someone coming and just covered as best he could quickly. Who knows?"

"So, what now? Is this everything?"

"My client said that there's a shovel in the back of the cave and that more artifacts are there. Let's go look."

Paul broke out his powerful flashlight and they walked twenty feet to the end of the cave. Paul wedged the flashlight into a crevice of the cave wall, where it illuminated the back of the cave. There, flat on the ground and partially covered by dirt, was a standard wood handle round-point shovel.

"Great. This makes it much easier. I'm relieved I won't need to sneak a shovel in here. The second batch of relics are supposed to be buried a few feet from the shovel. Let's take turns. I suggest we start digging back here and work our way to the entrance of the cave."

"It's about eleven o'clock now. When do we leave for lunch?"

"Rick, that's a good question. I think we need to improvise. My original thought was to test if we could make it here undetected by the park employees, make sure there really is treasure, then leave for lunch, to come back near closing to get the carvings. Now that we've made it here, I don't want to risk someone seeing us leaving and coming back. What do you guys think about starting with the uncovering while I go back and bring back some food and water? We can finish before dark, but will still need to wait for dark to carry everything out."

Gary and Rick agreed to the new plan. They emptied their backpacks that were filled by the laundry bags. Paul took the first turn digging, stopping after thirty minutes, already working up a sweat.

"No more digging for you until you're back with our food and water. You're already pretty sweaty," observed Gary, "and you need to be presentable for your role. We'll take it from here on the digging."

Gary carefully shoveled as Rick and Paul sifted through the dirt, and before 1:00 p.m., they had uncovered twenty-three relics.

"How much do you think what we've uncovered is worth?" asked Rick.

"It's hard to say," answered Paul. "There could be wide variability among the pieces. Hopefully my client's estimate of about $10 million for everything is accurate. We'll just have to wait and see."

At 1:15 p.m. they were all hungry, but primarily thirsty.

"I'll step out to bring us back some food and water. Don't overdo it while I'm gone."

Paul stepped cautiously out of the cave and worked his way back to the fringe of the trail beneath the chairlift. It was a wide expanse until he could reach the platform. Seeing the workers above, he knew his chances of making a dash for it unseen were slim. He needed a distraction, but the next one was not scheduled until 3:00 p.m. He decided to walk down the mountain and emerge at the far point of the parking lot. He hoped for an opening to dart back among the customers arriving for the attraction without calling attention to his movement from the woods. He began the trek down.

THIRTY-EIGHT

LEKHA REACHED THE parking lot and scurried in DK Gems. She still felt flustered.

"Good morning," said Jeff looking up. "Everything okay?"

"Yes, I was just delayed by a motorist who had broken down in my neighborhood. Where's Jason? I need to talk to him."

"I'm right here," Jason responded, coming out from the back room when he heard Lekha's shaky voice.

As he stepped into the showroom, he could immediately see that something was wrong. His ears had not deceived him.

"Jeff, I'm sorry to do this, but I need to step away to talk to Lekha. We'll be back out in just a minute."

The two walked into the back room where Lekha stood, closing her eyes, and shaking her head side-to-side trying to make sense of everything.

"It happened again. There was a broken-down motorist near our house. He seemed nice; I went out to check on him as I was leaving for work. He didn't have a phone and asked me to call for a mechanic to come out. As

I turned to leave, he asked about that night. He said he had heard about it too. And yes, it was a different person than the customer who came in yesterday."

"That's uncanny. What did you do?"

"This time I didn't deny it. He asked a few times, and I finally told him who we picked up. I didn't know what else to do. I was getting very uncomfortable, and it was the easiest way to stop talking about it. When I talked to Lisa last night, she said it would be okay to tell the truth and that I could give their names."

"You should call her to let her know what happened."

"I already have. She didn't answer, so I left her a message. I'm worried about her, and frankly, us. Let me try her again now."

She dialed Lisa's number, but she went immediately to her voice mail. Lekha left her another message.

"Hey Lisa, it's me, Lekha. I saw another person today who heard about that night when we saw you and Paul. I didn't deny it this time. I hope it's okay, but when he pushed the matter, I told him your names. He seemed nice enough, so I don't know that there is anything to worry about. But it's the second person in two days, so I wanted to let you know. Please be careful and call me when you get this message."

Lekha ended the call and turned to Jason.

"I think you've done all you can. Lisa and Paul already know to be careful. Try to relax. Do you want to go home?"

"No, I don't need to go home. I'll be fine. It's just pretty eerie how two people in the last two days have asked me about it. I hope there's nothing more to it than a coincidence. You can go back out with Jeff. I'll be out in just a minute."

Jason walked back into the showroom and began helping a customer. Lekha joined Jeff and Jason a few minutes later and resumed her normal routine. She prayed there would be no more discussion about that night by her customers.

As Lekha was telling Jason about the strange encounter, Samuel was finishing his call with Antonio.

"I've got the names. I think you know them, Paul and Lisa. I'm ready for my money."

"Yes, I know them. And you'll get your money."

"Thanks. You know Paul has a reputation as somebody not to mess with, right?"

"I've heard stories. I'm not about to back away from what will be a big pay day, and you shouldn't either. Are you still in to make some more money, or are you a big, tough guy on the outside, and chickenshit on the inside?"

"I can take you down any day," he scowled. "What do you want me to do, and how much is it worth?"

Antonio knew Samuel would take the bait, defending his honor and not say no to a request.

"You've got two grand coming to you, for another two you need to find Lisa and get that statue."

"How am I supposed to find her?"

"Do I need to earn your money for you? Go where she lives, see if she's home. If she's not there, wait for her, go in and get the goods. This needs to be finished today, no more delays."

Again insulted, Samuel responded to the challenge with a steely resolve and no concern about any danger.

"You'll get your dumb statue today. I want you to bring me the four grand at the Red Piano tonight. Do we have a deal?"

"I'll be there with the money. We'll see if you can do your part to earn it."

"It's done. Just be ready to pay. I don't want to have to club you with that statue to get you to pay, but I will."

"You're the man, Samuel, you're the man."

Samuel hung up and drove to the Cliff to try to find Lisa. He still wanted nothing to do with Paul. He was glad he was wearing his disguise.

He parked at the Cliff and walked to the reception area. The attractive clerk greeted him as he walked in.

"How may I help you?"

"I'm here to see Lisa, do you know if she's in?"

He gave the receptionist her condominium number.

The friendly receptionist prided herself on knowing all the residents by sight, especially long-time residents like Lisa and Paul.

"I'm sorry, but she's not in."

"Thanks, but would you mind calling up to check?"

"That won't be necessary. I was on duty this morning and saw her before she left. She was dressed for the beach. She's not back, and probably won't be back until late this afternoon. Do you want to leave a message?"

"Oh, that's right. Now that you mention it, I remember her telling me that. Oh well, I missed her. You wouldn't happen to know which beach she went to, do you?"

"No. But if you want to leave a message, I'll be sure to pass it along."

He believed the receptionist was becoming suspicious.

"No, I'll try calling her again. If I still don't reach her, I might come back later. Thanks."

Having ended the conversation, he turned and walked back to his car. Scanning his phone, he found Lisa on social media, and convinced he could recognize her in a crowd, called Antonio.

"Did you run out of gas on your way to find Lisa?"

"Very funny. But I got an idea and could use your gas."

"What is it?"

"There's a lot of security at the Cliff. I'm not going to be able to just watch her walk in the door and follow her. She'll likely park under the building where non-residents don't have access. So, I got a better idea than yours of sitting here waiting on her."

"All right, what do you want from me?"

"I'm going to get a beach towel and swimsuit and be back here at the Cliff in fifteen minutes. I need to leave my car here for when I walk out with the statue. But I need you to give me a ride. The receptionist here said she's at the beach, and based on her social media posts and where she lives, she's probably at Cupecoy Beach or Orient Beach. I want you to pick me up here and drive me to those beaches.

When I find her, you can go ahead and leave. I'll be catching a ride with her to her place. I'll get the statue, walk out to my car and drive away."

Antonio was tired of waiting to get his hands on the statue.

"I'm on my way," he sighed.

They ended the call and Samuel was back and parked at the Cliff in twenty minutes. He wore swim trunks, a t-shirt and tennis shoes. The prosthetic nose would not withstand time on the beach, so he reluctantly left that part of his disguise and the padding around his waist at home. As he parked, he saw Antonio's car pull into the parking place beside him. He hopped in Antonio's car to find Lisa.

THIRTY-NINE

PAUL REACHED THE bottom of the mountain with the goal of getting food and water for himself and his co-conspirators working in the cave. With his empty backpack on his back, he exited the woods near his car and marched purposefully to the attraction entrance, showed his park ticket, and leaned back as the chairlift moved under him. He rode the chairlift to the top and walked over to the mountaintop bar. He saw the girls relaxing with a drink and was waved over.

"What are you doing here? Where are the others?" asked Sylvie.

"They were digging for treasure when I left them," whispered Paul. "I'm here to get us some food and water. We decided it made more sense for me to get the rations while they continued to work. We had no problem sneaking to the cave, but this will reduce the risk of being seen before the job is finished."

Paul ordered a sandwich and water at the bar. He tipped the water bottle back and drained it. His sandwich came and he ordered a second water, then walked over to sit with the girls to eat.

"So, how did it go this morning? We made it unseen, or at least nobody came after us, but what happened when we left the platform?"

"We gave them a little show," answered Erica. "We took off our shirts for the ride in the inner tubes. I'm wearing a little bikini top, Sylvie had on some kind of fishnet top where the holes were about as big as my hand, and Karen just decided to let the girls fly free. It was a success," she laughed.

"I'm sure it was," he said smiling.

Paul looked admiringly at his friends for helping out without a second thought.

"You did great. Thanks for stepping outside your comfort zone to make it work," he said kiddingly. "Are you set for one more performance to get me back to the cave?"

"Oh yes. The second act begins around three o'clock. We should have a very attentive audience."

Paul wolfed down his sandwich and sat sipping his water. Feeling refreshed, he was eager to get back to the cave with food and water for Rick and Gary.

"I'm going to order the stuff for the guys. I'll be right back."

He walked to the bar, ordered two more sandwiches, and half a dozen bottles of water. Placing them in his backpack, he returned to the table with the girls.

"It'll be time in a few minutes. I'll ride the chair lift down to the level with the schooner ride and you three need to ride down a few chairs later. I'll hang around, waiting for my chance to make my run for it. The attendants may be more alert on who is there with getting everyone cleared out before the show. You may need to do some more persuasive acting to distract them when I make my dash, and also convince them that everyone is gone and accounted for."

"Don't worry. We'll do whatever we need to do," assured Sylvie.

"All right, let's do this. I'm counting on you to be on your distractingly best behavior."

Paul walked over to the chairlift and joined a couple in the next chair as it descended to the platform halfway down the mountain. They slid off and were greeted by a park attendant on autopilot, who yet again gave directions to those wanting to continue the chairlift to the bottom, as well as for the other zip line and schooner rides. Paul ambled toward the continuation of the chairlift ride. The couple continued well ahead of him. Another chair with four passengers arrived, and they passed him as they were set to continue their ride down in the chairlift.

Paul watched them pass, and seeing no one else nearby, moved to the edge of the walk surface. There, he slid down the side of the mountain, dropping just off the path before any other tourists could come up behind him. He was in position to make his way across the clearing that stood between him and the woods to the cave. He would wait in hiding until the next distracting performance began.

Sylvie, Karen and Erica jumped out of their chair on the platform near the schooner ride. It was no surprise that the attendant stood waiting for them. He radioed his co-worker at the top to stop passengers from riding the chairlift as the agreed upon favor to the schooner ride attendant. For the next ten minutes, the attendant at the top instructed would-be riders that a test of the chairlift system was underway. The chairs would continue to run, but needed to be empty, during the short test. The tourists were thanked for their understanding and cooperation for the ten-minute delay.

"We're back," announced Erica as the three girls approached the ride. "Are you ready for us?"

The schooner ride attendant smiled. He radioed to his friends who were finishing with the last of the riders on the four nearby zip lines.

"My buddies are on their way over. We're ready for the show."

The girls' concerns for Paul returning unseen to the cave were minimized when none of the attendants asked any questions, or even looked to confirm all riders to the platform, had continued down the mountain.

Erica turned toward Sylvie, her hands out to her side, her jaw dropped questioningly, communicating her wonder that none of the workers were confirming that no other tourists remained.

"It's the islands," responded Sylvie as she shrugged her shoulders in Erica's direction. "As they say in Jamaica, *no problem, mon.*"

"We've arranged for a ten-minute intermission for your show," the lead attendant said. "Are you girls ready?"

"We're not," responded Erica. "But we're getting there," she teased as she lifted her t-shirt over her head.

Sylvie and Karen followed Erica's lead, and the three stood with their t-shirts by their sides.

"Sylvie, why don't you hang on to all of the clothes for us until we reach the end of the ride? Is that good with you, Karen?"

"Sure." Karen handed Sylvie her shirt, put her hands on her hips, and posed topless for the workers.

"I'll put everyone's clothes in the bottom of my innertube," responded Sylvie. "Now, could you guys tie three innertubes together? We thought it would be good if we formed a naked train down the mountain."

She lifted off her fishnet covering and held out her hand for Erica's bikini top. Erica untied her top and happily tossed it to Sylvie.

The attendant walked over to the inner tubes, wanting to please the girls.

"I'll hook the innertubes together now. We'll set them at the top of the chute, you can all board on flat land, then we'll give you girls a push down."

The tubes were tied together and ready for the girls to board.

"Right this way," the lead attendant stated, holding his hand out in the direction of the first inner tube.

"That one is mine," said Sylvie as she took three steps and stood next to the tube. "Is this it? You're ready for us to hop in now?"

"Yes," the attendant responded. "Hop on in."

Sylvie wanted to make sure Paul had enough time for a clean getaway. She had more in store for the workers to keep their eyes unwaveringly fixed on the girls.

"Erica, Karen, we can do better than this. These guys have gone to a lot of trouble to help us today. We need to keep our shoes and socks on for our run out of the park, but other than that, let's get real here."

She pushed her shorts down and stepped out of them. Tossing them onto the small growing pile of clothes, she stood naked and did a little twirl.

"All right girls, get with the program, time's a wasting," she instructed.

Erica and Karen slithered out of their remaining clothes and handed them to Sylvie.

"Now the naked train begins," announced Sylvie, placing the rest of the clothes in the bottom of her inner tube. "Let's boogie."

She sat on the small pile of clothes and looked back as Karen and then Erica settled into their inner tubes. They formed a line, each holding the grab bars on her tube, feet resting atop the opposite side of the tube. They were set, each positioned headfirst looking back at the attendants, their full femininity on display, as they waited for the push to start them down the chute.

Each of the attendants desperately wanted to participate. They all had a hand in the initial shove to start the train of innertubes on its downward journey. The girls yelled in delight as they bounced through the curves of the ride to the bottom.

The ride glided to a stop, and the three naked girls scrambled out.

"That was unreal," called Sylvie, waving back up to the helpful attendants, giving them one last eyeful. It was met with loud cheers and whistles from the guys. She picked up the pile of clothing from the inner tube.

Not diminishing the event by dressing, they decided to remain naked on the short run back to Sylvie's car. They dashed across the parking lot and piled into the car. Opting to dress later, Sylvie cranked the car and the naked trio sped off to the sailboat *Eclipse* to meet Brad.

FORTY

PAUL RACED ACROSS the clearing to the woods hiding the treasure cave. The park employees were oblivious to his movement as their brains shut down during the girls' diversionary performance. A little past 3:00 p.m., Paul entered the cave where Gary and Rick, dirty and sweaty, sat just inside the opening.

"Welcome back man. I pray you have water in that backpack," greeted Rick.

"Here you go."

Paul removed the backpack and handed each a water. They slugged the water back, looking for more.

"I got you both sandwiches, looks like you could really use some food too."

He looked deeper into the cave as he handed them their sandwiches.

"Other than the obvious, that it was too hot, how was it while I was gone?"

"We worked pretty steady, counting on you bringing water." Rick waved deeper into the cave. "Walk back there and check it out."

Paul walked to the furthest recess of the cave. The dirt had been smoothed and a stack of carvings were neatly piled along the western cave wall.

He walked back to them amazed and grateful for what they had accomplished.

"You guys did great. It looks like you've completed everything back there."

"Yep," answered Rick. "We dug up what we think is everything. After the last one we found, we kept digging for another two feet. We decided if there were more statues down there, the treasure gods didn't intend for us to get them."

Paul smiled. He did not count the statues, but he was pleased by the hefty pile his friends had erected.

"We also took some pictures as we dug. We tried to document our finds at the different layers."

"I'd say you got it all. You guys eat and rest. I'll dig for a while. You've earned a long break."

Paul began shoveling at the entrance. It was clear that someone had dug two large holes, one at the front of the cave and one at the back, dumped the statues into the holes, and covered them up.

"With what you guys have already done, we should be finished in a couple of hours. We'll load up our bags and wait for dark to leave with them."

Feeling guilty about how much was accomplished by Gary and Rick, Paul worked without stopping for the next hour.

"Let me take another turn," Gary volunteered. "Have some water. You need to rest. We can't have you too tired to carry some of this stuff to the cars."

"Gladly," replied Paul. "I'm going to sit outside and catch some breeze. I'll let you guys finish up."

Paul stepped outside and looked around. Everything was quiet. He hoped it stayed that way.

Gary and Rick took turns, alternating the shoveling every fifteen minutes. An hour later, they felt confident there were no more artifacts to unearth. Gary walked out to notify Paul.

"Come check it out. I think we're done. We've stacked everything up, but haven't shoveled the dirt back to fill the hole. We want you to see it first. If you agree that we've got everything, it won't take more than ten minutes to fill and smooth it out."

Paul followed Gary just inside and once again marveled at the second stack of artifacts.

"It looks good to me. You guys fill the hole and I'll start putting everything in the bags. When we're done, let's step out for some fresh air, have a water, and wait for dark."

FORTY-ONE

LAUREN AND BEN were on their way for a day at the beach. After shopping most of the previous day, they planned to take advantage of what they found most special about St. Martin. They parked near the Perch and found two chairs for the day.

"There's nothing like Orient Beach," remarked Lauren as she set down the beach bag and placed her towel on the chaise lounge.

Ben set his towel on the adjoining chair, undressed, and tucked his clothes into the bag. Lauren adjusted her chair to lay flat, undressed, and sprawled face down in the sun.

"I definitely know your happy place. If we're ever asked on the *Newlywed Game* television show, we'll both know the answer to the question of each other's favorite place on earth."

"That's an easy one," responded Lauren. "The more interesting question would be 'What would your husband or wife say if you asked him or her to sunbathe nude at the beach?'"

"Yes, that would be an interesting question. We probably need to practice answering that one. Lauren, what would you say?"

"I'd probably say something like, you've got to be kidding, neither of us would ever consider doing something like that."

Ben loved her answer and howled laughing.

"I thought that might be your response," he said, still snickering.

Lauren adjusted her chair, sitting upright to continue the conversation.

"Well, Ben, so that I could match your answer to get the ten points toward that brand new washer and dryer, what would you say?"

"I'm pretty sure I would lie just like you. I know we both have clients who might not understand or appreciate our full enjoyment of Orient Beach. So, I'll go with your answer and hope that my nose doesn't grow."

They both had a good laugh.

"This is simply the best way to enjoy a beach. I wish everyone would give it a chance on a nude beach, but they'll probably need encouragement from someone other than me," giggled Lauren. "Maybe one day my response will be different, but probably not, at least not yet. Instead of telling the world, I'll opt to be selective on who I tell."

"All right, I think we've adequately covered that topic and we're on the same page. What else should we discuss?"

"I have another question. This one's a real question."

Ben chuckled. "I thought the last question was a real one."

"Maybe it was, but this one is more real. It's not a question preparing for a game show. Can you believe how lucky we are with all the great friends we've met on this island?"

"That is a great question. Before visiting this island, I would not have believed it. However, very quickly, on the first trip to this island, it was clear that this island has a way of helping people make friends. It truly is a friendly island, as their marketing slogan says, with people who live here and people who visit. Now, I would find it hard to believe someone saying they visited this island and didn't make friends while here."

"Speaking of friends, I see some. There's Lisa, Kris, Carol and Shelly. Let's walk over and talk to them."

"Okay, let's do it. But let's just stay for a minute and come back. I don't want us to interrupt. We can let them know we'll be going to lunch around noon. If they don't have plans, we can ask them to join us."

"That's a deal."

Lauren and Ben walked over to the four girls sprawled in their chairs and soaking up the sun. A few minutes later, they excused themselves with plans for a group lunch. Lisa promised she would wave Lauren and Ben over when they were ready to eat.

"Now, back to why we came here this morning," Lauren said. Adjusting her chair down a notch, she reclined and surveyed the calm ocean. "I'll never get tired of this view. It looks like another perfect day in St. Martin."

She sighed contentedly as she basked in the sun.

FORTY-TWO

ANTONIO, DRESSED FOR a trip to the beach, drove to Cupecoy Beach with Samuel in the passenger seat. He parked at Dany's Beach Bar, paid Dany five dollars for parking, and walked to the entrance of the biggest of the beaches comprising Cupecoy.

Samuel walked down the hill to the beach while Antonio took a seat at the open-air bar and ordered a Corona from Dany. Samuel walked the length of the beach before returning to the bar.

"She's not here. Finish your beer and let's get out of here."

Antonio nodded to Dany, drained the bottle, and left money for the beer on the bar. They walked back to the car to make a quick check of the other Cupecoy beaches. After scouting out the other lightly populated beaches, they were satisfied Lisa was not at Cupecoy, and it was time to drive to Orient.

"I'll park at one end of the beach. We'll start at the most populated southern end and work our way to the Mont Vernon on the other end, if needed. If we don't spot her, I'll drive you back to the Cliff. You can just wait for her there. I'm counting on you being very persuasive to get her to tell you where she has that little statue."

They drove to Orient and turned in to the southern-most end near the Perch Restaurant and Bar. Samuel rushed out of the car to walk down to the beach while Antonio lingered back. In two minutes, Samuel returned with a huge smile.

"She's here. She's with a group, so I'll need to wait a bit before I approach her, but I've got this."

Antonio returned Samuel's grin.

"Maybe I'll hang here with you for a while. We can watch and wait for the right time to get her alone. Let's get some chairs down the beach from them."

"That's not needed. To prove it, you can leave now, I'll get a ride and have the statue before the day is out."

"My, my, what confidence. I'll leave it with you, then." Antonio turned and walked back to his car.

Samuel watched as Lisa walked away from her three girlfriends and heard her call to Lauren and Ben.

"Are you guys ready for lunch? We've worked up an appetite catching up this morning and we're ready to go."

"Sure," answered Ben. "Where do you want to go for lunch?"

"Aloha is open again. If it suits you guys, we'd like to go there. Meet us at our chairs when you're ready."

Knowing the waiters and waitresses at Aloha wore sarongs as the standard restaurant uniform, Ben wrapped a short sarong around his waist and Lauren fashioned a dress out of a pareo. Dressed in their wraps, they walked over to their four friends. Seeing Lauren and Ben dressed, each of the girls also wrapped in a light-weight sarong for lunch.

They walked as a group to Aloha. A sarong-clad waitress sat them at a table for six. When their waiter came to the table to take their orders, Ben asked a neighboring diner to take a photo that included the waiter and waitress.

Feeling celebratory, they had pre-lunch drinks, during lunch drinks, and after-lunch drinks.

In addition, complimentary rum shots, customary in better restaurants in St. Martin, were brought to the table after the lunch plates were cleared away and the bill was paid. Shelly held her shot glass and looked in Ben's direction.

"You should be feeling very special. You're the only man at the table."

Ben reached for Lauren's hand, gave it a squeeze and grinned. "You're right, I am feeling very special."

"You're also the only one baring your chest," continued Shelly playfully. "That doesn't seem right. What if I wanted to eat topless?"

"Yes," chimed in Carol. "Why is it accepted for men and not women? That doesn't seem fair," she teased.

Overhearing the comments, the Aloha waitress returned to the table, surprising them by placing a full bottle of complimentary passion fruit rum on the table.

"Enjoy. If you finish that, another bottle is waiting for you. And by the way, I agree with you girls," she said grinning as she re-wrapped her sarong around her waist, leaving her chest uncovered.

Needing no further encouragement, the girls joined Ben in topless rum shots. A toast to Hawaii in St. Martin completed the outstanding dining experience. Feeling the effects of their alcohol consumption, the group made their way back to their chairs.

Lauren and Ben pulled their chairs over to join the others, and the party that began at lunch continued most of the afternoon. Ben brought a final round of drinks to their chairs from the Perch Bar to end the day, and by 4:00 p.m., the party began to break up. They gathered their clothes and towels before sharing goodbye hugs.

Ben refrained from drinking between lunch and the final round. Feeling capable of safely driving, he asked if anyone wanted a lift.

Kris, Shelly and Carol were in one car, as Kris felt sober enough to drive. Lisa, who after lunch also moderated her alcohol consumption, planned to drive. Satisfied everyone would be safe, they walked to their cars.

Samuel sat watching the girls all afternoon. As the group passed by him, he allowed them to reach their cars. Ben and Lauren sat in their car and Kris, Carol and Shelly in the other. Samuel called out to Lisa before she could open her car door.

"Hey, Lisa?"

Lisa turned to see who called out her name.

"I thought that was you."

She paused at her car as Samuel slowly walked toward her, giving time for Ben and Kris to pull out of the parking lot before getting within a few feet of Lisa.

"Hey, how are you? I'm sorry, but I don't remember meeting you. I feel awkward that you remember my name, but I'm drawing a blank."

"Oh, no problem. Don't feel bad. You're a celebrity."

Lisa, puzzled at his remark, wrinkled her nose at his comment.

"A celebrity? I hardly think so."

"Oh yes, you're part of the famous naked couple that people are talking about."

"What?"

She looked at Samuel, a look of concern beginning to replace her smile. Samuel continued despite her change in demeanor.

"Oh yes. I'm pleased to meet you. If you don't mind, I have a favor to ask. It's about a little statue. I'm here to pick it up from you. It seems the owner misplaced the statue and wants it back."

"Look, I don't know what you're talking about."

"I'm going to make this real easy," he said sternly. "I'm not going to debate you. You know, and I know, you have it. And I know you're going to give it to me. If you give it to me now, we can both just go our separate ways. If you insist that you don't know what I'm talking about, someone I know will be very effective at fixing your memory. Take my advice. It will be much better for you if you stop talking and hand over the statue."

Reality began to sink in, and Lisa recognized she was in a perilous situation with no one around to come to her rescue. She feared he could hurt her, or worse.

"I'll cooperate. You can look in my bag and car, and you'll see for yourself I don't have anything you want."

"So where is it?"

"At home. It's at home."

"Unlock your car. I'll ride with you. This won't take long, and if we get there and you give it to me, this is over. If we get there, and there's no statue, or you don't give it to me, this isn't over, but you are."

He lifted the tail of his t-shirt for effect. She saw the handle of the small gun tucked in the waistband of his swimsuit.

She obediently climbed into her car as he slid in beside her. Her mind was racing as she began driving to the Cliff.

FORTY-THREE

LISA TYPICALLY CHECKED her telephone for messages when returning home from the beach. Certain that the stranger sitting next to her would not allow her to use her phone, she left it untouched at the bottom of the beach bag.

She pulled out of the Orient Beach parking area and, in the quiet of the car, could hear her phone vibrating. Samuel heard it also.

"Let's ignore that."

When the vibrations ended, he reached back for her bag, and fished out the phone.

"What's your access code?"

She gave him the code, he tapped it in, and scrolled through recent messages.

"You've gotten new voice and text messages today. I'm sure you're curious. I'll check them out for you."

Samuel played three voice messages from Lekha expressing concern after her encounter with the stranded motorist.

"My oh my, it sounds like I'm not the only one who heard about you running around naked at night. How many people know about you? As I said, you've become famous," he lied. "Now let's check your text messages."

Samuel read all of the missed messages to her as she continued driving. He wanted to find out about Paul's whereabouts, nervous that Paul could be waiting at the Cliff.

"It's interesting that of all the messages you received today, there are no messages from Paul. Why is that?"

"I don't normally get messages from Paul."

"Where is Paul?"

"I don't know. He was at home when I left this morning."

"As a couple running around naked together, I'm guessing you're on pretty good terms," he said sarcastically. "So, he probably said where he was going and what he was doing today." Samuel lifted the tail of his shirt and tapped the handle of the handgun. "Why don't you share with me what he said?"

Lisa gripped the steering wheel tighter, feeling her heart beat faster.

"I told Paul that some friends of mine asked me to meet them at the beach today. He said I should go and have fun. He would keep himself busy and see me tonight," she said in a shaky voice.

"He didn't tell you what he was going to do to keep himself busy or where he was going?"

"No, it was all about me this morning. I've been stressed and he knows it. I told him what I wanted to do, and he told me to go enjoy myself. I kissed him goodbye and said I'd see him tonight. That's it."

Samuel did not press her. He decided that she had enough time to make up something and that it was unlikely he would be able to find out his whereabouts with certainty from what she said. Satisfied there were no messages indicating Paul would be at the Cliff, he would continue with the plan. If Paul was there, he would press his advantage with a gun trained on Lisa. Paul would be powerless to do anything other than hand over the artifact.

They reached the Cliff and Samuel directed Lisa to park in the guest lot. He carefully followed her out of the car and in through the lobby. The receptionist on duty was not the one Samuel met earlier in the day and merely glanced up while on the phone. Taking the elevator, they exited at Lisa's condo. She unlocked the door and he pushed her inside.

Relieved at not finding Paul there, Samuel pulled the gun from his waistband.

"Forgive me for this," he said, pointing the gun at her. "I don't plan to use it, but I don't like surprises either. If you'll bring me the artifact, I'll be on my way."

"It's in the bedroom on the nightstand."

"Fine, I'll go with you to get it."

She led him into the bedroom, and he saw a small statue standing as she had described.

"I'll get it, you stand right there."

Samuel walked over to the statue, picked it up, and motioned her out of the bedroom with the gun.

"Now, that wasn't so bad. I'm leaving now. Unfortunately, I need to inconvenience you one more time. I can't leave your phone with you."

He pulled the phone back out of the beach bag and shoved it in the pocket of his swimsuit.

"I think it would be nice if you see me out. Walk back with me to your car and then you can park in your normal place. Once you're parked, walk over to where your car was first parked. Because I'm a nice guy, I'll leave your phone right there. But hurry back to get it, somebody could be tempted to take it. Not everybody's as honest as me."

Lisa nodded her understanding of what he said.

They stepped out to the parking lot and Samuel watched as she drove to the residents' parking area. He wiped the phone clean of prints and placed it in the middle of the vacated parking space. He walked the short distance to his car, pulled away and removed his wig. He would darken his eyebrows to their natural color once safely back in his home.

Samuel was out of sight when Lisa rushed over to retrieve here telephone. She was relieved to see it sitting in the parking place as promised. Carrying her phone inside, she locked the door behind her and sat on the balcony overlooking the ocean. No longer in imminent danger, she refrained from calling Paul, waiting for him to contact her. She sent a short message to Lekha stating that all was well, Paul was out, but that she would call after she had a chance to talk with him. She set her phone down, continuing to gaze at the ocean below. Her body relaxed with relief from feeling safe following a day of sun and alcohol. Listening to the lullaby of the breeze and ocean, she closed her eyes and fell into a deep sleep.

FORTY-FOUR

SAMUEL CALLED ANTONIO as he drove.

"I've got it. If you have the cash, I'll bring it to you now."

"I'm ready for you. Come on over."

Not wanting to take any chances on something going wrong, Antonio waited until he had the statue in his hands before calling Wendall. He stood in his doorway as Samuel pulled up and waved him inside. Samuel walked in and smiled broadly as he held the artifact out to Antonio.

"Have a seat. I'll call the boss now and then get your money."

Thrilled at the good news, Wendall authorized the payment to Samuel, and instructed Antonio to bring the artifact to him within the hour.

Antonio stepped into his bedroom and returned with the cash, handing over the $4,000.

"Sam, it's been a pleasure doing business with you. But as you heard, the boss wants this now. I'll walk you out."

Samuel drove home to darken his eyebrows and Antonio drove to see Wendall. Wendall ushered him into his house and examined the statue.

"Well, look what you have here. Outstanding, I'll get this evaluated immediately for authenticity. You'll be rewarded in your next paycheck."

Antonio left, pleased that he proved his value once again.

Wendall uncapped a celebratory beer and called Gregorio. He was finishing up his workday but was still in his office and answered the call.

"Good afternoon Wendall. Does this call mean you're ready for my help?"

"Yes, it does. I need your expert to give me an evaluation of an Arawak artifact I've uncovered. If this is authentic, there are many more where it came from."

"All right, my expert is in Anguilla. It's a small community of people familiar with these things. Do you want her to come to you, or do you want to go to Anguilla? For me, I'm sure she will meet with you as soon as tomorrow. I'll call her to make the introduction, let her know you'll be in touch. Wait fifteen minutes, then give her a call. Here's her number."

Gregorio hung up from the call and placed the promised call. Fifteen minutes later, Wendall called the contact and made arrangements to take the artifact to her art studio the next morning.

FORTY-FIVE

THE SUN HAD set as Paul, Rick and Gary finished the last of their water. The artifacts were packed in the laundry bags, and they were ready to begin the hike down the mountain. Paul cautioned Rick and Gary again of the possibility of encountering others after his experience when bringing the first artifact down from the mountaintop.

At 7:00 p.m. they began the trek down, staying under the cover of the surrounding foliage. They refrained from talking as they concentrated on maintaining their footing on the uneven terrain.

Every few minutes Paul stopped to listen for any unwanted sounds. Gary and Rick followed closely behind, stopping with him, waiting for his whispered okay to continue.

They worked their way to the bottom, and as Paul had feared, several men patrolled the area of the parking lot. They did not appear to be associated with the Flying Dutchman attraction, as they were dressed in dark clothing and were difficult to discern.

"We need to hang here. I don't know how long they'll be patrolling, but we can't make it unseen to our cars as long as they're here. If they don't leave soon, we'll need to create a diversion."

Fifteen minutes later, Paul grew impatient.

"We could be out here all night. Gary, I'm putting you in charge of my bag. I'm going to work my way around to the other side of the field and make some noise. With any luck, they'll follow my noise up the mountain. I'll look for a way to circle back, but when you hear the commotion, wait one minute and make the break to your cars. Throw the artifacts in and drive over to Orient Beach as planned. Continue with the plan, but without me. No matter what you might hear, keep going. Don't hesitate. Hopefully I'll meet you later."

Gary nodded and pulled Paul's bag over to him.

Paul soundlessly moved away from Rick and Gary. When he was a hundred yards away, he walked to the edge of the foliage, looking out over the field where some cars remained. It was time to implement the makeshift plan. He purposefully made some noise, attempting to attract the attention of the three men patrolling below. He saw the movement of the men stop. Believing they heard him, he picked up two small branches at his feet and snapped them, the sound carrying to the open field. The three men started moving in his direction. As quietly as possible, he crept up the slope thirty feet before intentionally stomping on some brittle underbrush. The three were moving rapidly. Paul watched as they spread out over seventy-five feet and began to pick their way up the mountain.

"You, up there," the leader called to Paul. "Come down now and show yourself."

Paul kneeled quietly, trying to stay hidden.

The leader called to the other two. "I think I see him. Up there," he pointed.

Hearing he was possibly spotted, Paul's mind shifted to full combat mode. He silently made his way up the mountain as quickly as possible, increasing the distance between him and his pursuers. He stopped to assess how much separation he had gained, when he heard the crack and felt a stinging pain at the same time. With an exhale, he reached for the burning, feeling the wet area on the outside of his arm. Relief flooded him as he tested his arm and still had full movement. His fingers explored the area, confirming he was grazed, but no bullet remained. He moved more rapidly up the mountain and again stopped to listen. Although he had increased the distance between them, he could still hear the men talking in hushed tones.

"I might have hit him. Let's keep running him. You guys go about forty feet either side and let's continue up. Don't give him any room to double back."

Paul used their words for additional inspiration. He quickened his strides, keeping noise barely detectable. A few minutes later he stopped to listen, and this time could not hear them trampling the underbrush. He did his best to run, knowing the sound might be heard, but was determined to increase the distance even further. Finding a patch of trees to his liking, he stopped and climbed up. About ten feet off the ground, he found a broad branch where he stood with his back flush against the tree trunk. He believed it was unlikely they would be scanning up in the trees to find him. He waited, his breath shallow, for them to travel by his hiding place.

Ten minutes passed before he heard someone moving through the underbrush. Rigidly still, he watched as a pursuer with gun drawn, crept to the base of the tree and just past.

Looking down, the man was a little further away than ideal, but close enough. Paul pushed away from the tree, launching himself in the air, his arms poised one above the other as he took aim. His body crashed down on the unsuspecting pursuer, who dropped the gun with the contact. They hit the ground with Paul's vice-like grip around the stalker's head and neck. The impact of the ground beneath his adversary jarred Paul, his grip twisting more than intended. Paul stood and appraised the man who lay motionless at his feet.

With stealth movement, Paul began his descent back down the mountain. Even if his attack was heard, Paul counted on a minute or more passing before the other two found their fallen comrade. Paul moved efficiently down the mountain, pausing only for a second as he approached the clearing, then broke into an all-out sprint to his car. He climbed in and drove to the main road, only then turning on his lights and allowing himself to tap the brakes. Rick and Gary had a thirty-minute head start, but he decided to drive straight to Orient Beach. He called Lisa ten minutes into his drive.

"Everything is fine," he began when she answered. "Sorry it's later than I expected. I was delayed, but the others went ahead of me. Right about now Brad should be in his dinghy meeting Rick and Gary, and loading Brad's boat with a huge haul of artifacts. I'm on the way there now. I hope to be home in about an hour. How is everything there?"

"Everything is fine. It's been an interesting day, but I think you'll be pleased. The day may have been better than hoped for. Be careful. I'll be waiting for you."

They ended the call, with Paul's next call to Gary. When Gary answered, Paul began talking.

"All well here. I'm on the way to Orient. How is everything there?"

"The treasure has been stowed on Brad's sailboat. Brad and Sylvie are aboard, and Erica and Karen are leaving with us now. Do you want us to wait on you?"

"No, it sounds like everything is done. I'm going to turn around and go home. We'll talk tomorrow."

Paul turned his car toward home and called Sylvie. Sylvie immediately answered.

"Are you okay?"

"Yes, I'm fine."

"The boys said they might have heard a gunshot. Are you sure you're fine?"

"Yes, no problems. And the loot?"

"Wow, the dinghy could barely hold it all," she exaggerated. "Brad will be on guard, it's stowed, so you can sleep soundly tonight."

"You did a great job today. Everybody did a great job today. With luck, we'll receive our payout soon. Let's talk tomorrow."

"Paul, I know I don't have to say this, but be careful. We're not letting our guard down, and we don't want you to either."

"You'll never have to worry about that," he assured her.

They ended the call. Paul was grateful when he finally reached the security of his garage. Lisa opened the door before he could use his key. They had a lot to talk about during their late dinner.

FORTY-SIX

PAUL AND LISA were awake as the sun came up. Paul's arm had been attended to by Lisa, the bleeding had stopped, and they realized how the night could have turned tragic had the bullet's trajectory been slightly different.

The original plan for the treasure was for Paul to present the Arawak artifact he retrieved from the mountaintop to the museum curator for authentication, thereby giving credibility to the other pieces in the cave. Augustus, as the finder of the artifacts, would have more negotiating power when selling the entire collection of found artifacts.

After Paul and Lisa were pursued, Paul decided to change the plan. The artifact created by Marcus Richards would be determined to be of little value by the museum curator, and the danger of others wanting the artifacts would go away. A sale of the collection could occur without fear of theft and without danger to him, Lisa, Lekha and Jason.

"It looks like the plan has changed again," sighed Lisa. "I'm sorry I wasn't more careful at the beach."

"I'm glad you weren't hurt. You handled the situation well. The only change in plans is that instead of me having the curator determine the artifact is of little value, the person taking the replica yesterday will determine that for himself. it's like cutting out the middleman. Hopefully the result is the same, they cool their heels for what will be presumed as a worthless collection, and we can negotiate a sale without continuing danger."

"So, you took the real artifact in your backpack yesterday?"

"Yes, I figured it was safest with me. It also made for an easier delivery to the boat with all the other artifacts last night."

"So, what do we do today? When do you think we can go back to normal life?"

"We need to play it safe a while longer. Today is a good day to stay in. Right now, you and I are the only ones known to be involved, and possibly Augustus. I'll call him, he needs to stay in hiding for at least one more day. I need to convince him that I'll sell everything, all he needs to do is stay put to collect his money, but that we're now fifty-fifty partners."

"I want to call Lekha this morning. I think everything should be back to normal for her and Jason."

"I agree. They can tell everything they know if pressed, even that we had an artifact. It will soon be determined to be worthless."

"I'm going to call her now before she goes into work. She'll be relieved that we're both fine and they can have their normal lives back."

As Lisa called Lekha, Paul walked into his office to call Augustus. After thirty minutes of discussion, the two men reached an agreement as equal partners; Augustus accepting that Paul had all the treasure and the power to dictate terms. They agreed that Paul would oversee selling the collection. Paul assured him the treasure was safe but would not divulge its location. If Augustus decided to come out of hiding despite Paul's recommendation to stay out of sight, Paul emphasized Augustus would not be his concern. He would take no action to help him if he were captured. Augustus fully understood the warning, and that if anything happened to him, Paul stood to be the sole owner of the treasure. Augustus promised to remain in hiding.

Satisfied that Augustus would stay put, Paul called the potential artifacts buyer he had lined up. Martha, the owner of a large horse farm in Anguilla, had accumulated great wealth. As an avid historian, she was the best candidate to pay top dollar for the collection of artifacts. Despite the early hour, and the fact that she maintained an early schedule for her horses, she answered his call on the first ring.

"Martha, this is Paul. I'm following up with you on the Arawak artifacts. When we last talked, I planned for the collection to be ready for you to view today and we are right on track. It's all set if you can make it to St. Martin to take a look."

"That sounds great. I was hoping we were still set."

Paul, upon hearing her comment, had the feeling she had more to say.

"Sure, everything's set. Is there a problem?"

"I was hoping not, but you can't be too sure. Tell me the time and place in St. Martin and I'll be there."

Paul, still feeling somewhat unsure about her comment, wanted to know more about her concerns before sharing the location of the treasure.

"Martha, as we discussed, this transaction is to remain very quiet. It would not be good if word of your purchase snuck out before the deal is done. You've piqued my curiosity. Has something happened that you're having second thoughts?"

"Oh no, I'm not having second thoughts. I was just afraid that you might not have the collection."

"Why would you say that?"

"Well, it's very coincidental, but my daughter, Sue, was recently contacted by someone to evaluate an Arawak artifact. It's not every day there's a potential Arawak find, so to have two people with a find at the same time made me wonder if you had lost the collection to someone else."

"Rest assured, I have not. Did you tell your daughter about the deal we're working on?"

"Absolutely not. I love my daughter, but business is business. I understand the nature of our relationship and the confidentiality required. I would never jeopardize a deal by talking, and that includes discussing with my daughter."

"I trust you're telling the truth. Sharing with anyone, even your daughter, could put you in danger."

"Paul, this isn't my first deal, and it won't be my last. Let's get on with it."

"Fine but I have another question. Do you know how the person came to know about your daughter as an expert?"

"Just as I won't share anything about our deal, I won't share the name of the person who contacted my daughter. But I can tell you she was recommended by Gregorio."

"Thank you, Martha, do you need anyone else to corroborate your appraisal?"

"Nope. I'm the best there is. Once I see them, I'll tell you immediately what I'll pay you. I won't negotiate. I'll give you my best price, and if you accept, we'll have a deal. If you want to shop the material, I understand, but there'll be no need to come back to me. If you reject my offer, I won't make another one."

"I understand. Let's work out the details for you to see the artifacts today."

FORTY-SEVEN

AFTER SPENDING A great day together as a couple, Dean listened as Debi presented her idea. After some discussion, he was agreeable but far from enthusiastic.

"Dean, are you sure you're still willing to do this?"

"I guess so, but it seems a little extreme to me. The wedding on Saturday will be special enough without us doing something strange to make it more special."

"It definitely will be special no matter what. But I was reading in a magazine about the new trend for engaged couples living together to be apart a few days prior to their wedding. It's supposed to serve as a reminder of single life and how special marriage truly is."

"Even if I believed the value in that, why would it apply to us, we're already married?"

"Yes, in Canada. But we're not in Canada, we're in St. Maarten, and about to be married in St. Maarten. So, it makes sense for us to give it a try."

Dean shrugged, knowing he was wasting time if he tried to change her mind.

With the agreed upon temporary separation, Debi packed a small bag to stay at La Playa for a few days sunning on the beach, while Dean opted to spend his time working at the casino. They could call and text but would not see each other again until the day of the wedding.

Debi sent a text message to Lauren, asking if she and Ben would meet her at Orient Beach. Lauren replied immediately that they could make it and for Debi to save them beach chairs.

"Dean, I'm going to leave now. I'm meeting Ben and Lauren at the beach. Remember, this is your last chance to live the single life and be the most eligible bachelor in St. Maarten," she kidded.

"Right dear, even though we're already married."

He thought it was so crazy that it was almost comical. He looked at her questioningly.

"Is it acceptable for me to get a goodbye kiss?"

"Sure. Do you want me to make it a quick sweet one, or one where you'll be taking a cold shower as soon as I walk out the door?"

"I've already showered for the day. Better make it a quick sweet one."

She put her hands on his chest, leaned toward him, and planted a quick peck on his cheek.

"There, that was my sweetest. You have fun in the casino. And remember, you're single and married, so don't be scoping out any women while I'm away."

"You are too funny. Have fun and thank Lauren and Ben again for hosting the wedding. You know you're crazy, don't you? But I guess that's one of the reasons I love you."

"I love you too. You can start looking forward to the wedding night. Don't work so much at the casino that you're all tuckered out on Saturday night."

She turned to leave, tempting him with an exaggerated shake of her hips.

"Miss me, but don't miss me too much," she called back to Dean. "This separation is really working. I haven't even left, and I can hardly wait to get my hands on you," she teased.

She walked out the door, and Dean felt the same way about already missing her.

"Maybe this crazy separation idea isn't so crazy after all," he said aloud to himself. "But I'll never admit it to her."

FORTY-EIGHT

WENDALL RECEIVED A full report of the activities of the prior night of how his men had chased someone up the mountain. It had not turned out well. Not only did the person escape, but Wendall suffered a casualty. The body would be quietly disposed of with no police involvement. It was just another unexplained case of an islander disappearing, never to be heard from again.

Disturbed about the prior night's events, Wendall nevertheless arrived in Anguilla early Wednesday morning to meet with Sue, the Arawak artifact expert recommended by Gregorio. He knocked on the door to her studio. The door opened and a young woman reached out her hand.

"Good morning, you must be Wendall. I'm Sue, pleased to meet you. Come on in."

"Yes, thank you for meeting me so quickly. I'm really excited about what I've found."

He delicately took the statue out of a bag and handed it to her.

She walked it over to a long examining table and set it down under the bright overhead light.

"This is very nice work. Have you been a collector for a long time?"

"No, this is my first piece. I discovered this and a friend suggested I bring it to you to size up. I'm glad you think it looks good."

She turned the small statue, squinting as she leaned in for closer looks on all sides. She lifted it, checked out the base, and set it back down.

"Done."

"Wow, that was quick. I had no idea you would finish so fast. So how does this work? Will I get some kind of certificate of authentication? Do you provide a value?"

"I don't provide an official certificate. I do provide my opinion, though."

"Okay, I'm eager to hear it. What do you think?"

"Well, as I said when you first handed it to me, it is very nice work. I've seen similar work before, so it's a nice piece. I'm guessing it's worth a couple hundred dollars."

Wendall broke into a big grin.

"I know Gregorio thinks highly of you," he chuckled. "He didn't tell me what a good sense of humor you have. So, what do you think the real value is?"

She stood eye to eye with him.

"I'm sorry. I wasn't kidding. Although it's a nice piece of work, I would set the retail value at about two hundred dollars. This is not an authentic work by the Arawaks."

Wendall realized she was serious. His emotions quickly spiraled from confused and disappointed to mad.

"How can that be? It's been buried for hundreds, maybe thousands of years. It's got to be worth a thousand times that."

"You're welcome to get another opinion. I'm quite certain, however, that this has not been buried for hundreds of years. The clay has not been set for even a hundred days. It's an attractive piece, but an Arawak artifact it is not."

"So how do you explain how it came about? I'm almost certain it has been buried for at least hundreds of years."

"Wendall, I'm so sorry to disappoint you. Let me give you a name of someone also on island here in Anguilla. He's a sculptor and very knowledgeable on Arawak artifacts. He can give you his opinion, and perhaps shed some light on its creation. I assure you this is a relatively new work."

"Thank you. I'd love to talk with the person you're suggesting. Would you mind giving me his contact information? In fact, maybe you could give him a call, see if he's available for me to bring it by since I'm already in Anguilla."

"Sure, it's a small community of us who have any interest in historical finds. In addition to being a talented sculptor, he's a friend. Wait here, let me get his number and I'll give him a call."

Sue stepped away into a small room. He could hear her talking on the phone. A few minutes later she returned.

"I have good news for you. I was able to reach him. His name is Marcus Richards. He said he'll come over and take a look at it, if you don't mind waiting about fifteen minutes."

"That will be great. Thank you."

Wendall took a seat in her studio and waited to meet Marcus. Fifteen minutes later he stepped into Sue's studio.

"Hi, I'm Marcus," he said, holding out his hand and shaking Wendall's hand. "My friend here tells me you have an art piece you'd like me to take a look at."

"Yes, that would be great. It's over there," Wendall added, pointing to the statue on the examining table.

Wendall watched Marcus's face, and thought he saw a look of recognition.

"So, what do you think? Is it an authentic Arawak artifact?"

Marcus walked over to the statue and held it at different sight lines. After a few minutes, he placed it back on the counter.

"No, I'm certain it is not. I think it's a nice piece, but it doesn't have any historical significance, other than a similarity to how a genuine artifact might appear."

"Is there anything you're not telling me that I should know?"

"No, I don't believe so. If there's nothing further I can help with, I'll be heading back now."

Wendall looked at Sue.

"Thank you very much for your help. Marcus, do you mind if I walk out with you?"

Feeling inwardly nervous, Marcus believed he had no choice but to agree to his company. The two stepped out of Sue's studio.

"So, tell me the story behind this statue."

"I don't have anything else to tell. My opinion is consistent with Sue's, that it's not an Arawak artifact."

"Have you seen this statue before?"

"No, I've never seen it."

"You're a sculptor, right?"

"That's right."

"So, you've never seen it before. Because you've never seen it, then of course you didn't make it, is that right?"

"That's right," responded Marcus.

Wendall could tell he was lying. Knowing the only person likely to have requested Marcus make a phony statue was Paul, Wendall stopped grilling the young sculptor.

"Marcus, thank you for your time. You've been very helpful."

Wendall left for his boat to return to St. Maarten. He was encouraged that a genuine artifact existed, prompting the production of a fake to try to dissuade his pursuit. He needed to find Paul and get the treasure trove before it was too late.

FORTY-NINE

DEBI ARRIVED AT La Playa, was allowed an early check-in, and threw her suitcase inside, before walking to her favorite area of Orient Beach near the Perch Restaurant and Bar. She selected a beach chair and saved two adjacent chairs for Lauren and Ben. She sat back and was excited when she heard Lauren's voice.

"Good morning, Debi," called Lauren. "Thanks for saving us chairs. What a great surprise when I got your text."

Lauren and Ben undressed and settled into their lounges. Debi settled in as well, eager to talk.

"Dean and I started a trial separation, just until Saturday. It's something I read about, and we wanted to try, to make our wedding day even more special."

"So, you two won't have any contact until Saturday?"

"We can call and text, but we won't be staying together or have any physical contact until Saturday. Dean thinks it's dumb, but he's being a sweetheart and going along with it."

Wearing a conservative cut yellow bikini, Debi reclined in her chair with her beach bag beside her, but without the usual cooler.

"That doesn't seem to be the only change," remarked Lauren.

Debi smiled playfully before responding.

"Are you referring to my usual eleven o'clock champagne brunch? I intentionally left the cooler and champagne this morning. I decided it was too much work to pack and store champagne for the next three days. I'll just rely on the Perch until Saturday."

"Yes, that's part of the change I noticed, but I'm sure Ben hasn't noticed anything else," Lauren added with good-natured sarcasm.

"Are you referring to my swimsuit?"

"Well, yes, I've never known you to wear a swimsuit on Orient Beach. What's up with that?"

"I don't know if I'll be able to keep it on or not. It feels so strange. But I'm toying with the idea of having some tan lines for the wedding night. Lauren, what do you think?"

"That might be a question better answered by Ben. Ben, instead of commenting on Debi's tan lines or no tan lines, I'll make it easier for you, so you don't get yourself in trouble. We're engaged and it's getting close to time for our wedding. On our wedding night, do you want me to have tan lines or no tan lines?"

"I can honestly say that's something I've never thought about. I can't speak for any other men, but my guess is most won't give it much thought either way."

Ben put his hand to his chin, pretending to still be in deep thought pondering the question before continuing.

"Okay, you don't have tan lines, so I'll go with no tan lines. As I've heard contestants say on the Gameshow

Network, that old program *Family Feud* with Richard Dawson, that's my final answer, Richard. But in this case, it's not my final answer to keep the show moving, but my final answer because I don't want whatever I say to be the wrong answer."

Ben gave Lauren a silly smile, making sure she knew not to take his response seriously.

"Thanks for your input, and yes, well played, you're not in trouble. So, Debi, does that help? What will it be, tan lines or no tan lines?"

In response, Debi untied her top and slipped out of the bikini bottom. She placed them in her beach bag and leaned back in her chair.

"He fell in love with me with no tan lines, I haven't seen any disappointment so far, so to be on the safe side, I better make sure I don't have any unsightly tan lines on Saturday. Plus, I like it better and it's way more comfortable. We all know it's no fun to sit around in a wet swimsuit."

"Good decision. We're glad to be on the beach with you, but what is Dean doing today?"

"When I left, he planned to go to the casino. I think he'll be working until the wedding."

Debi held her hands out, palms up, as if weighing her options.

"Work, beach, I pick the beach every time. As Ben said, that's *my* final answer, but I'm glad one of us is industrious. A reason I wanted to come to the beach today, in all seriousness, is to thank you again for providing the place for the wedding. You guys have been great friends, and that makes it even more special to me."

Lauren was moved by Debi's serious statement.

"We're really looking forward to the wedding. From the plans we've heard, it sounds amazing."

"I know the wedding is not far off, but with my separation from Dean, it seems like too long. Instead of taking a cold shower, maybe it's time for me to take a cooling dip," she laughed.

"I'll keep you company," responded Lauren, looking at the blue sky atop the water. "It looks like it's going to be another perfect day on Orient Beach."

FIFTY

WENDALL HAD PAUL'S address and believed he and Lisa would be at home. He struggled to come up with a plan to get the treasure. Not knowing that the artifacts had already been moved for appraisal and sale, he called Antonio to keep a watch on Paul and Lisa. Antonio answered the call immediately when he saw it was Wendall.

"Antonio, I still need your help. The artifact you got from Samuel is a fake."

"What! How can that be?"

"It is. I just finished having an expert look at it. Not only is it a fake, but I'm also almost certain it was planted to throw me off. The real one is still out there."

"What do you want me to do?"

"I need you to find Paul or Lisa. We can't be picky. Whichever one you find first, get them and get the real artifact. There are more, and we need to find where they're hidden. Did you get any leads on finding Augustus?"

"No, nothing. He still hasn't been back at work."

"Call Baldo, get him to check for friends, family, neighbors, anybody who may know where he is. We need to move soon."

When Wendall ended his call with Antonio, he called Gregorio. He was pleased when Gregorio answered.

"Gregorio, thank you again for lending me use of Baldo. I hope you don't mind, but I just asked Antonio to reach out to him as I could use his help again."

"That's not a problem. I'm glad you're pleased with his services. In addition to Baldo, you asked for assistance with an appraisal. I trust my contact Sue provided the service you wanted?"

"Yes, thank you very much. I just finished meeting with her."

"I'm glad she could help. I've heard a few rumors about a collection of Arawak artifacts for sale. As you've just had a piece appraised, are you in touch with more items you are trying to sell?"

"I have some hope, but that hope is dwindling. I learned of a large find, but I'm afraid someone has beaten me to it. Any suggestions?"

"I assume you have tried the usual means of persuasion to acquire what you are after?"

"Yes, but so far without success."

"Then your next attempt could be through diplomacy. If you tell me the name of your competition, I may be better able to help you."

"You know him. He has historically flown under the radar but has created quite a reputation for himself. I think he may have brokered a deal involving one of your energy companies."

"I know who you're describing. If he has what you're after, he provides a formidable obstacle. You will need to be very creative to successfully make a claim with him."

"That's what I'm finding out. I would appreciate you sharing any ideas."

"I don't have any suggestions. As I do work with both of you, I'm not inclined to pick sides. I think you both expect that from me."

"Yes, Gregorio, I understand. Wish me luck."

"That I can do."

FIFTY-ONE

MARTHA ENDED THE call with Paul. She planned to boat from Anguilla to Brad's sailboat *Eclipse* around two in the afternoon. Paul called Sylvie and Brad and updated them on the plan. He would not board their boat, but Brad and Sylvie would lay out all of the artifacts for Martha's inspection. Paul hoped her evaluation would take no longer than a few hours, but mostly hoped she would declare them authentic and of great value. A lot of work and planning had gone into this, and everyone would be extremely disappointed if the artifacts were determined to be of little value.

Paul walked into the den where Lisa sat, staring vacuously out the patio window.

"It looks like you're wishing you were somewhere else. What are you thinking about?"

"I was just thinking that if I hadn't wanted to go up the mountain with you, you would have been much quicker. You would have made it down without leaving our clothes as a clue," she said smiling somewhat sadly, "and we wouldn't be trapped here today."

"I was just thinking the opposite."

Lisa looked at him, an accusatory look that he was just trying to placate her.

"No, seriously, I was. First off, it was a great night running around without clothes. Second, we're becoming much better friends with Lekha and Jason, which might have happened anyway, but not as soon. And third, and most importantly, the timing was about perfect." He spread his arms. "Let's say you're right and I would have been faster without you. I wouldn't have been twice as fast. I would have gotten the artifact and would have made it only part way down the mountain when they arrived. They could have gotten the artifact from me, and I could have been captured or killed. So, I think it's turned out the best possible way."

"Thanks. I don't know if you're right, but I like the story. Anyway, we're stuck here for the day and I'm already getting cabin fever."

"That's something else I want to talk to you about. The artifacts are safely loaded on Brad's boat. The hoped-for buyer will boat to *Eclipse* today around two o'clock, and Brad and Sylvie are going to show all the artifacts. I won't be meeting Martha, the buyer. But now that everything has been worked out, which is sooner than I expected, a change of plans for you and me might be okay."

"Really? Like getting out of here?"

"Yes, why don't we get ready and go down to the car, safely parked in the downstairs garage, and go to the beach. I think it's an acceptable risk to be on the beach. We'll be with other people, we won't have any valuable stuff with us, and I don't think we'll be easy targets there. Plus, I can watch from the shore to see if Martha, the buyer, makes it to look at the artifacts."

"Fantastic, I'll be ready in fifteen minutes."

Lisa jumped up and stepped into their bedroom, packed the beach bag, and stood at the front door ready to leave.

"Let's go," she beamed. "I'm going to appreciate the beach today even more than usual."

Paul opened their door, poked his head out making sure no one was lurking outside, and called the elevator to take them to the garage. Lisa scurried into the elevator with Paul, and they were soon driving to the beach.

"I'm watching to see if anyone follows us," assured Paul. "You relax, we'll stay with others, and I'll be alert. It should be a great day."

They parked at the dirt lot near the Perch Bar and Restaurant and saw Debi, Lauren and Ben.

"See?" said Paul. "I love it when a plan comes together."

"This is great," exclaimed Lisa. "Hey guys," she called out to them, "Is there room for us to bring two more chairs?"

Debi hopped up and ran to greet them. Ben nodded to Cedrick, who maintained and oversaw the beach, for two more chairs. The two of them undressed and stretched out to relax and catch up with the others.

The talk quickly turned to Debi's upcoming wedding. Although Debi did not know much detail, her excitement was apparent.

"I can't wait. It's going to be the best wedding ever."

"Where's Dean?" asked Paul.

"We've decided not to see each other until the wedding day; I know it sounds crazy, but before you say anything, you should know it was my idea," Debi smiled. "But anyway, he'll be spending time working in the casino, and I'll be on the beach with friends. Speaking of which, I'd like to have a beach day tomorrow with all of my bridesmaids. Would you two be willing to come?"

Lisa looked toward Paul to see his reaction. He nodded and smiled in her direction.

"Count me in," squealed Lisa.

"Yes, me too," said Lauren. "Ben, this will be official bridesmaids' business. I hope you understand."

"I do; I'll find something to occupy my time."

"Ben, since Lisa and Lauren will be with Debi, you could always hang out with me. What do you say?"

"Thanks friend, you've got a deal."

As Paul talked with Ben, the three girls chatted with excitement.

"I'm going to call the others now," said Debi. "Not to put any pressure on them, but I'll put the calls on speaker and let them hear from you two on how much fun we're going to have."

Debi placed calls to Jodi, Karen, Terri, Sylvie, Michele and Erica. They all accepted without hesitation.

"Time to celebrate. I don't have champagne today for a liquid brunch, but I'll get everybody a glass of wine from the Perch. Is it too early or are you ready to join me?"

Lisa and Lauren agreed to a glass of wine with Debi, but Paul and Ben decided to wait a while longer before beginning a day of drinking. Paul planned to greatly limit his consumption.

The group sunned and swam until noon. Now hungry, Ben motioned toward the Perch to Lauren, and she nodded her readiness for lunch.

"Is everyone on board with getting some lunch?" asked Ben.

With everyone in agreement, they decided to walk the short distance to the Perch and sat on towels under the roof of the open-air restaurant. It was the perfect solution to take a short break from the sun while not needing to dress.

From his seat at the Perch, Paul continued to watch for anything unusual as well as monitoring for any activity on Brad's sailboat. Paul continued to refrain from drinking.

After lunch, the five returned to their chairs, with Paul continuing to keep a close watch over Lisa. She appeared relaxed and fully enjoying the day.

"I'd like to take a walk on the beach," mentioned Lisa. "Would anyone like to go with me?"

"That sounds great, I'll go," answered Lauren. "Debi, you can't stay here without us. Come on, let's go."

"Where are you guys walking?" asked Paul.

"I'm thinking the usual, to the Mont Vernon on the north end and back."

"Okay, have fun."

Paul waited a couple of minutes, letting them have their girls' walk, before beginning his walk to follow and keep an eye on them.

"Ben, I could use a walk myself. Do you want to get a little exercise?"

"Sure. I've got a few things going on at work I'd like to tell you about. It won't be much business talk. I'm trying to do none around Lauren. We're having a great time just focusing on vacation."

They matched the pace of the girls, staying a comfortable distance for Paul, while still allowing the girls to have their time without male company. Fortunately, the walk to Mont Vernon and back was uneventful.

Back at their chairs before 2:00 p.m., Paul saw a boat pull alongside Brad's boat. He watched Brad throw a couple of lines to the motorboat and saw him help Martha aboard. It was time for her to view the Arawak artifacts.

FIFTY-TWO

AFTER WENDALL ENDED his call with Gregorio, he considered his options to retrieve the treasure of artifacts. He had not been able to find Augustus, and to add insult to injury, Antonio had gotten a cheap fake from Lisa instead of the sought-after article. He was not sure he could gain control of the artifacts by force. Perhaps Gregorio was right when he suggested using diplomacy.

Wendall called Paul but his call went to voicemail. Wendall decided to leave a message.

"Paul, this is Wendall Thomas. We have a mutual friend, Gregorio. He suggested I give you a call. When you get this message, would you mind giving me a call. I have a business proposal for you to consider. I'll send you a text message with all my contact information. Look forward to hearing from you soon."

Leaving the message for Paul left Wendall feeling unsatisfied. He did not like being in a position of sitting around waiting. In addition to diplomacy, he would continue to try gaining control of the artifact by force, and phoned Antonio.

"Antonio, have you made any progress?"

'I'm working on it, but I've got nothing to report."

"Have you seen Paul or Lisa today?"

"No, I'm outside their place, but I haven't seen them come out."

"Where was Lisa yesterday?"

"At Orient Beach."

"It's unlikely she's there again today, but why don't you check? Ride over there, or have someone ride over there, with instructions to get the real artifact."

"Will do, I'm on it."

Antonio called Samuel to help.

"Sam, I just talked to the boss. He's sounding desperate to get what he wants. He wants you to go back to Orient to find Lisa or Paul."

"I can't do that. She'll recognize me. You need somebody else this time."

Antonio knew Samuel's reluctance to go to Orient Beach was justified. He ended the call and began driving to the beach.

FIFTY-THREE

"RIGHT THIS WAY."

Brad ushered Martha inside the cabin of his boat. Sylvie sat at the table with the treasure of artifacts laid out before her.

"Martha, this is Sylvie. She and I are helping Paul."

Martha acknowledged Sylvie but was eager to begin her business.

"This looks like quite a collection. Is this everything?"

"That's it," responded Brad. "Is there anything we can do to help you?"

"No, I'll be looking it over. But to be sure, you're not looking to get a bid on individual pieces, are you? You're looking to sell the entire collection?"

"Yes, the whole lot. Paul didn't mention wanting individual prices or keeping any of the pieces. But if he wanted to keep a piece or two, would that be a problem?"

"No, I just need to know if I'm expected to give a separate bid on each piece. There's a certain swag involved with this, and as long as he'll accept that basis for the bid, then I'll just take a stab at one or two based on the total if he wants to keep a few."

"Okay, I'm sure he wants the entire collection sold as quick as possible."

"They always do. I should have a price before I leave today. Am I supposed to tell you or tell Paul?"

"That's not been discussed. Just tell us, and I'll pass it along to him. I'm sure he'll call you no matter what price you offer."

"Then it's time for me to get started."

She pulled out a chair, sat down at the table, and reached for the first sculpture.

Paul was watching from the beach. He saw Brad and Martha disappear inside. After thirty minutes, the temptation to call for a progress report loomed as a thought, but he decided to wait. Nearing the end of happy hour, Paul decided to have a beer since he refrained from any earlier drinking.

"Happy hour is about to end. I'm going to have a Coors Light. Ben, would you like the second one in the two-for-one?"

"Sure, I'll do that. I'll walk up there with you. Ladies, what would you like?"

They continued with their white wine. Lauren and Lisa were content with one glass each, so Ben ordered the happy hour two for Debi, with Lauren and Lisa splitting the other two.

When he and Paul returned, they all dipped in the water with their drinks.

"A Coors Light always tastes better when standing in the ocean," claimed Paul.

They toasted to that, agreeing that a drink anywhere on Orient Beach was better than the same drink elsewhere.

Paul noticed that he never saw Lisa looking out toward Brad's boat and it pleased him that she was relaxed and enjoying the day. Martha's boat was still rafting with the *Eclipse*. Paul had no guess as to how long it would take for Martha's appraisal, but he planned to leave the beach around 4:00 p.m. knowing that the appraisal was underway, and nothing could be accomplished by staying late on the beach watching Martha's boat.

At 4:00 p.m. Martha's boat was still there.

"Lisa, are you about ready to head on?"

There was a groan from Debi. She had just started another glass of wine.

"Hey, I'll be back again tomorrow. We're all meeting here at nine, right?"

"Yes, let's get started at nine. No champagne again tomorrow, so the eleven o'clock champagne brunch will have to wait for another day. But the good news is, there will be a white wine brunch, and it'll start early," she smiled. "So be ready. I'm planning on it being an amazing day."

Paul looked around and did not see anyone hanging around looking problematic, but knew there was added safety in numbers.

"Are you guys getting ready to leave too?"

Ben looked at Lauren for her response.

"Yes, Ben and I probably should be heading out, too. Debi, we'll wait for you to finish that glass before we go."

Debi tilted her glass back and drained it.

"I hope I didn't hold anybody up too long," she laughed. "I'm gathering my stuff now."

They all gathered their belongings and walked as a group to the dirt parking area.

"Hop in, Debi. I'll drive you to your room at La Playa," offered Ben.

"Sure, just in case I've had too much to drink to walk it," she kidded, climbing into the back seat.

Following Ben, Paul and Lisa hopped in their car and pulled out. As they turned onto the main road, Paul smiled over at Lisa.

"That was a good day. Martha has been there for several hours and hopefully she will make an offer for the artifacts before we go to bed tonight."

"That would be super. I'll make us some dinner when we get home. Maybe it will be a celebration dinner."

FIFTY-FOUR

ANTONIO CALLED WENDALL with an update. Wendall had been impatiently waiting for his call.

"Antonio, was Lisa at Orient Beach?"

"I'm leaving Orient Beach now. Yes, I saw Lisa and Paul, but I didn't have a chance to get them or the statue today. They were on alert and always with a group. But I have some good news."

Wendall was losing hope, and his voice reflected his disappointment.

"Okay," he said sighed dejectedly, "What is the good news?"

"I heard them talking as they were leaving the beach. There's a girls only outing planned for the beach tomorrow. Lisa will be there without Paul. I should have a great chance to get her and the statue tomorrow."

Wendall allowed a little optimism to creep back into his voice.

"So, what time will she be there? Are you going to get the statue tomorrow?"

"I should be able to take care of business sometime tomorrow. They're meeting in the morning. I don't know that I can get it done first thing tomorrow. Most likely It will be when they're all leaving at the end of the day, but I will have her tomorrow, and she'll hand over the real statue this time."

"Antonio, we're running out of time. Do what you need to do, but get it done."

Wendall ended the call and sat back in his chair to think about his plans. He decided to wait a little longer before calling Paul again. He had two parts to his new plan. Antonio would continue to pursue Lisa and Paul to get the artifact by a show of strength. While Antonio pursued using that approach, Wendall would distance himself from Antonio and would place another call to Paul, using diplomacy instead. He would be happy with whichever method worked.

Wendall next placed a call to Gregorio. He would not ask for any advice but hoped Gregorio would volunteer something of value. Gregorio answered as usual, expecting a follow-up call from Wendall.

"Good day, Wendall. How might I help you?"

"I wanted to thank you again for your help on my last call. I've reached out to Paul, with an approach of friendly diplomacy."

"And did it work?"

"I'm still waiting. I left a message for him to give me a call, but I've yet to hear back from him. I'm planning to call again in a bit if I don't hear from him soon."

"Do you think you have something of value to offer?"

"I think I can offer my support, knowing the treasure will be in demand, and that if he joins forces with me, he can better defend against others who may not be as cooperative."

"So, your diplomacy is a veiled threat?"

"I wasn't thinking of it as such."

"Paul will. He won't be persuaded by a threat. I advise you tread lightly. If that is your approach, things may not go well for you."

"Okay, I'll suggest I can assist by finding a buyer and with any needed transportation, and will do it at a minimal cost."

"I don't know if that will be successful either, but you have a better chance. Paul may view you as a friend, but you certainly do not want to encourage Paul to become your enemy."

"Thanks, Gregorio. I appreciate your thoughts."

Wendall ended the call. He needed to better his approach with Paul before making his next call to him.

FIFTY-FIVE

PAUL WATCHED FOR anyone following his vehicle as he drove Lisa to the Cliff. He pulled into his reserved place in the garage and looked around before getting out. Seeing nothing unusual, he and Lisa stepped out and walked with urgency to their door, unlocked it and slipped in.

Lisa reached her arms around Paul.

"Thanks for a great day. I know you were on full alert and let me totally relax. I needed that. I'll whip up some dinner and we can get comfortable for the night."

She gave him an inviting smile before moving into the kitchen.

As Lisa prepared dinner, Paul received his anticipated call from Sylvie and Brad. Sylvie began immediately, interrupting Paul as he began to say hello.

"You got what you wanted. Martha is done and the total is twelve million dollars," she screamed. "Can you believe it?"

Lisa stopped with the food preparation when she saw Paul answer his phone. He signaled her over and she sat on the couch beside him. Paul put the phone on speaker.

"Lisa, we got more than we hoped. This is amazing news. Sylvie, you and Brad tell us the details."

Sylvie relayed the events to them. If Paul agreed to the price, Martha would be back before sunrise to load the artifacts onto her boat.

"You need to give Martha a call to arrange the payment. She's expecting your call."

"Sylvie, you and Brad were awesome. You've certainly done your part. I'll give her a call now."

As soon as Paul ended the call, Lisa could no longer contain her excitement. She clung to Paul, pinning his arms to his sides, making it impossible for him to dial Martha. Paul did not mind the delay.

"We're definitely going to celebrate tonight. Let me call Martha. I'd love for us to go out for dinner tonight, but I think we should stick with eating in. We'll have lots of celebration dinners soon."

"Sounds good to me. I have something special in mind. And, you'll love the dessert," she called over her shoulder as she headed for the kitchen.

Paul made a short call to Martha accepting her offer. He provided her with the information of his special account used for unconventional transactions. Martha agreed to transfer the funds tomorrow after the pickup.

"Please make the pickup in the morning. I trust the payment will be in my account tomorrow. I know where you live, I'm not concerned that the payment will be a few hours after you have the items. But I have one more thing to discuss."

Paul finished his business with Martha. When the call concluded, he and Lisa phoned Brad and Sylvie, confirming the deal was complete. Paul next had a three-way call with the other two couples, Erica and Gary, and Karen and Rick. They immediately began celebrating the incredible news. Walking out of his office, Paul met Lisa coming toward him.

"Paul, this is just too good to be true. I'll finish making dinner, then we can sit back and let this sink in."

"Okay, I need to call Augustus to let him know he's about to be a multi-millionaire."

Paul returned to his office and called Augustus to work out the details for his payment of half of the money from Martha.

"You'll have the money tomorrow. I recommend you stay put for another day, but you should be free then to do as you please. But remember, you're now a rich man. With money comes responsibilities and an awareness that you can always be a target because of your money. I suggest you not flaunt it."

"I understand Paul and I want to thank you for how you handled the sale. I'm pleased and ready to get my money."

Paul ended his call with Augustus and returned to the living area as Lisa completed preparation of their meal. She served dinner, Paul with a Coors Light and Lisa with a glass of red wine. They continued with after-dinner drinks when Paul's phone rang. He set down his beer and answered the call.

"Paul, this is Wendall Thomas. We have a mutual friend, Gregorio. I'm sorry for bothering you, but I'm following up on my earlier call."

"Wendall, hello. I'm sorry, if you called earlier, I didn't pick up your message. I normally check for messages regularly, but today has been very busy. What can I do for you?"

"I'm aware that you've come into possession of some valuable artifacts. I'd like to propose a deal with you."

"Wendall, thank you for your call, but I'm not in possession of valuable artifacts."

Wendall was not expecting Paul's comment and struggled as he continued with his call.

"The information I received came from very reliable sources. I've never received incorrect information from these sources."

"Your sources are wrong this time, Wendall. I *was* in possession of valuable artifacts, but no longer am."

Not accepting Paul's response as ending the discussion, Wendall pressed on.

"I'd like to help you find the highest bidder. I'm also in a position to help you with transportation issues that are common with moving that type of inventory."

"Again, thank you for your call. As I said, I am no longer in possession. A transaction is already complete. Transportation is complete. There's nothing you can possibly do. If another opportunity arises at some point, I'll definitely keep you in mind."

"Is it possible to void your transaction? I have a very interested buyer who will pay top dollar," he lied.

"I appreciate your persistence, but the answer is no. I will keep you in mind with future opportunities, but this one is closed. Our mutual friend, Gregorio, knows me well. Perhaps you should give him a call and share our conversation. He may be able to help you understand that there is no business for us, and no additional discussion is warranted."

Wendall was steamed but saw no way to continue with the discussion. He was confident Paul was telling the truth.

"Thank you, Paul, for your time. Perhaps there will be a future deal."

Wendall ended the connection. Paul was glad that Martha would be picking up the artifacts before dawn.

"So, does this mean it's over?" asked Lisa.

"I think so. We were lucky. All arrangements have been completed and we'll have the money tomorrow. I don't think there's anything left. There's probably more to the call from Wendall than we know, but you can go to the beach tomorrow and relax. You girls should have a great day."

"I want to call Lekha and let her know the update that it's all basically over. We should be back to normal."

"Okay, while you're calling her, I have a couple of other calls to make. I'll go in my office to take care of those while you call Lekha."

Paul stepped into his office as Lisa dialed Lekha. Lekha, worried and hoping to hear from her, answered when she saw the call was from Lisa.

"Lisa, it's so good to hear from you. Are you okay?"

"Yes, that's why I'm calling. Everything couldn't be going better. Since we last talked, I had a run-in with someone wanting that crazy artifact, but I'll give you all the particulars when we get together. More important, I think it's all over. All of the artifacts were gathered and have found a happy home. We're done with it all. All of our lives can get back to normal."

"That's awesome news. But don't make me wait until later, tell me all the details now."

Lisa glanced towards Paul's office, and hearing him on the phone, was happy to oblige. They talked for another thirty minutes.

"Do you think you and Jason could meet Paul and me at the beach on Friday?" Lisa asked as the conversation wound down. "Tomorrow I'm meeting with Debi and the other bridesmaids, but I'd love for us to get together the next day."

"I think we can do that. I'll talk with Jason to make sure he'll agree to both of us being out of the store on Friday."

"Great, we've never gotten together at the beach. I'm looking forward to it."

"What beach do you want to go to?"

"Are you willing to go to a clothing optional beach?"

"I guess. Clothing optional means I decide once I'm there if I want to stay dressed, or not?"

"Absolutely, you dress however you want. Have you ever been to one of the clothing optional beaches?"

"No, we usually go to Mullet, and sometimes to the main part of Pinel Island."

"Then let's try something different for you. Why don't we go to Happy Bay? It's quiet with not that many people. I think you'll like it. Just think back to when you held the naked statue, and let the feeling take over. If you decide to not wear your swimsuit, I'm almost certain you'll love it. And with fewer people around, you might feel more comfortable quicker."

Lekha did not plan to go naked on the beach, but the thought did seem somewhat appealing. She liked thinking that if she did try it, she could hide behind the thought of doing it to please Lisa, instead of it being her idea. She was not sure she wanted it known that she would even consider being naked on the beach.

"Okay, that sounds good. I'm sure Jason will go wherever. After I talk to Jason, we can make it final, but plan on meeting us Friday."

As Lisa was talking with Lekha, Wendall replayed in his mind the conversation he had with Paul. He did not think of anything that he could have said differently and decided to call Antonio.

"Antonio, you've done an excellent job for me, but it's over. There's nothing more to do."

"But I'm going to Orient Beach tomorrow. I'll be able to get what you want."

"It's too late. They don't have any of the artifacts. It's time to move on."

"All right, you're the boss."

Wendall ended the call, but Antonio was not ready to move on. He planned to be at Orient Beach. Once he captured Lisa, Paul would do whatever Antonio told him to do, including the retrieval of the artifacts. Antonio would continue without Wendall.

FIFTY-SIX

SYLVIE AND BRAD were sleeping on the boat. Brad was awakened and saw that it was still dark. He lay very still, listening while being mindful for any change in the motion of the boat. Looking at the clock, he saw it was 3:00 a.m. He was expecting Martha to come for the artifacts, but that was not to be for another hour and a half.

Slipping out of bed, he looked down at Sylvie, still soundly sleeping. He reached over for his pistol before slipping on a pair of gym shorts. He felt both nervous and eager to offload the artifacts, and realized his waking up suddenly might be from nerves instead of an intruder. Debating if he should wake Sylvie, he decided to leave her sleeping.

He slipped topside and immediately saw the boat. It slowly approached, closing in to about twenty feet away.

The name of the boat was clearly visible, and it was not Martha's boat.

Brad stayed low and out of sight, prepared to fire if there was any attempt to board *Eclipse*. He waited for the visitor to announce his presence.

Ten minutes went by without any further activity. The boat simply idled nearby.

He crept back down and awakened Sylvie.

"It may be nothing, but an unknown boat has pulled close to us. I'm checking it out. Get up and put something on."

Sylvie became immediately wide awake. She slipped out of bed and stood beside him, hurriedly pulling on shorts and a t-shirt.

"Here, take the gun and stay behind me. I'm going to acknowledge the boat. If there is anything unnerving, shoot. Don't hesitate."

The two slipped topside, Sylvie remaining in the shadows. Brad stood and made a visible target of himself.

"Good morning," he called out. "Can I help you?"

"Good morning. I'm way early and didn't want to disturb you."

Martha stood and waved. Brad felt a flooding of relief.

"Come on over and tie on. Is anyone with you?"

"No, just me."

She threw a line and he helped her aboard.

"What are you doing on this boat? It's not the boat you came in yesterday."

"I know. If there were any prying eyes, I elected to use a boat other than my standard."

Sylvie heard the discussion and came forward.

"Hey Martha, welcome aboard."

Martha looked at Sylvie, the gun still in her hand.

"I'm sorry if I alarmed you. I was trying to be considerate, but I see I had the opposite effect."

"Not a problem," responded Brad. "I'll have your items topside in a few minutes. The sooner these things are off my boat, the better." He went below and began handing them up to Sylvie who lined them up on deck. Brad returned and they loaded the artifacts into Martha's boat.

As Martha turned to board her boat, she shook hands with both Brad and Sylvie.

"I'll be on my way. We can have a social visit at another more reasonable time."

"Be safe," called Brad as they watched Martha pull away.

Turning to Sylvie, he motioned to the cabin below and she nodded in agreement. With the stress of the artifacts now gone, they fell asleep immediately.

FIFTY-SEVEN

DEBI AWOKE EARLY Thursday morning in anticipation of meeting her bridesmaids for a day of celebration on the beach. She quickly dressed, packed her beach bag, and walked down from her room to the beach.

She waved to Cedrick as he was setting up chairs for the day. He agreed to place nine chairs together for her group. The girls in the wedding party were Jodi, Karen, Erica, Michele, Sylvie, Terri, Lisa and Lauren. The chairs were set up at Debi's favorite area of the beach near the Perch Restaurant and Bar.

"For all your loyal business, the first round for you and your friends is on me," offered Cedrick.

"Great. You know we appreciate all you do, maintaining the beach, providing chairs, and dealing with any of the cruise shippers who try to sneak pictures without asking. My friends will be here around nine. We'll probably form a line at the bar for those free drinks around nine-oh-one," she laughed. "I normally bring champagne to the beach each day, but didn't today. I'll walk with you to the Perch to purchase a couple bottles of pinot grigio. Once those are gone, we'll be collecting on your offer."

Cedrick cared for all of the regulars at his area of Orient Beach and tried to ensure everyone had a good time. He looked forward to greeting Debi's friends as they arrived to celebrate her upcoming wedding.

As the girls arrived, the group of nine settled in for a day of full body sunning. Debi passed out plastic cups to her friends.

"I know I always wait for eleven o'clock to start, but this is a special day, so I hope you don't mind getting started a couple of hours early."

She poured the pinot grigio for everyone.

"A toast for the new bride," began Jodi. "May the married life be everything you always dreamed of, but don't forget your single friends."

"Hear, hear," the others chimed in as they toasted to Debi.

When their cups were empty, Debi was quick with the refills. After polishing off the remaining pinot grigio, it was time to cash in on Cedrick's offer.

"Cedrick is buying each of us a drink, a thank you for our loyalty. I'm ready to collect my glass of wine. I hope you'll all keep me company."

"That's what best friends are for," answered Karen. "Why don't we serve you today? If a few of you will come with me, we'll be back with the drinks."

"I'll be waiting right here. You have permission to serve me for the rest of the day," kidded Debi as she stretched out on her lounge chair.

Karen, Jodi and Michele bounced out of their chairs to fetch the first round. When they returned, Michele offered up the next toast.

"To Debi, who immediately befriended me when I moved to St. Martin. She made me feel at home and is now one of my most treasured friends. To many more wonderful days. Cheers."

They all drank. With the first round completed, Erica stood and cleared her throat.

"Okay," she began, waving her hands over her head, "now that I see we're going to get all liquored up today, I have a suggestion." She broke into a teasing smile. "Knowing some of you girls may not be able to handle your alcohol as well as me, I suggest we record this day for our memories. I may not remember everything tomorrow, so I want some pictures, you know, to let me know I was here. I'm going to see if I can get someone to be our photographer. Don't do any great poses while I'm gone."

She approached Cedrick, who was watching over the beach in front of the Perch and walked over to him.

"I need your help. My friends and I want some pictures made of us and we need a photographer. Could we hire you for this important job?" she asked, smiling broadly.

"Sure, I'll be happy to help you. There's a section of the beach a little further down where there's nobody else. I'll take a few pictures for you there."

"That is so kind. We'll take up a collection to pay your photographer fee."

"No fee, this gig is on me."

"All right. It's a special group. We have lots of things in common. One thing, which you'll probably notice, is that we like to go skinny dipping. That's why we're called the Naked Nine. We're naked and we're nine, so Naked Nine."

She looked at Cedrick with mock seriousness.

"Now that I see you understand who we are and the important job at hand, let's do this. Right this way."

Erica took a few steps and looked back to make sure Cedrick was following.

"And when you get there, before taking the pictures, you can seem like a professional photographer, like you can say something, maybe break a leg before you want us to say cheese."

"I'll do my best," grinned Cedrick, ready to play along.

"Girls," he began when he reached the other would-be participants in the photo shoot.

Before he could continue, Erica cleared her throat, shrugged her shoulders, and looked inquiringly at Cedrick.

"Oh, I'm sorry. Naked Nine," he corrected, "if you'll follow me, there's a good area right over there where I can take some pictures for you."

The girls jumped up and cheerfully followed Cedrick for the picture-taking session.

"Okay, here's what we want first." Erica was continuing as the decision-maker for the pictures. "Debi's the star. The rest of us are going to lay down in the sand and form two capital 'Ds' for Debi and Dean. Karen, you and Jodi can be the straight line in the first 'D' and Michele and Terri, since you're both beautifully curvy, you'll make the curvy part of the letter."

The four girls smiled and took their positions in the sand.

"I'll be part of the next 'D' and I'll need your help Cedrick, to make sure the 'Ds' look good. Lauren and Lisa, ya'll can be the straight line and Sylvie and I will be the curving line."

"Since I'm supposed to be the star, what do you want me to do?" asked Debi.

"You have the most important part. We're forming the letters close together, where you kneel in the sand, just above us. You'll be right in the middle."

Debi kneeled in the sand, looking confused.

"That's good, but now for the double meaning. You lean forward, and put your hands under your boobs, highlighting your own DDs. So, our picture is honoring you and Dean, but also paying respect to your perfect figure."

Debi laughed and posed. Cedrick took several pictures.

"Okay eight of the Naked Nine, does anybody else have any picture ideas?"

"What about a normal picture, like the nine of us standing and smiling with Debi in the middle?" asked Lauren.

"That'll make for a good picture," answered Erica. "A little boring, but still good."

They stood, arms around each other's waist, and Cedrick snapped pictures from the front and behind, with the ocean in the background.

"Any other pictures you girls want?" asked Cedrick.

No one spoke up right away. Hearing no other requests, Debi spoke for the group.

"Well, I think that does it, Cedrick. Thanks for your help taking pictures on my day with all my closest friends."

Cedrick handed Debi her phone back and turned to leave.

"Well, if nobody has any other requests, I have one more," piped up Erica. "It's a good thing the Naked Nine has me for my creativity."

To conclude the photography session, Erica had the girls form the words "WE LOVE" with Sylvie and Michele forming the "W" by laying on their backs in the sand, rears to the camera with their legs in the air, Sylvie's left foot touching Michele's right. Next was Lauren forming an "E" by standing with feet to knees on the ground, twisting her body with one arm down from the shoulder and then out, and the other arm out parallel with the ground at head level. Lisa formed the "L" in "LOVE" by standing straight on her knees, her knees to feet forming the bottom of the letter. Jodi volunteered to form the "O" by laying on her back, rear to the camera and legs in the air, the bottoms of her feet touching.

"Oh, what the hell," exclaimed Karen, laughing at her friends in compromising positions on the ground. "I'll spread 'em to form a 'V' for the picture. Debi, this is for you," she said as she lay back in the sand.

That Left Terri to form the final "E". Debi looked at Erica.

"Well Erica, that completes 'WE LOVE', but what are we going to do?"

"You're the queen, and a queen deserves a throne. I'm going to get down on my hands and knees and you're going to sit on my back. The message is we love Debi. You smile into the camera and tell me how you want the chair angled."

"Debi, if you don't mind," interjected Karen while on her back in the sand, "I suggest your chair be angled toward the camera same as me, with Erica's butt with a full-on smile."

"I can do that, but where will Debi's legs go when sitting on her throne."

"I can figure that out," insisted Debi. "Cedrick, you'll need to take the pictures, one where I remain the lady everyone knows me to be," she laughed, "and one for Dean. Erica, he's going to love your picture idea."

"I aim to please," she said, getting on her hands and knees. "Let me know when I'm angled just right."

"That's perfect. This reminds me of that song 'Save a Horse, Ride a Cowboy' but Erica, I'll change it to 'Cowgirl' in your honor."

Debi sat sensuously on Erica while Cedrick obligingly took a series of pictures capturing the moment.

"Okay, I think we're done," Debi said, lifting off of Erica.

She smiled at the beachgoers who had gathered around.

"I think we've provided enough entertainment for the morning."

The girls got up from the sand, brushing themselves off and laughing as they thanked Cedrick for his help.

"Wow, all the work during the photo shoot has me thirsty. Servants, are you ready to serve your queen her next drink of wine?"

The girls walked back to their beach chairs, and Erica, Lisa and Lauren took the next turn bringing the group their drinks. As the girls began their next glasses of wine, Antonio retreated from the circle of admirers during the photo shoot and returned to his beach chair. He sat on the beach north of the Perch but kept the group of girls in sight. Although he enjoyed the antics of the girls, and especially Debi, he was primarily keeping an eye on Lisa.

Earlier, Antonio had called his friend, Baldo, to meet him on the beach. Baldo sat in the beach chair next to him, both wearing their swim trunks on the clothing optional beach.

"Baldo, thanks for coming today. I'm still working the artifact deal, and it helps me to not be sitting here by myself."

"No problem. I didn't know there was going to be such a good show today."

"Yeah, that was a bonus. Before the day's out, I'm going to have a meeting with Lisa. I'll handle that when the time comes. I just need you to hang out for a while."

"Sure, I'm here for you. Besides, the entertainment is worth it," he added with a laugh.

FIFTY-EIGHT

AFTER LISA LEFT Paul for the beach, Paul decided to call Ben.

"Good morning, Ben. Lisa is spending the day at the beach, and I've got some free time. With Lauren in that group of girls spending the day together, do you have any plans?"

"No, we had mentioned getting together today. I thought you might call."

"Are you at your house? I can come by and we can get some breakfast."

"That's a great idea. Come on over, I'm hungry."

"I'll be there in fifteen minutes."

Paul picked up Ben and the two drove to the Croissant Royal for breakfast.

"I know you love this place. Lisa and I started coming here recently and have made it a regular spot for either breakfast or lunch."

The two ate their breakfast mostly in silence.

"It's strange being in St. Martin and not having Lauren with me. I appreciate you rescuing me today."

"No problem. I just finished a major assignment and am taking a little time off. As you know, I'm still helping Sylvie with her company. I'll tell you a little about my last job, as it involved Sylvie, and she's going to want you to make another investment for her. She just earned a hefty amount of cash."

Paul gave Ben a high-level summary of the past days with the artifacts and concluded by telling of the large amount of money Sylvie was receiving.

"I can get her money invested right away. I'll give her a call and discuss what's needed."

"That's great. Sylvie wanted me to let you know about the additional money. Selfishly, I wanted to tell you about what's been happening. I could use your help."

"Sure, what can I do?"

"Why don't we take a ride after breakfast. I'll tell you all about it."

Paul signaled for the bill and paid for their breakfast. They walked to Paul's car, and as Paul drove, he told Ben how he could assist.

FIFTY-NINE

AFTER THE GLASSES of wine, the Naked Nine laid back in their chairs feeling very relaxed. They passed around Debi's phone and took turns looking at the pictures. The alcohol they consumed increased the volume of their laughter.

"I know we've had a lot to drink already, but I'm going to have one more glass of wine before lunch. Does anybody want anything? I'm buying and will bring the drinks back," offered Sylvie.

"As queen for the day, I'm charged with making the rules. There's one important rule that I need to make sure everyone knows, and that is, when one person drinks, everybody drinks. So, Sylvie, nine glasses of wine please. We can change the rules after lunch, but I hope everyone will go along without too much complaining."

Sylvie looked around the group, and seeing no signs of disagreement, turned to begin the wine run.

"Don't you want some help?" asked Lauren.

Sylvie stopped to respond. As she did, she noticed Antonio at the bar.

"No, I'll handle it. Who knows, there might be a handsome man at the bar who will help me."

Sylvie walked up to the bar and placed her order. As she waited for the wine, she began some good-natured flirting with Antonio to encourage him to help her carry the drinks to the girls.

"So, what's a handsome man doing hanging out by himself at the bar?"

Antonio grinned in response. Sylvie clearly did not know he was involved when she was robbed at La Playa on a prior trip to the island. He was relieved.

"Are you talking to me?"

"I don't see any other strong, handsome man. What do you say? Would you help me carry these drinks to the girls?"

"Sure, anything to help."

He cast a glance at Baldo, hoping Baldo could read his face and not acknowledge being with him.

The bartender placed the cups of wine in several carry-cartons. Antonio grabbed two cartons and followed Sylvie to the rest of the Naked Nine.

"Hey, I see you did find a handsome man to help you. Thank you very much, handsome man," greeted Jodi. "You can bring me wine anytime," she snickered.

Antonio smiled and handed out the cups of wine.

"But your service could be better," continued Jodi. "What's up with those swim trunks? This is a nude beach."

"Oh, I don't know. Just being professional with my delivery, I guess."

"Well, enough of being professional. Hand me my beach bag please."

Antonio did as he was instructed. Jodi reached into her bag and pulled out a twenty-dollar bill.

"Here, here's your tip."

Antonio was not sure what to do. He decided to play along.

"That won't be necessary. It was my pleasure."

"Okay, suit yourself." She put the money back in her bag. "But I must insist, you've got to ditch the shorts. You're in the company of nine naked women, and I'm starting to feel uncomfortable with you the only person dressed."

"Yeah, this is Debi's special day," echoed Karen. "If you won't do it for Jodi, do it for the bride-to-be. You can be the hunk for our bachelorette party."

The rest of the girls joined in, imploring him to get rid of the shorts.

"Oh, okay," he said, sliding his shorts down and stepping out of them. When he did, Jodi grabbed them off the ground and stuffed them in her beach bag.

"I'll hold onto these for you," she grinned. "You can come back later, and I'll let you have them before you leave the beach."

"Antonio, you're being such a good sport, come with me back to the bar and let me buy you a drink," offered Sylvie.

Antonio left his swim trunks with Jodi and followed Sylvie to the bar, leaving the eight girls behind howling with laughter.

"Jodi, I can't believe you did that," gasped Terri. "But it sure was fun. I loved the look on his face when you grabbed his shorts and put them in your bag."

That started another round of laughter at Antonio's awkward experience.

Back at the bar, Sylvie ordered a beer for Antonio.

"Antonio, please forgive my friends. We've all been drinking, and it was intended as harmless fun. I'm sure they'll turn your pants over to you later today, but I think they want you to play along a while longer."

Antonio took a big drink of his beer.

"That's all right. I know they're just having fun. You can go back to your group, and I'll visit a little later."

Sylvie waltzed back to the other members of the Naked Nine, where they finished their latest glass of wine.

"I know it's a little early, but I think we should get a bite of lunch while we can still walk. Does anybody disagree with the queen?"

Everyone agreed that it made sense, and because no one wanted to get dressed, even in a swimsuit, they decided to have lunch at the Perch Restaurant and Bar. They took towels to sit on and made their way there, stopping at the first outside table they came to. They crowded around and waited for the waitress to take their lunch order.

After finishing his beer, Antonio walked down the beach to his lounge next to Baldo. Baldo was grinning broadly when he returned.

"I've heard of losing your shirt gambling, but what happened to your pants? Was coming back to your chair naked part of your plan?"

Baldo could not contain his laughter as he watched Antonio's face contorted in anger.

"Yes, that's real funny. Now you're figuring in the plan. I'm going to need to borrow your shorts."

"What do you mean, borrow my shorts? You want to wear them?"

"I can't very well take a hostage while I'm naked."

"I love you, Antonio, but like a brother. I don't want you getting in my shorts," he laughed.

"Well, get used to the idea. There's a lot of money on the line. When the time is right, I need them. I'll make it up to you."

They watched the girls eat their lunch and consume more wine.

"It won't be long and none of them girls will even be able to stand up. They might not even notice you don't got no pants on."

This time Baldo burst out in laughter, thinking he was very witty. Antonio, tired of the ribbing, decided to ignore the comment. If Baldo thought it was not bothering him, he would probably stop with the kidding soon.

The girls finished their lunch and walked unsteadily back to their beach chairs. After spreading their towels back on the chairs, they dipped in the ocean for a swim. Fifteen minutes later, they were back in their chairs, some of them looking as if they were about asleep. The sun and alcohol had calmed down the group.

Antonio, seeing the girls on the verge of sleep, turned to Baldo.

"I think it's about time for me to make my move. I'm going to walk down there and I'll be back up in a few minutes. When I start toward them, you take off, but leave your shorts on the chair. I'm going to get Lisa to come back up here with me, get my phone, wallet and keys, put the shorts on, and the two of us are going for a short ride. If she can't give me the damn artifact, I'll tuck her away safely and make Paul bring it to me. He'll do whatever he has to do to get Lisa back safely."

"All right, Antonio. I'll do it. Good luck. Just remember when you get all that money, your best friend Baldo made it happen."

Antonio began walking toward the Naked Nine. He glanced back over his shoulder and saw Baldo walking naked on the beach, his shorts on the chair as directed. He reached the girls, now sprawled out on their chairs next to the water's edge.

"Well, if it's not my favorite naked server," grinned Jodi. "Welcome back."

"Have you still got my shorts in your bag?"

"I sure do. I'm holding them for ransom. If you bring us another round, I'll take that into consideration for getting out early for good behavior."

"I'll do it. But I need this one to come with me." He pointed to Lisa. "I can't bring them all by myself."

Lisa pulled herself out of her chair.

"I'm a team player. If you need help, I'll be there for this fine group."

Lisa began walking away from the water toward the Perch with Antonio beside her. He looked over to his chair where he planned to grab Baldo's shorts, but they were missing. Instead, he saw a man dressed in shorts, t-shirt and ball cap picking them up and walking away with them.

Knowing he needed those shorts, he turned to Lisa.

"Wait here, I'll be right back."

Antonio picked up his pace, walking purposefully toward the man who was carrying the shorts into the parking area. Increasing his pace to just under a jog, Antonio gained on the shorts thief.

"Hey, you. I know you. Stop."

Ben glanced back and saw Antonio gaining on him. He broke into a full sprint, dashing between cars.

"Now," coughed Ben as he approached the next line of vehicles.

Ben had agreed to keep Paul company for the day as he kept a distant watch on Lisa at Orient Beach. Paul was familiar with Antonio and Baldo from their prior robbery of Sylvie. He was also aware that Antonio worked for Wendall Thomas. After the call from Wendall, he decided it was more than a coincidence when he saw Antonio watching the girls and especially making a second trip to talk to them. When he saw Lisa get up from her chair to walk with Antonio, it was time for Paul to act.

He sent Ben to grab the shorts and take them through the parking area. Pleased when he saw Antonio begin following Ben in pursuit of the shorts, Paul moved between two cars to wait, looking between car tires to track the progress of Ben and Antonio. Ben made sure Paul was ready by barking "Now" as he raced past.

Antonio bolted after Ben, intent on taking him down. He made an easy target for Paul to trip the unsuspecting man, who came down hard on his head, knocking him woozy. He eased out of consciousness as Paul applied a headlock.

"What do you want me to do?" Ben asked, breathing heavily as he came back to stand over Antonio.

"Drop the shorts on the ground here. If Baldo comes back soon, I don't want him to see them. If Antonio was intended to take them, he'll think all is well. If he wasn't, he'll be reluctant to leave the beach without his shorts."

Ben dropped the shorts.

"Now, go on the beach and talk to Lisa. You're smart, play it by ear. She most likely will be wondering where Antonio is and when he'll be back."

Ben left Paul and Antonio to meet Lisa. Paul grabbed a spare towel from his trunk, placed it in the passenger seat, and rolled down the car windows. He reached back into the trunk and prepared the syringe in his tool bag. The injection in Antonio's hip that followed would keep him from waking for quite some time. Paul placed Antonio in the passenger seat, head back on the head rest, appearing to take a nap.

Three late arrivals to the beach walked near the car with quizzical looks. Paul gave them a smile and a thumb's up sign.

"Day drinker. If he doesn't come around soon, I'm going to have to take him home."

The looks of concern changed to knowing smiles as they continued past to the beach.

Lisa stood, gazing out to sea. Ben was standing almost beside her before she noticed him.

"Hey, Ben. What are you doing here?"

"I saw you standing by yourself and came over. Without Lauren, I wasn't sure what to do with myself, so just stopped by for a minute. Looks like your group is having a blast, or maybe blasted is more like it. I better be on my way. I don't want to interrupt."

"At least come down and say hey. I'm sure Lauren will be touched that you were admiring her from afar. I'll be down in a minute. I'm waiting for someone who is helping take our next drinks to our chairs."

"I saw the guy walking with you. If it's him, he left the beach in a hurry. I don't think he'll be back."

"Well, then I will need your help in bringing everyone a fresh glass of wine."

"I'll be happy to."

Ben walked to the bar and placed the order. Lisa carried two glasses of wine, and he carried the others in two carry-trays.

"Look who I found," announced Lisa as she handed a glass of wine to Debi.

"I'm here only for a bit. Just going around the island and decided to stop at the Perch for a minute. I'm not staying, so go back to having fun."

Lauren stood up and wrapped her arms around Ben. She then kissed him deeply.

"Wow. It looks like you two need to get a room," laughed Debi.

"Today is your day," responded Ben, breaking free from Lauren's grasp. "Lauren, I'll see you tonight. You girls have fun."

"Hey, what happened to the guy who was bringing us drinks? I have his shorts."

"It looks like there was a change of plans. I saw him leaving the beach in a hurry. I guess you can keep his shorts as a souvenir."

The girls were all laughing as Ben left the beach to meet Paul in the parking lot.

SIXTY

PAUL SAT BEHIND the wheel of his car next to the slumping Antonio. He dialed Brad and was relieved when he immediately answered.

"Brad, it's great to hear your voice. I'm in a bit of a pickle and could use your help."

"It's good to be needed. I'm sitting back on my boat catching up on some reading. I'd love to do something. What's going on?"

Paul gave Brad a quick summary of the day's events.

"Ben should be back with me in a few minutes. Would you be able to meet us in your dinghy at the northernmost point of Orient Beach?"

"Sure, when do you want me to be there?"

"Let's say thirty minutes. That should give Ben more than enough time to be back, and we'll drive over there. We'll meet you on the beach."

Paul ended the call and waited for Ben. He was back twenty minutes later and saw Paul sitting in the car. With the front passenger seat occupied, he slipped in the back seat behind Antonio.

"Did everything go okay with Lisa?"

"Yes, everything is fine. All of them have had plenty to drink, so nobody had any tough questions for me. I left them drinking wine on the beach."

"All right. We're going to meet Brad. He's bringing his dinghy to meet us the other end of the beach. We'll be bringing our friend with us."

Paul drove to the far end of the beach and parked in the paved lot.

"This is going to be the tricky part. Antonio is out and won't be able to walk, plus he's naked and we're dressed. Take your shirt off and leave it in the car but leave your shorts and shoes on. You'll need them."

Ben and Paul peeled out of their shirts and stepped out of the car.

"I'm going to get Antonio out of the car and try to wrap that towel securely around his waist. You'll get on one side of him and I'll be on the other. We'll hopefully look like we're helping a drunk friend. Let's do this as rapidly as possible. The fewer people who see us the better. Thankfully, this northernmost point of the beach is normally pretty quiet. I'm going to take a quick look before getting Antonio out."

Paul walked to the edge of the parking area and peered out over the beach. Walking back to Ben, he pointed down the beach.

"There's only two couples, and they look pretty involved with each other. Brad is waiting. I waved to him; he knows what to expect. Let's do this."

With no one nearby in the parking lot, Paul wrestled the naked Antonio out of the car and draped him over the hood. He wrapped the towel around his waist.

"Hope that holds. Let's get going. The sooner we're on the boat the better."

With each holding Antonio up, they drunk walked him to the edge of the paved area and onto the white sand below. No one who may have taken notice of the trio said anything to them as they crossed the beach to the water's edge. In less than one minute Antonio was slumped in Brad's boat.

"Thanks Brad, you know what to do. Thanks for picking up Ben and me and our new friend."

Brad motored slowly away, steering the small boat toward Green Key, the small uninhabited island across from Orient Beach. There was no one on the beach when they arrived. They hopped out on the smooth sand. They pulled Antonio onto the sand, leaving the towel that had been wrapped around him in the boat.

"We're close to a good spot for our new friend to continue his nap. Ben, help me with him. We'll cut across the interior and find a nice resting place. Wearing shoes, it won't be too bad, but watch your step. The coral rocks can be loose and are sharp. There are also small spiny cacti to deal with."

They hoisted Antonio and found an area of rock and cacti, but with a view of the ocean on the other side.

"Let's drop him here."

Ben lowered Antonio down to the ground with Paul's help.

"What do you think will happen to him after we leave?"

"Well, he'll sleep for a couple more hours. When he wakes up, he won't feel too good and he'll quickly see the terrain is not good for bare feet, or for bare everything for that matter. It won't necessarily hold him, but it will be painful for him to get down to the water. Especially if it's dark and he can't see where he's stepping. If he's a good swimmer, he might be able to swim back to Orient Beach. There's also the chance that someone coming along might see him and offer help. I don't have any other ideas on what to do with him. Let's head back to the boat. I'm ready for Brad to take us to the car. I'll be thinking on if there's anything else we should do."

They carefully treaded their way back to where Brad waited for them with the boat.

"All aboard. I imagine you're eager to get back to Orient. You want to be dropped off where I picked you up?"

Paul responded with an affirmative nod. Brad motored them back.

"Thanks for all the help," said Paul as he and Ben climbed out of the boat. With a wave, Brad turned the boat and headed back to *Eclipse*.

Paul and Ben walked back to Paul's car.

"Well Ben, that should take care of our adventure for the day. Thanks for your help. I'll call someone to check on Antonio in a bit. For now, I'm ready to go home. I'll drop you at your place."

"That sounds perfect. That was enough adventure for me today."

SIXTY-ONE

LAUREN LOOKED AT the others in the group of girls celebrating Debi's upcoming wedding.

"Debi, I'm having a super day, but I don't think I can drink any more. I don't mean to let the group down, but I've got to at least slow down."

"You've all done a great job. I think I'll slow down for the rest of the day, too. I want everyone to make it home safely. Thank you all for making this an unbelievably good day, one I'll always remember."

"Instead of having another drink, why don't we have a walk down the beach? I could use a little exercise to help clear my head," suggested Michele.

Meanwhile, Baldo returned to his chair and saw that his swim trunks were missing. Although he wanted his shorts, he was pleased for Antonio, believing Lisa had been captured. He wondered when he would get his share of the money from the artifact. He settled in, thinking he would lounge peacefully in the sun until Antonio returned.

The group of girls began their walk, a slow promenade toward the northern end of the beach. The small waves washed over their feet as the bevy of beauties caught the attention of many, including Baldo. Stunned to see Lisa without Antonio around, he quickly rose from his chair to follow the group.

After fifteen minutes, they were still traipsing along the beach. Baldo elected to go back to his chair to think, knowing the girls would eventually return. Soon the girls came into his sight as they retraced their steps to their chairs and resumed lounging.

Baldo, now concerned, wondered what had happened to Antonio. He wanted the money he earned for coming to the beach. He also wanted, and needed, his swim trunks.

When it was approaching three-thirty, he knew he needed to do something, but was not sure what. He wandered down the beach to pay a visit on the group of girls.

Sylvie saw him approach. She recognized him but could not remember his name or where they had met.

"Hello. Are you girls having a good day?"

Baldo's feeble attempt at small talk was met with a couple of unapproving glances. Sylvie spoke up.

"How are you today? You look familiar, but I can't remember your name."

"I'm Baldo. My friend Antonio was talking with you earlier."

"Oh yes, I remember you now. You're Antonio's friend."

"Have you seen him lately? I thought he would be back, but he's been gone a long time."

"Yes," Lisa piped up, "He was going with me to the Perch. He told me to wait a minute, I stared out into the ocean, and he never came back. I don't know what happened. I asked somebody and was told he left the beach in a hurry. I don't think he's coming back."

"That's strange. I don't know why he would do that."

"Hey, since you're a friend of his, let me give you his swim trunks. I was going to give them back to him, and not knowing if he'll be coming back, can I give them to you to pass along?"

"Yeah, sure," Baldo responded, relieved that he would at least have some pants to wear as he left the beach. "I'll let him know I've got them."

He turned and walked back to his beach chair.

"That was one strange visit," said Karen.

"Yes, it was," agreed Lisa, becoming suspicious of the chance meeting with Antonio, then his disappearance, right before Ben turned up. "I think we should be careful for the rest of the afternoon. Let's keep an eye on him. When we leave the beach today, let's all go as a group."

They ordered snacks from the Perch and laid back in their chairs enjoying the food. Believing most of the alcohol had worn off, they pronounced themselves fit to drive. They continued sunning until the beach chairs were beginning to be gathered for the day.

"I think that's our signal. You guys are the best. Thanks so much for making this day special for me. I love you all, you're the best friends ever."

They gathered their belongings and dressed to leave, except Sylvie, who, after hugs from everyone, began her swim back to Brad's sailboat *Eclipse*. The rest of the group watched as she reached the boat and climbed aboard.

They then shared their own parting hugs, walking Debi to her room at La Playa before continuing as a group to the parking area. Remaining vigilant at Lisa's urging, they made sure everyone was safely in their car before leaving.

On her drive home, Lisa called Lekha to confirm their beach date for the next morning. She was eager to talk to Paul about the unusual visitors that afternoon but would wait until she got home.

SIXTY-TWO

PAUL WAS INSIDE when he heard Lisa unlock the door. He ended his phone call with Gregorio as she entered his office.

"How was the big celebration with Debi today?"

"We had a blast. I drank too much trying to keep up with the others. But I felt fine by the time I drove home."

Lisa looked at Paul, waiting for him to tell her about his day. When he did not, she pressed on.

"Although it was a great day, there were a couple of strange moments this afternoon."

"Oh?"

"Yes. So, tell me, did you take care of those 'strange moments' before they became a problem?"

"I did."

"I thought so. It didn't occur to me right away when I saw Ben, but I figured it out later. I assume you and Ben spent much of the day watching over me?"

"Yes. It became obvious that Antonio was a real threat. With Ben's help, I took care of it."

"Should I know how you did that?"

"It's up to you. I can tell you the details, you deserve it. Or you can just accept that it's been taken care of."

"You know what? I fully trust you. I'm going to accept that there was a problem and you handled it. I'm ready for all the problems to be over. At this point, I prefer to not know any details. But what about Lauren? Is Ben going to tell her?"

"We didn't discuss it. He might, but if she doesn't ask, he probably will let it be without talking about it."

"You look fine. Ben's fine too?"

"Yes, we're all well. Oh, and Brad also helped and he's also fine."

"Okay, that's enough on that subject," she replied, rolling her eyes.

"For a happier topic, you should know we now have our money. I need to call Augustus to complete arranging for his payment."

"Why don't you do that while I start supper?"

"I've got a better idea. Why don't you put your feet up and relax while I make the call, then we can go out to celebrate?"

"That sounds wonderful. I'll go shower and will be ready in thirty minutes. I love you."

"I love you too. This call won't take long."

Paul placed a call to Augustus and ironed out the details of his payment which went smoothly. Feeling relieved that everything was now behind him, he was ready for a fun dinner out. He walked into the living room to wait for Lisa.

Lisa eventually emerged from the bedroom in a sexy island dress and sat next to Paul.

"Are you ready?"

"Wow, you look beautiful. What about dinner at O Plongeoir in Marigot?"

"I love it. Great food, setting, service and easy parking. It's in my top five restaurants, if not my favorite. It will be perfect."

"While we're there, I want to talk about some of our newfound money. I had an idea that I've already partially acted on. I think you'll like it. But if you don't think it's the thing to do, I can easily undo it."

"Anything you want is good with me. I'm sure I'll like your idea."

She grabbed his hand and pulled him up.

"Come on, let's go. I'm starving, and when we get back, I hope you'll be ready for dessert."

"Sounds like the perfect ending to a great day," smiled Paul as they stepped out.

SIXTY-THREE

LEKHA AND JASON were up early on Friday morning. They planned to meet Paul and Lisa at Happy Bay for a day on the beach. It would be their first visit to Happy Bay.

As Lekha packed a beach bag, she heard her phone signal an incoming text message. It was from Lisa asking Lekha to call her. Concerned that something had come up changing Lisa's plan to meet at the beach, Lekha immediately called.

"Good morning, Lisa. Jason and I are getting ready. Is everything okay?"

"Oh yes, everything's great."

"Good. I was hoping so as we're really looking forward to a day at the beach."

"Same here. But I have a special request and wanted to catch you before you left."

"Okay, what's your special request?"

"Well, Paul and I are celebrating the end of problems with his last assignment. We did a lot of celebrating last night," she snickered. "He wants to do something special for me, and I thought, what's more special than jewelry?"

Lekha laughed. "Jason and I might want to hire you as a spokesperson for our store."

"My pay as spokesperson can be you doing me this favor. Paul wants to buy me a new piece of jewelry, and I want to get a new piece of jewelry. I'm looking for something shiny and sparkly, but I don't have anything in mind. If you'd feel okay about it, would you mind bringing some pieces of jewelry to the beach?"

"We can do that."

"Fantastic. Paul assured me that he'll keep everything safe. There are quiet secluded areas on the beach, I'm thinking in particular of a small, protected section between some rocks, that might be a great setting for a mini jewelry show."

"I'll talk to Jason. We can stop by the jewelry store to pick up some pieces on the way to the beach. It won't take long."

"That's awesome. There have been plenty of worries, for you too, starting with your act of kindness. It's not every day when you give a ride to a couple of crazy, naked people. Today will be a celebration of everything good that came out of it."

"Great. We'll be heading out in a few minutes."

"Okay, we'll meet you at the entrance to the beach near the basketball courts. We can all walk down together."

Lisa ended the call and saw Paul ready and waiting for her.

"They agreed to bring some jewelry. This day is going to be perfect. I'll grab my bag and be ready."

Paul started toward the door when she returned with the bag.

"The big cooler is already packed and in the car. Let's go," he said cheerfully.

Arriving first, they parked and waited for their friends. When Lekha and Jason arrived a few minutes later, there were still no other cars at the entrance.

"Welcome to Happy Bay," greeted Lisa as she hopped out of the car. "About ten minutes down this path will open up to one of the most beautiful beaches on the island. I'm glad you'll see it for the first time with us."

They crossed through the barrier blocking vehicular traffic, and pulling the large cooler on rollers, hiked down the path to the beach.

"This is beautiful," exclaimed Lekha as her feet hit the sand. "What a phenomenal beach. Thank you for introducing us to it."

They stepped a little further from the path on the way to their private slice of the beach.

"Over here is Danny's Bar. It's tucked away to where you might not notice it at first. Let's go there. I want to introduce you to Danny."

They walked to the bar, empty other than Danny, who looked up with a welcoming smile at their approach.

"Danny, I hope you remember us. I'm Lisa and this is Paul."

"Oh yes, I know you. He is Mr. Coors Light, but he gets Corona here."

Paul chuckled. "You do remember me."

Paul reached his hand out, Danny took it with a hearty handshake.

"And these are our friends," continued Lisa. "This is Jason."

The two men shook hands as Danny turned next to Lekha.

"And this is my special friend, Lekha."

"You have a very beautiful friend," smiled Danny. "It's great to meet you, Lexy. A beautiful name for a beautiful woman."

"Thank you," blushed Lekha, choosing to ignore his mispronunciation of her name. "You're very kind."

"The next time you come, Lexy, you won't have to ask if I remember you. Can I get any of you something to drink?"

Although they had a cooler of drinks, Paul and Lisa wanted to support Danny. They appreciated what he did by always manning his bar.

"I'll have a Corona, Danny. But you knew that. In fact, give me four. If they don't drink them, I will."

They decided to stay a few more minutes, taking seats on the wooden stools, talking with Danny and drinking the early morning beers.

"Danny, that was perfect," offered Paul as they pushed away from the bar. "We'll be back."

The group floated as if in a dream as they made their way to their spot on the beach. Lisa broke into a huge grin as they walked.

"Was that not a great way to get the morning started? You're not going to find another bar like Danny's anywhere else on the island. It's as good as it gets."

She stopped walking, the others doing so as well, as they waited for Lisa's next comments. She turned to Lekha.

"You've been kind of quiet today. What do you think so far, *Lexy*?" she teased.

"I couldn't correct him. Especially after he said my name is beautiful. And to answer your question, yes, I agree, we're off to a great start to the day. I've *got* to go back to the bar later today, you know, to make sure he remembers me."

Everyone enjoyed the light-hearted banter. They continued until Lisa pointed to her spot and announced they had arrived. They set the cooler and beach bags down and spread their towels on the warm sand.

"I think it fits. Jason, what about you? She's your wife, but I like it."

Jason smiled as his response.

"Lexy, that's your name," Lisa said addressing Lekha. "Do you mind if I call you Lexy? New beach, new life, new name, it's you."

"Lexy, I think I like it, too. Please, call me Lexy. I hope my other friends will too."

"Well, Lexy," began Paul, "It's early, and we've already had a beer, but I'd like you to take a look in the cooler and decide what you want next. We need to toast to a phenomenal day with special friends."

SIXTY-FOUR

DEBI WAS LOOKING forward to meeting her photographer, Chantelle, who had arrived on island late Thursday night. She would drive the two of them to Villa Islandtude to check it out for photographing the wedding. Although Ben and Lauren had given the key to Debi, she insisted they be there to meet Chantelle.

Lauren and Ben made a quick breakfast trip to the Croissant Royal but arrived back in time to greet Debi and the photographer.

"Good morning," Lauren called out as they arrived. "Come on up."

When the two reached the top of the stairs, Debi introduced Chantelle to Lauren and Ben. Chantelle looked around in wonder.

"This is beautiful. I want to walk around to see what everything will be like for tomorrow. Can you show me where the vows will be exchanged, as well as location for food preparation and the guest seating?"

"Sure, we can do that. This afternoon everything will be set up if you'd like to take another look then. Debi, you know everything here, would you like to give the tour?"

"No, you go ahead. I'm going to sit back and just envision the day unfolding tomorrow. Ben, if you'd like, you can keep me company as Lauren shows her around. I'm sorry to be imposing on your day."

"You're not, we're excited about the wedding. I'm glad the photographer is here to make sure she'll be ready for tomorrow."

Ben and Debi sat on the pool deck next to the spa, overlooking where the ceremony would take place. Chantelle and Lauren walked around with Lauren pointing out each area and answering her questions. They soon made their way back to the pool deck.

"I think I'm good. It's a beautiful setting for a wedding. Debi, thank you for offering me the opportunity to be your photographer."

"Lauren, do you guys have plans for today? It's the last day of my separation from Dean, and I thought I'd show Chantelle around the island for a bit. Would you guys like to come along?"

"Sure, what do you have in mind?"

"Since we're so close, maybe we could go into Marigot for lunch at Rosemary's. I was thinking of a driving tour this morning before lunch. And if you're willing, I would like to come back here when everything is set up."

"Yes, I'd like that, too," added Chantelle.

"Sure. Why don't you take Chantelle on your sightseeing tour of the island this morning, then Ben and I can meet you at Rosemary's for lunch. We can come back here after lunch when everything will be ready for the wedding, and if you'd like, we can swim here this afternoon."

"Chantelle, does that sound okay with you?"

"That sounds great. Debi, thanks for the tour offer, I'd love it. Rosemary's for lunch and time at the pool after that sounds like a vacation for me."

"Then it's settled," responded Lauren. "We'll meet you at Rosemary's at twelve-thirty, have an authentic island lunch, then come back to see the final layout and have some pool time. That's a great day on vacation for me too."

Debi and Chantelle left for the tour while Lauren and Ben decided to swim in the pool until time to meet for lunch.

SIXTY-FIVE

LEXY LOOKED IN the cooler and saw the gallon of rum punch.

"I don't know if it's good after beer, but I'd like some rum punch. Is it made with Topper's rum?"

"Oh yes," answered Paul. "Equal parts white rum, coconut rum and spice rum. It's Ben's recipe, I hope you like it."

"Oh, I do. I've had Ben's rum punch before."

Lisa broke out the plastic cups and Paul poured. They still stood as they tapped cups in a toast.

"Now that we've had the ceremonial drink of rum punch, it's time to settle in for the day. I know you don't do nude beaches, but seeing as you've already seen Paul and me naked, I'm going back to my normal lack of attire."

Lisa slipped out of her t-shirt and shorts and sat back on her towel. Seeing no objection from Lexy and Jason, Paul also undressed and handed his clothes to Lisa, who placed their clothes in her beach bag.

Lexy and Jason sat on their towels wearing their shorts and t-shirts. Lexy lifted her t-shirt over her head and stepped out of her shorts, revealing a modest two-piece swimsuit underneath. She sat on her towel as Jason sat beside her in his shorts that doubled as swim trunks.

Lisa suspected Lexy wanted to experience clothes freedom, but felt reluctant, not sure she wanted to take the step.

"If you guys don't mind us," Lisa continued, "you're good wearing your suits. It's a clothing optional beach, not clothing mandatory or nude mandatory. Everybody does what they enjoy and feel comfortable with."

"I'm a little jealous," responded Lekha. "It's great that you are so comfortable."

"There's really nothing to it. It took me maybe five minutes, if that, to feel comfortable the first time I went without a swimsuit. It quickly became natural, where I now do everything I would otherwise do, but with no swimsuit."

"It's just the four of us. I feel a little funny looking at you two without your clothes. So, here goes."

She untied her top and also dispensed with her bottoms, leaned forward, and put her swimsuit in her beach bag.

"There, done. Jason, what are you waiting for? You can't be the only one clothed at the nude beach."

Jason grinned and stepped out of his trunks. He handed them to Lexy.

"You can put those in the beach bag. I don't think I'll be needing them again until we leave."

Pleased, he sat back on his towel and reached for his cup of rum punch.

"To great friends, rum punch and nude beaches," he toasted, grinning broadly. "This is continuing to be a special day."

SIXTY-SIX

....

LAUREN AND BEN pulled into a parking place at the Marigot Market and found Debi and Chantelle already seated at Rosemary's.

"How was the driving tour?" asked Lauren.

"I loved it. I want to come back soon. It's got everything I want for a vacation."

"It was unfortunately a quick tour. If I wasn't going on my honeymoon after the wedding tomorrow, I'd try to convince her to extend her stay."

"You've been very kind. In addition to giving me this fantastic work opportunity, I'm beginning to think of you as family. I promise I'll do my best for your wedding tomorrow."

"I know you will. The photos from Orillia are beautiful. But enough of that, I'm hungry. Let's order some lunch."

The four soon finished their lunch, and sat enjoying the atmosphere of the open-air restaurant. When finished, Ben signaled for the check and paid the bill.

"I don't want to rush you, but if you want to see the set-up at the villa, it should be done now. They were working on it when we left."

"Let's go. I'm anxious to check it out now that it's ready. I'm expecting to still be taking pictures this time tomorrow."

Ben and Lauren led them back to Villa Islandtude. They walked up the stairs to the pool deck.

"I said it this morning and I'll say it again. This view is stunning. What a great setting for a wedding."

"There have been some fun times here. As you can see, the chairs for the guests are out, the area for the preacher is over here, and the band will be set up in that corner outside of the master bedroom. Each bedroom is named for a beach on the island. The master is Orient Beach, which is where the girls will be getting dressed and their hair and make-up done. And over here is Happy Bay, the bedroom next to the spa. The guys can get dressed for the wedding in there."

Lauren walked around with her and answered questions. After fifteen minutes, the girls returned.

"All right Debi, I'll be ready. It will be my favorite wedding of those I've photographed with these amazing backgrounds. I'll want to put some of the pictures up on my website."

"You're welcome to post any pictures you want. I know they'll all be beautiful. Now, who wants to go swimming? I'm certain we won't mess up the pool or anything else before the wedding."

"Sounds good to me," answered Lauren. "Ben, will you get us some towels?"

"Sure, I'll be right back."

"Thanks for the invitation. When I left my room this morning, I wasn't planning on going swimming today. I'm not prepared, but you guys go ahead and I'll sit back and enjoy the view."

"What do you mean, not prepared? What do you have to do to go swimming?"

"Thanks, Debi, but I didn't bring a swimsuit. You guys go ahead, I'm enjoying just being here. I will enjoy sitting and looking out over the pool."

Ben was back on the pool deck with four towels. Debi reached for the towels and grabbed one.

"Thanks Ben. Now I'm almost prepared for a swim."

She walked over to the nearest lounge chair and laid her towel on it for sunning. She made sure Chantelle was watching.

"This is the next step," she said, lifting off her t-shirt and stepping out of her shorts. "Oh my, I must have forgotten my swimsuit in the room," she said in mock modesty, covering herself with her hands. "Oh well, I'll just have to make do."

She dropped her hands and smiled broadly.

"This is the way it's done on the island. Ben, hand Chantelle her towel. Chantelle, you're now only one step from being prepared. Get your clothes off and get in the pool."

Debi tested the pool water with her foot.

"It feels amazing," she said, walking the length of the pool to its steps, then submerging.

She popped back up, rubbed her eyes, and focused on Chantelle.

"Come on in, don't let the chance slip away from you. The water is perfect. Ben and Lauren, does she need a swimsuit to swim in the pool?"

"Of course not. Ben and I don't care. We've got swimsuits, but if no one is offended, we weren't planning to put them on."

"Don't change anything on my account. I'm happy sitting back with my feet up."

Lauren and Ben undressed and joined Debi in the pool. After Chantelle settled back into a reclining chair to enjoy looking over the pool and the view, Ben climbed out and got floats for Lauren and Debi.

"Chantelle, while I'm out, do you want me to get you something to drink?"

"Sure, why not? What are my choices?"

"We have a variety. There's beer, wine, sodas, water and rum punch. I'm going to get some rum punch. Debi, do you want your usual pinot grigio?"

"That would be perfect. Chantelle, what do you want?"

"Either a glass of wine or rum punch. I'm easy. Debi, what do you suggest?"

"I'm not a big rum punch drinker, but people who are say they love Ben's rum punch. It's made with Topper's rum from the island. To get the full island experience, I recommend you try it if you like rum."

"Ben, please bring me a rum punch. I'm eager to have an authentic St. Maarten drink in St. Maarten."

Ben went inside and poured three rum punches and a pinot grigio for Debi. The girls climbed out of the pool to enjoy the sun and their drinks in their lounge chairs. They clinked their glasses together as Debi gave the toast.

"Here's to Chantelle and her maiden St. Maarten rum punch drink!"

"To Chantelle," said Ben and Lauren in unison.

Chantelle took a healthy swig of her drink.

"Ben, you have some smart friends. This is the best rum punch I've ever had. You and Topper have done good. Thank you."

The afternoon wore on and the group lounged until just before sunset. The swimmers dressed and sat back with Chantelle watching the sun descend toward the horizon.

"I can't believe I didn't bring my camera. It looks like it's going to be a beautiful sunset, and I'm a photographer without a camera."

"You'll have another chance tomorrow at my wedding. But for today, use your phone like everybody else. And while you're at it, how about getting a picture of me with my two hosts. St. Martin friends truly are the best."

They posed at the railing with their drinks for an early sunset shot.

"Okay photographer, come on over and get in the picture. I'll set my phone up on timer and get all four of us. Ben, Lauren, make room for Chantelle."

A few group pictures were made as the sun quickly descended.

Chantelle checked out the pictures.

"Oh my gosh, these are beautiful. Debi, you've set a high standard for me when I have my camera tomorrow. This has been great, but is it time for us to be leaving? I don't want you to be too tired for the ceremony tomorrow."

"That won't be a problem. That's what photo shop is for. Make me beautiful," laughed Debi.

"If you guys don't have dinner plans, you're welcome to come with Ben and me. We're planning to go to Pizza Del Sol. It's close by and is our favorite Italian restaurant."

Chantelle looked to Debi for her to respond for the two of them.

"Thanks for the invitation. Chantelle and I would love to go to Pizza Del Sol."

"And after dinner, would it be okay if I invite myself back for a little time in the hot tub?" asked Chantelle. "I may be bolder with the sun now down."

"It will be a perfect ending to another wonderful day celebrating in the islands," answered Ben.

"Today we celebrate new friendships, and tomorrow we'll be celebrating Debi's marriage and my good luck having Debi pick me as her photographer. Do we need to go back for different clothes, or can we wear what we have on?"

"It's casual, what you're wearing is fine," answered Lauren.

"That's super, because I don't want to waste time going back by my room. I'm glad we're coming back after dinner. You guys are the best. This definitely won't be my last trip to St. Maarten."

SIXTY-SEVEN

PAUL HAD SOMETHING he wanted to tell Lexy and Jason. He saw everyone was having a good time, so he decided to wait a while longer before sharing his news. Lisa finished her rum punch, pleased that Lexy and Jason appeared to have overcome their initial discomfort from disrobing.

"I've got an idea. Lexy and Jason, you've now basked on the beach and have ditched the swimsuits for the first time. What about another first? Let's all dip in."

Paul stood, ready for the first skinny-dip of the day. Lisa glanced at Lexy, who appeared unsure about leaving the shelter from others' view that the rocks provided.

"You can put your bottoms on if you'd be more comfortable. Or your whole suit, for that matter. You should do what's comfortable for you," encouraged Lisa. "Nobody on the beach cares or will even notice."

Lexy stood, looked at Jason, then glanced at the beach bag with their swimsuits.

"Come on Jason," Lexy said, reaching for his hand, "Let's go skinny dipping."

Jason also appeared hesitant, but with Lexy's encouragement, was the first to reach the water. Finding a calm area with smooth sand, they all waded in.

"The water feels amazing. I can't believe I'm doing this. Jason, I'm about to be a convert."

She was beaming, proud that she had taken the leap.

"It wasn't all that bad. I really like the feeling, and it *will* be way better not having to sit around in a wet swimsuit."

"Welcome to the club, Lexy. I'd say you're living into your name, you've earned it. The next time there's a girls trip to a nude beach, you'll have to come with me."

"If you invite me, I'll go. Let's plan a trip."

Lisa laughed out loud at hearing her words. Lexy sounded like a full convert, not one in name only.

"We have a wedding to attend tomorrow. Lexy, we can talk to some others there and see if anybody is interested, and maybe bring our husbands along."

"All right, let's see if we can put together a group tomorrow. Hopefully, I won't chicken out. But first, I have something I really want to do."

Lexy waded out onto the sand and squeezed the water from her hair.

"Jason, will you get some money? I want to go to the bar."

"Don't you want to dry off first?"

"No, I'm going to drip dry. But bring my towel, will you? I might be there for a while and want to sit down. I'm going to see if Danny remembers me."

Jason dutifully started toward the shore.

"It looks like I'll be going to the bar. Do you guys want anything?"

"No, you go ahead. Lisa and I will go back to our stuff in a few minutes. We'll wait for you. You two can have a little fun at the bar without us."

Jason was fumbling in the beach bag for their money when Lexy reached Danny's Beach Bar. Danny came over and greeted her with his smile.

"I would like two Coronas, please," she said, sea water dripping off her arms. "I'll have the money in a minute."

"No rush on paying. You can run a tab and pay me later today."

"Thank you, Danny."

"You're welcome, Lexy."

"You do remember me."

"Yes, I remember. How could I forget the beautiful lady with the beautiful name?"

"Thank you. Danny, this has already become my favorite beach bar."

He handed her a Corona and she took a drink. He placed the second beer on the counter. While she waited for Jason, Lexy did a little shake as if to speed the water from her body, then used her hands as a makeshift towel. She smiled at Danny as he watched the show.

"Here's your towel babe. Sorry, it took a few minutes to find my wallet."

"That's okay. We can pay later. I ordered a beer for you, too."

Lexy placed her towel on the wooden bar stool and climbed up on it.

"This is heaven. Danny, after this beer, we'll need to get back to our friends, but I'll be back."

Danny gave his best smile.

"I know you will, Lexy. You and Jason have fun today."

They finished their beers and Jason placed a fifty-dollar bill on the bar.

"We'll be back later. If we don't have more beers, keep the change."

They merrily returned to where they had set up for the day. Lexy was radiant.

"I take it you had fun?"

"Lisa, it was great. The beer tasted better and even seemed colder."

"That might have been because you were cold from being naked and not drying off," teased Jason.

"If it was, I'll want to do that every time," she teased back. "My first naked bar beer and I loved it!"

Lexy tossed her towel over her beach bag and sat directly on the sand.

"I love it. Jason, try it. If you get too much sand on your bum, I'll help you sweep it off," she said playfully. "I feel like I'm five years old again. Lisa and Paul, thank you for suggesting this beach."

"I'm glad you guys are having such an enjoyable day," smiled Paul. "I have something for you that I hope you'll like."

He reached into the giant cooler and pulled out a white plastic bag. Making a presentation out of the movement, he reached in and slowly drew out its contents.

"Oh my! You've got to be kidding," exclaimed Lexy.

"It's for you. It was my idea, but when I asked Lisa, she agreed it was worth taking a chance on giving it to you. You don't have to keep it if you think it would be better to do something else with it."

Paul handed Lexy the artifact he retrieved from the mountaintop that she first held the night of the rescue.

"I love it," she said, staring at why they had dubbed it the fertility god. "But I'm not sure it's something friends and family would understand me liking. They may think it's over the top, and up, it's way up," she snickered. "Do you think it would be safe if I keep it?"

"I think so. The danger was before anyone claimed ownership. A suggestion is you could take it to the local museum and let them have it for display for a few months. You'll be established as its owner. After a few months, you could take it home and do whatever you wanted with it. By the way, it's appraised value is about $250,000."

"Oh my gosh, that's what I'm going to do. Jason, is that okay?"

"Yes, but Paul, that's a lot of money. We shouldn't accept such a valuable gift."

"Nonsense. Lisa and I got a lot of money from that project. You helped us, and we may not have been able to do it without your help. That's why I have an equivalent amount in cash that I'll be giving you later."

"Absolutely not. We've not done a thing for the fertility god and definitely not for money, too. We can't accept it."

"I thought that might be your reaction. We insist we're giving you the statue and the money. We want you to enjoy at least some, but you can always make a sizable contribution to the charities of your choice. You'll at least accept the tax help from your charitable giving, won't you?"

"You must have made a *lot* of money on this. Thank you for your amazing generosity. Lexy and I will talk about it later. But this definitely calls for a drink. Let's break open one of those bottles of red wine."

Jason opened the bottle and poured before handing each of them a wine glass. Lisa accepted her glass, but then held it out for Paul.

"Before we drink, Paul, will you hold my glass a second?"

Lisa stood and gathered her towel from the sand, stepped away about ten feet, and shook most of the sand from it. She then tossed the towel on her beach bag and sat back down directly on the sand. She took her glass of wine and reached for Paul's glass, also.

"Paul, I suggest you not be a prima donna and ditch the towel like the rest of us. We're going for total freedom and new beginnings here."

Paul obliged, added his towel to the stack on the beach bags, and plopped down in the sand.

"Okay Jason, now we're ready." Lisa nodded at Jason to begin.

"To an amazing day, I can't even begin to describe it, so I won't try. You have to live it to believe it and understand it."

They clinked glasses and drank to the toast.

"Just like the Corona I had at Danny's Bar," Lexy offered, "This is the best glass of red wine I've had in a long time."

At noon, they took their towels and glasses of red wine to Danny's Bar and ordered lunch.

"Danny, do you mind if we continue drinking our wine at lunch?" requested Jason. "We'd like to sit at your table to eat."

Danny held out his hands toward the table inviting them to sit.

"You are good customers. Your food will be out soon."

The friends ate, laughed, and drank wine until after one o'clock. Jason placed two more fifty-dollar bills on the bar top as they left.

They sat in the sand near their beach bags, tossing their towels aside. Jason nodded toward Lexy.

"That was a great meal. Now, it's time for me to provide the afternoon entertainment."

Lexy reached into her bag and pulled out a jewelry box.

"Who's ready for a jewelry show?"

Lexy modeled the many pieces she had brought to the beach, offering to help Lisa try them on. The afternoon passed quickly with Lisa selecting a necklace and a bracelet.

"What a unique way to shop for jewelry."

"I agree with that," added Paul. "The modeling show and jewelry were super."

"Thanks," replied Lexy. "But before you suggest it, this won't become part of our regular marketing strategy," she giggled.

"You two have been ridiculously generous, so before you say anything, we want you to have the jewelry as our gifts. It doesn't come close to matching your generosity. Lexy and I can't thank you enough for this unbelievable day. I don't like thinking it, but it's probably getting close to time to leave."

"Let's have one more glass of wine," suggested Lisa. "Then we can dip in and get the sand off before we go."

SIXTY-EIGHT

SATURDAY MORNING FINALLY arrived, and Debi, too excited to sleep, was out of bed early. She was wide awake and eager to begin the day. She picked up her phone from the bedstand and called Lauren at Villa Islandtude.

"Lauren, how are you and Ben this morning?"

"Everything is great. Are you ready to start your big day?"

"I am. I can't wait to get started. Is it too early for me to come over?"

"Of course not, come on over. We have some croissants and fruit, and you can have breakfast here with us."

"Thanks, I'll be right over."

Debi had already packed her bag for her hair and make-up. By the time she arrived at Villa Islandtude, Lauren was outside waiting and greeted her with a big hug.

"Debi, I'm so glad you're having the ceremony today where your island friends can be a part of it. It's special for all of us. I know you had an amazing ceremony in Orillia, but we're praying this one will be equally as amazing."

"I'm sure it will be. This is my new home, and I can't thank you enough for hosting this for me."

"It's an honor to be part of your wedding. Come on in and let's eat breakfast. The rest of the girls will be here soon."

Ben ate but then left the girls to themselves. It was not long before the others began arriving. The girls made the main house and connecting master bedroom theirs until the ceremony began. They would serve as traditional bridesmaids, dressing in yellow pareos dotted with pink flowers. Lauren laid out the look-alike pareos in the master bedroom.

Dean's groomsmen also arrived early. Paul and Gregorio arrived first. Ben greeted them as they gathered on the pool deck. The groomsmen were Ben, Brad, Gary, Rick, Paul and Gregorio.

"Good morning, Gregorio," greeted Paul. "I trust everything is good this morning?"

"Oh, yes, Paul. I assume you're inquiring as to our call on Thursday?"

"Yes, you're right. I appreciate your willingness to help when I called. Antonio is very resourceful, as I know you're aware. There was a time when you employed him."

"Antonio has always been very capable, but his determination tends to become insubordination. And you're right, Antonio and I parted ways."

"I had concern when I called you that I possibly had not done enough when I left him on Green Key. I had second thoughts, fearful that it may not be the last I'll see him."

"I understood your concern."

"So, you're comfortable he will not interrupt today's marriage ceremony?"

"Anything is possible, but the chances of that happening are much less than when you left him."

"Thanks, Gregorio. I don't want today to be ruined for any of us."

"Dean is my friend. I will also be disappointed if anything interferes with today's plans."

SIXTY-NINE

ANTONIO WAS LAYING down. He found the water and beef jerky that sustained him but was still hungry and thirsty. It was dark and he had lost track of time.

Not sure what had happened, he could remember falling while chasing someone he recognized. He was just at the point of catching him and grabbing the swim trunks he was after when he stumbled. He was now certain someone had waited, cowardly tripping him while hiding under the cover of a parked vehicle.

He hit his head hard. He remembered feeling woozy, when someone jumped on his back and put a wrestling hold on him. The next thing he could remember was waking up in the dark.

Engulfed in total darkness, he explored to the limited amount he was capable, reaching out with his hands and stretching his legs. He was on his back. Reaching up, he touched the ceiling of wherever he was being held. He could slide only about a foot beyond where his head lay, and only about that same distance beyond his feet. He could breathe normally but kept his breaths shallow.

Antonio reached to the ceiling and pushed, but did not feel the ceiling move. He flipped onto his side and pulled his knees up above his waist. He wanted to kick the constricting walls, but did not have enough room to put the required force into the movement to break free.

He lay back, trying to remain calm, when he felt movement. He believed he was on water and could feel movement as if a calm sea of rolling waves provided some motion. He heard no voices or other distinguishable sounds. As he lay there, he looked as best as he could toward his feet. There seemed to be slivers of light flashing, indicating several small openings at the end of his constricting box. He decided someone had captured him and the small holes in his wooden prison allowed him to breathe. He searched with his fingertips for any indentation where he could potentially pry the lid off the box.

Unsuccessful, he had little choice but to wait. He could find no more food or water. He hoped his captor would soon check on him. He was determined, that when the slimmest of chances occurred, with only a tiny lifting of the lid, he would spring into action. He would wait, gather his strength, and be ready given the smallest opportunity to escape.

SEVENTY

AS DEBI STEPPED out of the shower, her handmaids waited to help her finish getting ready.

Chantelle stood by to photograph the bride and bridesmaids preparing for the ceremony.

"I just finished taking pictures of the guys. They're ready whenever you girls are finished."

"I know I agreed to do whatever they wanted," Debi said, referring to her girlfriends, "but I'm having second thoughts."

"Nonsense. What are you talking about? Is there something that's troubling you?"

"I see the pareos laid out for my bridesmaids, and I know they'll look great wearing them. But sarongs for the groomsmen? I'm not so sure that was a good idea. Shirts and pants wouldn't be all bad."

"Well, it's too late now. That's what they're wearing. And rest assured, they look very handsome. The groomsmen are wearing solid royal blue, and Dean will be in midnight blue. They all look very masculine. Don't let that worry you."

"Thanks for your reassurance," Debi laughed and gave her a quick hug. "Everyone will know this wedding is a little different when a man in a skirt greets them to be seated."

"They're not skirts, they're sarongs, and they look great. After this wedding, everybody getting married on the island will be copying you, and those already married will be envious that they didn't do it."

"Okay, I trust you. Hopefully no one will step on a sarong, and we have an unveiling during the ceremony."

"That won't happen because they're not that long. Now, enough on that. Let's finish getting you ready."

Debi quickly painted her fingernails as Jodi insisted on painting her toes. Debi stretched out on the king bed and enjoyed the attention as her toes were decorated in blue.

With her nails dry, Karen brought the pareo selected for the bride. Similar to the yellow pareos worn by the bridesmaids, Debi's white pareo had only a few pink flowers so she would be dressed primarily in white and adorned with a white veil.

"I'm going to step out and make some pictures of the wedding decorations. I'll be back in to capture you wrapping your pareo. Sit back and relax for a few minutes. It's still too early for the guests to arrive."

Chantelle stepped out to take the photos. Debi sat back on the bed and admired her friends' beaming faces staring at her.

"I can't believe I'm doing this. I know, I just did this in Orillia, but it still doesn't seem real. I'm marrying the man of my dreams, and I'm surrounded by the best friends I could hope to have. I guess I'm nervous. Is there any advice you can give me for my wedding night?"

That caused an eruption of laughter.

"I think you'll be okay," giggled Karen. "I'm reassured that you mentioned wedding *night*. Just remember, dessert follows the entrée, and the wedding night follows the ceremony. You and Dean have been separated a few days, but still try to hold off until the guests have left."

The joking and laughter continued until Chantelle returned to take the final photographs of Debi and the girls as they finished dressing. The contrast of Debi's pareo amidst her bridesmaids made for some amazing pictures.

"All right, I'm stepping out now. The guests are arriving, and I'm going to capture some of it. When I come back in, it will be show time. Debi, you all look gorgeous. Remember to have fun."

The Northeast Florida Tiki Hut Association had arrived. The group of ten was on island when Dean spotted Debi for the first time, and they spent meaningful time with her during their vacation. They were all helping with today's wedding. Chris, Mark, Paulie and Dale had the task of handling their version of valet service. Tammy and Catherine oversaw the wedding book, directing the guests to sign in registering their attendance. The other girls, Jeanne, Mary, Sara, and Kathy, greeted the guests with nets of flower petals for after the ceremony.

After making it through the gauntlet of the Tiki Hut Association, the groomsmen stood at the top of the stairs to seat the guests. A few guests exhibited looks of surprise when greeted by young men wearing the low-slung sarongs, but only because it was not expected wedding attire.

As the last of the guests took their seats, the members of the Tiki Hut Association joined to watch the wedding. Island Dreamers began playing "Something" by the Beatles as the bridesmaids made their walk out to the landing area of the pool deck. Next came the groomsmen followed by Dean, walking out as Dave and Kerry performed "You Make My Dreams" by Hall and Oates. Dean stood waiting for Debi to join him. After a short pause, the band started again, this time capturing Debi's taste in country music, by singing "Forever and Ever, Amen" by Randy Travis. Debi looked radiant as she glided next to Dean in front of the minister.

The minister looked out over the assembly of friends.

"We are gathered here to witness the marriage of our good friends, Debi and Dean. They are blessed to have found one another, two wonderful and unique individuals, who wish to express their love and commitment to each other here today. They each have a few words they would like to share, and they thank you as the witnesses of this special time."

The minister looked at Debi and Dean and nodded for Dean to begin.

"Debi, I recall as if yesterday the first time I saw you. I was looking around the casino, and there you were. You sat at one of the slot machines, easily the most beautiful woman in the casino. In fact, you were the most beautiful woman I had ever seen. I was spellbound, distracted from my work. I couldn't take my eyes off you."

Dean paused, passionately looking into her eyes.

"But there was more. You had an unparalleled spirit. You radiated joy, and the combination of looks and your inner spirit commanded the attention of everyone around you."

"I watched as you engaged your friends, and I loved your overwhelming enthusiasm. I found myself in the unusual position of pulling against my casino, wanting you to win on every spin."

"Little did I know how I and others would be rewarded each time you won."

Dean looked at her again, but this time with amusement. She broke into a broad smile, remembering how with each winning spin, she had opened her dress, cupped her breasts, and pretended they were cheering her on. She was pleased when Dean did not share that additional information during the ceremony.

"I knew I had to meet you. I was almost nervous to approach you, fearful of rejection. But I was prepared to win you over, no matter what I might need to do. And when we did spend time together, it was magical. Debi, you complete me in so many ways, as a partner in every aspect, pleasure, facing the unknown, and as my equal in all endeavors. I pledge my love to you."

Dean gave her a slight nod, and it was time for Debi to share her thoughts.

"Dean, I too, remember our first meeting. A handsome, cultured man approached me, firm in his approach yet still gentle. I'll admit, I wasn't disappointed to think that you had money," she smiled.

"I came to know you as smart and charming. I realized you had many choices and it thrilled me that you chose me. You've accepted me as your partner, and I never want to disappoint the faith and trust you've put in me."

"We have been tested, and my love for you has grown. I am so pleased to think of you as my husband, and I want to always make you proud."

"Dean, before all our wonderful friends here today, I pledge my love to you."

The minister turned briefly from Debi and Dean to address their friends.

"With the pledge of love we've heard today, it's time for the recitation of their wedding vows. Dean, will you begin?"

"Debi, I take you to be my wife, my one true love, for better or worse, for richer or poorer, in sickness and in health, forsaking all others."

Dean surveyed her with his eyes, a tropical beauty as his wife, his face reflecting his delight.

"Dean, I take you to be my husband, my one true love, for better or worse, for richer or poorer, in sickness and in health, forsaking all others."

"Debi and Dean, will you please hold each other's hands?"

Addressing the gathered friends, the minister continued.

"The word of God tells us that love is patient, kind and not jealous. Love does not brag and is not arrogant. It does not rejoice in unrighteousness, but rejoices with the truth, for love bears all things, believes all things, hopes all things, and endures all things, but above all, love never fails."

The minister turned his attention back to Debi and Dean.

"Debi and Dean, you have come here today before us and before God and have expressed your desire to become husband and wife. You have pledged your love to each other, forsaking all others. By the powers vested in me, I pronounce you are officially husband and wife. It's time for you two to publicly display your affection, with just a kiss, of course."

The minister smiled first at Debi and Dean and then the gathering of friends, as Dean and Debi kissed, demonstratively elated that their time of separation was over.

SEVENTY-ONE

VESNA AND YANNICK, the owner and chef of Debi's and Dean's favorite restaurant, Vesna Taverna, catered the event with a choice of beef and fish dishes for the guests. As the guests ate, the wedding party posed for Chantelle to capture more memories of the ceremony. At the conclusion of the photo session, the wedding party briefly mingled with the guests before sitting down to a delicious meal.

At Debi's insistence, Island Dreamers took a brief break from performing. Ben piped in music to fill the void while they ate. They rushed through their lunch, eager to resume performing. Dave, the lead singer, grabbed the microphone.

"Okay, everybody, we hope you're enjoying your time today helping Debi and Dean celebrate. Now it's time for our honorary couple to come out and have the first dance."

Dave began singing "Perfect" by Ed Sheeran. Friends gathered around as the newly married couple owned the dance floor. The song created a few moist eyes and loving looks among the onlookers. When the song ended, Dean looked lovingly at Debi, and they shared a kiss.

The band moved into the next song, inviting other couples to join the newlyweds. Several more songs were performed as the newlyweds continued to dance along with their friends. Seeing the signal from the caterers, Debi announced it was time to cut the cake.

Everything continued smoothly with no unwanted appearance by Antonio. The band played and everyone enjoyed the open bar. When not dancing, Debi and Dean enjoyed visiting with their guests. The serious portion of the wedding celebration was winding down.

Debi and Dean garnered everyone's attention.

"Thank you all for coming today," began Dean. "The bride and groom don't usually make the announcement we're about to make, but in keeping with the unique nature of the day, here goes. Instead of everyone gathering and throwing rice at us as we dash for a getaway car, we're going to do something different. Ordinarily someone other than the bride and groom would cue you in when it's time for the rice throwing, but Debi and I are handling that today."

Dean stopped talking to let Debi continue with the announcement.

"We don't want to leave yet, and we've still got some partying to do. But now we're going to have a variation of throwing rice at the exiting couple. Instead, there will be a ceremonial throwing of rose petals. But don't fret, this will be the kick-off of the party phase of the wedding. We're not really going anywhere. Get your rose petals ready. If you've lost your rose petals, we have plenty more. Help yourself and get ready to throw. We're stepping inside for just a minute. We'll be ready for you soon."

Chantelle followed Debi and Dean inside. She would video them from behind as they embarked on their version of a wedding getaway. Chantelle broke into laughter as Debi and Dean stood before her.

"Chantelle, we're about ready," announced Debi. "You know the path we're following, running along the pool deck from the shallow end toward the deeper end."

"Yes, I've got it."

"Our bridesmaids and groomsmen know what we're doing. Would you look out and see if they're ready and in position so that the others will fall in line?"

Chantelle peeped around the curtain and saw that they were ready.

"All good to go," she reported.

"All right. Dean, are you ready? But remember, we're running slow, very slow. Everybody knows the warning not to run on a pool deck."

"Yes dear," he smiled. "Let's do this. Chantelle, get the camera rolling."

Debi and Dean tiptoed out the large room and began their slow-motion run. Other than Debi's veil on her head, they wore nothing but enormous smiles.

Chantelle filmed as a line of rose petal throwers formed on either side of the streaking couple. They reached the far end of the pool and cannon-balled in. The serious portion of the wedding festivities had ended.

At the back of the crowd, Paul stood beside Gregorio talking in a hushed voice.

"Well, so far so good. I hate to do this, but would you mind checking on our friend? I'd like to join in the fun, but I want to know it's safe to do so before I can get in the spirit."

"Paul, for you, I'll check. I'll step inside to make the call."

SEVENTY-TWO

ANTONIO WAS CONVINCED he was traveling on a slow-moving boat. He tried to remain calm despite being trapped inside a small wooden crate.

As he lay waiting, he felt the forward momentum slowing, and what felt like an abrupt halt. Without the comfort of light or outside views, he was unaware of time of day or day of week.

He tried to stir himself, moving his fingers and toes to increase circulation and to try to be as alert as possible. He would be ready to escape given the slightest opportunity.

What he guessed was thirty minutes later, after the abrupt halt, he believed he heard muted voices. He considered shouting out for help, but decided to remain silent, in case the voices he heard were those of his captors. His silence would help him use the element of surprise to overpower them.

He continued to wait, and eventually the voices trailed off and he heard nothing further. He began to second-guess not screaming out, wondering if his possible rescuers had now left the area.

He listened intently, waiting to hear sounds and hopefully more voices. He would wait for a signal to determine if he should try making noise or remain as quiet as possible.

Then it happened. He was moving. There was no denying the motion of the crate, as it was swung up in the air, stopped, and he felt it moving again. Antonio remained still and quiet as he tried to mentally prepare for the unknown. More light entered through the end of the crate, enabling him to see his feet for the first time.

The motion of the crate stopped suddenly, as it hit hard on a solid surface, jostling him inside.

Outside of the crate, there was activity on and around the Blowing Point Dock in Anguilla. Some tourists ambled about as the ferry to St. Martin had just departed. The crate sat upon the dock. Then Antonio heard a conversation right outside his crate.

"I was planning to have them bring my boat and load up for me, take it to Sunshine Acres. Of all the times to be told they're delayed, that they're in the midst of the repair work. They volunteered to send someone with another boat in about thirty minutes."

"Mom, what do you want to do? We can sit out here and wait. There probably won't be too many questions about why we're hanging out here with this crate. Or, we can open it up and help our cargo out of there. You were assured he's fine, right? That he could be weak, but strong enough to walk?"

"That's right, Sue."

"Well, aren't you curious?"

"Of course, I'm curious. When Gregorio called telling me he had a delivery for me and that he wanted my help, he gave me very little information, so there are a lot of unanswered questions. He assured me that his present to me would not be dangerous, at least not right away. And even if it is, I've always been capable, and with old Tick-Licker here, I couldn't be more prepared."

Martha, the owner of an Anguilla horse farm, Sunshine Acres, was an old movie buff. She viewed herself as a latter-day Mae West, the film star born in 1893, who was a one-of-a-kind; a woman parading her sexuality, with style and wit. When she saw in an old movie that Daniel Boone had named his gun, bragging he could hit creatures as small as a tick with that rifle at thirty paces, she could not resist dubbing her handgun with the same name.

"Well then, I vote we do not wait another thirty minutes. I'll get what I need from the pickup truck to open this baby up. I'll be right back."

In five minutes, the two women readied themselves for the unveiling.

"Okay, Mom, it's time to see your gift from Gregorio. Sir, welcome to Anguilla," she said, sliding off the top of the crate, the lid falling to the dock.

Antonio was flooded with light. He was thankful for the small amount of light that that entered the end of the crate, but was still nearly blinded in the abundant sunshine. He was sweating profusely, but the rush of fresh air cooled and energized him. Struggling to see in the bright light, he jumped up from his prone position in the crate.

"Oh my!" exclaimed Martha. "That Gregorio, he's probably been laughing, wanting me to report my surprise when the crate was opened."

Antonio stood, relieved to no longer be pinned in the crate. His eyes were adjusting, and he could see the two women staring at him.

"Sue, an old Mae West line just popped into my head. But in this instance, the answer is clear. That's not a gun in his pocket," she chortled.

"Mom, behave yourself."

"Oh, I am, but why not enjoy the view," she responded. "Sir, I'm told your name is Antonio. I'm happy to see you, too. I'm Martha and this is my daughter Sue. We're here to help you. But this is Anguilla, not St. Martin. You can't be out in public without clothes, or at least not for long. Why don't you step out of that ridiculous crate and come with us? My Ford F-150 is waiting. Let's get you there before you cause too much of a stir and get arrested."

Antonio was trying to process all he heard. They appeared to be no threat, and even said they were here to help. He decided to willingly go with them. He walked between the two ladies to their vehicle.

"Why don't you hop up in the cargo bed? It's a short ride to my farm. We'll attend to you there."

Martha opened her driver's side door, reached in, and grabbed the bottle of water. She carried it back to Antonio, who still stood at the back of the vehicle.

"Here you go. I think you could use this."

He accepted the water and drank it all down before removing the plastic bottle from his lips.

Martha pulled down the tailgate for Antonio to climb in.

"Do you need any help? I can give you a boost."

"Thanks, I can do it," he uttered, his first words since being freed, as he climbed into the cargo bed and sat. He immediately felt his butt burning from the hot steel of the truck.

"We'll be there in a jiffy. Hang on. We'll talk there and get you attended to. I think we can work out an arrangement that we'll both like."

Martha climbed in her truck and drove Sue and Antonio to Sunshine Acres.

SEVENTY-THREE

OUT OF EARSHOT from the crowd of guests gathered at the swimming pool, Gregorio dialed Martha. When Martha saw the call was from Gregorio, she answered laughing.

"You crazy bastard. That was a good one. Sue and I were quite surprised. The poor man was left with nothing. You didn't even put a towel down to keep the splinters out of his butt," she howled. "He's in the back of my truck. We're on our way to Sunshine Acres."

A rare chuckle escaped from Gregorio.

"I'm glad you like the delivery. A business associate wanted my help, and it was my pleasure. I hope you make the most of his company."

"Oh yes. I've heard you shouldn't judge a book by its cover, but the cover of this book is missing. What I'm seeing is looking mighty fine, and if I have to, I'll read this one in braille." Martha tilted her head back in laughter at her joke, her vehicle veering over into the opposing lane. Sue glared at her.

"Mom! Get a grip, you're driving. You could kill us."

"Sorry, Sue," she said, only a slight chuckle this time, getting her vehicle back under control.

"So, tell me, Gregorio, when do I have to give him back?"

"You don't. My commitment was to keep him away for the day. My commitment will be over tonight, but I don't want him back. You're free to keep him as long as you like."

"Good, I have some ideas for this."

"Thank you, Martha. I'll reassure my associate that he will not be back in St. Martin today. But be careful."

"Oh, I will. Sue don't need any little brother or sister."

Martha was laughing as she ended the call.

Gregorio went back poolside to reassure Paul that they would not be disturbed by Antonio. As he spoke to Paul, Debi and Dean hung to the edge of the pool, watching as did all their guests, who were seated on the pool deck. Everyone's attention was focused on the Northeast Florida Tiki Hut Association.

Paulie addressed the gathering.

"We've got a game planned for the newlyweds, but we'll need your help. It's called the Newlywed Pyramid Game. We're going to provide the questions, but we need two volunteers to help us out in the pool. A couple, married or not, is needed to provide the competition. Do I have any volunteers?"

A lot of hands shot up to volunteer.

"Debi and Dean, I'm overwhelmed with how many people are willing to help. I'll ask you to pick from the volunteers who you want to compete against."

"Oh, I don't want to pick. Paulie, can't you please choose?" responded Debi.

"All right, on the count of five, the first couple who is naked in the pool wins."

Sylvie and Brad immediately slung their sarongs to the pool deck and jumped in.

"Well, you were supposed to wait until the count of five, but because this is a different kind of game where cheating is rewarded, I'd like to introduce Debi and Dean's competition. Sylvie and Brad, are you ready?"

"We're ready," hollered Sylvie from the pool.

"Okay, now I need one more volunteer to be the master of ceremonies. Terri, if you don't mind, come on over. You're it."

She untied the knot of her sarong and watched as it dropped to the pool deck.

"Your part is not required to be naked, but I don't think anybody is going to complain."

Terri did a little shimmy for the crowd and took her place next to Paulie.

"Chris, will you bring out the two cans of paint? And I'll need the final two volunteers. Who out there is a good painter? Erica and Karen, come on down."

They each dropped their pareos at their feet and Chris handed them paint brushes. Erica had the can of red paint and Karen the blue paint.

"This is special paint; it is water soluble and washes right off. It won't stain the pool deck and will wash off of everything real easy."

"Terri will ask all the questions, and when Debi and Dean give a correct answer, Karen will paint blue. When Sylvie and Brad give a correct answer, Erica will paint red. What do they paint, you ask? That's where us Tiki Hutters come into play. We're going to form a pyramid, four rows high. The couples take turns receiving questions, but since it's Debi and Dean's celebration, they go first. Tiki Hutters, assume the position! Chantelle, you need to get the video rolling. We'll want to send this to the major networks as the pilot of the next big gameshow."

Paulie put floats down for padding. The tiki members undressed, with Paulie, Chris, Mark and Dale on all-fours forming the bottom of the pyramid. Next were Jeanne, Tammy and Kathy. Everyone looked strong. The third row was Catherine and Mary. They managed to climb aboard amongst much laughter. Sara waited to be the point of the pyramid.

"I need a couple of strong men to place me up there. Are there any strong men who think they can handle me, I mean, handle the task?"

Michele and Lisa volunteered Gregorio and Paul to hoist Sara to the top. Sara wiggled her rear, milking the crowd as she settled in.

Paulie called back from his anchor position. "Erica and Karen, you're to paint butts only. Make it quick, we're not as strong as we look. When a question is answered correctly that team gets a butt painted their color. For an incorrect answer, a butt is painted in the competitor's color."

"Now before they get tired and somebody gets hurt, let's start," said Terri, assuming her master of ceremonies role.

She fired off the questions; the name of Brad's boat, if Dean owned a casino, the name of Ben's investment firm, the name of the villa where they sat, the correct spelling of the Dutch side and the spelling of the French side of the island. Derrieres were painted blue and red, with the questions all easily answered.

"Those were the easy questions," announced Terri. "But the final four get harder."

"Debi and Dean, how many of the ten Tiki Hutters here today sleep nude?"

Debi and Dean conferred briefly.

"We're going with ten, final answer," shouted Debi.

"Correct," responded Terri. "Karen, please paint another backside blue."

"Sylvie and Brad, just like the prior question, they're getting harder. Here you go. We all know Sara is a successful medical doctor. But the question is, has Sara ever gone commando at work?"

"Wow, that's a tough one. Brad what do you think? We need this butt to stay alive."

After a brief discussion, Sylvie was ready to answer for her team.

"Yes, Sara has gone commando at work."

"You're correct," shouted Terri. "In fact, it's rare when she doesn't, but that's just added info, no additional butt to be awarded."

"So now we are down to our final two, all-important questions. Two butts to go. Mary and Sara, get ready to be painted. Debi and Dean, how many times will you have sex tonight?"

"As many as possible," blurted Debi.

"Correct," shouted Terri. "Paint another butt blue. And under the rules, because you were first with five painted butts, you're officially the winner. But we'll still give Sylvie and Brad their final question. Sylvie and Brad, how many times will you have sex tonight?"

"One more than Debi and Dean," exclaimed Sylvie.

"I don't know if that's a correct answer, but I'm giving you credit for enthusiasm. Erica, paint Sara's butt red before the pyramid collapses. And with that, Debi and Dean, by being first to five, are the Newlywed Pyramid winners. Congratulations to both teams. Can I get a round of applause for everyone who helped today? And while we're at it, get those last pictures. I can see our pyramid scoreboard coming down soon."

Pictures were made before the Northeast Florida Tiki Hut Association went inside to quickly shower off the paint. There was a round of applause as each of them returned to the pool and jumped in.

As the applause waned for Jeanne, the last of the Tiki Hutters to jump in the pool, Dean commanded everyone's attention.

"All right everybody. The pool is open. Feel free to jump in."

Jason and Lexy stood watching as the guests undressed for swimming in the pool. Jason turned to Lexy.

"Well, what are you going to do, Lexy? Other than Lisa and Paul, none of your other friends are aware that you might join in without a swimsuit. What do you want to do?"

"Let's wait a few minutes and see what happens. There might be some others who don't go swimming. Or change into swimsuits."

Lexy and Jason stood back, as most guests began skinny dipping in the pool. A small minority remained as clothed onlookers.

"Do you want me to get you something to drink? A few people are leaving. We can get another drink, wish Debi and Dean well, then head home," suggested Jason.

"Are you kidding? And miss the party? But I am ready for another drink."

Jason went to the bar and returned with two drinks. He was surprised when Lexy reached for hers.

"Hey, Debi," Lexy called out. "Do you mind if I take my drink in the pool with me?"

Debi turned to look when she heard Lexy call to her. She focused on Lexy, standing naked, beaming with a drink in hand.

"That's a great idea," she called back. "How about bringing a pinot grigio for me with you?"

"On it's way! Jason, I'll be right back."

Lexy walked to the bar for Debi's drink, and with a drink in each hand, took the naked plunge.

After thirty minutes of additional partying, Debi got out of the pool, ready for the next part of the celebration.

"Hey, can I have everybody's attention. I want to have a ceremonial throwing of a bridal bouquet. So, if we can have all the single women who want to participate, I want to see who's going to be the next one to get married."

The others cleared out of the pool, leaving only the eligible girls to try to catch the bouquet. Debi came to one end of the pool, sat on the deck and turned her back to the girls in the pool.

"Hold on a minute, I almost forgot."

She retrieved her veil that had broken free when she dove in.

Everyone watched as she worked with her veil. Seeing her struggle, Gary rushed to her rescue and secured the headpiece. She adjusted the veil, sat back on the deck, and firmly gripped the bouquet handed to her by Dean.

"Now, that's better. That makes it official," she called out as she again turned her back to the girls. "Is everybody ready? Here goes."

The bouquet flew out of her hands and directly into the hands of her good friend Karen. Karen squealed, splashing in the water, as she held the flowers above her head toward Rick.

"Rick, it looks like it's going to be you and me next. If you'd like, I can check with Ben and Lauren now to see when we can use the villa," she joked. "I want a wedding just like this one."

Rick, standing on the pool's edge, tipped his drink glass at her.

Karen climbed out of the pool into the arms of Debi for her congratulatory hug.

"Okay," Debi began, "back in the pool everybody. It's time for the party to continue. The day is still young."

The party continued with everyone swimming and taking advantage of the open bar.

After another hour, guests began to leave. Lexy and Jason swam over to Lauren and Ben in the pool.

"Hey, it looks like the party is breaking up. Jason and I have had a fantastic day."

"Yes, what a fun group of friends. When Ben and I visit the island, there's so much to love. But at the top of the list is the fun friends we've met here."

"Are you guys going to the beach tomorrow?"

"I'm sure we are. Our base plan every day is to go to Orient Beach. It's not often we don't go there."

"With the jewelry store closed tomorrow, would you be up for company? Jason and I haven't been to Orient and would like to try it."

"Sure, that would be awesome. We set up on the beach near the Perch Restaurant. You can't miss us. We'll save you chairs."

"Great, we might see if Lisa and Paul want to join."

"Super, the more the merrier. They know where we sit. Just to make certain you know, we'd love for you to come there and sit with us anytime. Everybody just gathers, with generally no planning ahead of time, and whoever shows up has a party."

"All right, we'll see you tomorrow."

It took another hour for the last of the guests to leave, with Debi and Dean thanking everyone before they got away. As the last of the guests departed, the only ones remaining were Ben and Lauren, who were staying there, Debi and Dean, and Nico and Jenny, who would be captain and first mate on the sailing portion of their honeymoon.

"Debi and Dean, are you ready?" asked Nico. "The sailboat is waiting,"

"Oh yes," answered Dean. "This has been amazing and memorable, the best wedding I could have imagined. But now, I'm ready for some time with my wife."

SEVENTY-FOUR

MARTHA PULLED INTO Sunshine Acres.

"We're here. Let's get you some food. Come on in the kitchen and we'll make you some sandwiches."

Antonio felt angry but mostly weak. He had a lot of questions, but they could wait if he had an opportunity to eat. He gladly followed Martha's instructions, pulled out a chair at the kitchen table and sat.

"Sue, will you make our guest a couple of sandwiches?"

Martha brought him a bottle of water while Sue prepared ham and cheese sandwiches.

"After you eat, you can shower and then we'll talk."

Antonio wolfed down the food. He felt immediately better and became aware of the need for a shower.

"Right this way to the guest room. There's shampoo, deodorant, and even an unopened toothbrush. I think there are some disposable razors, too. We'll be in the den."

Antonio stepped into the shower and turned the water to hot. He lathered his body and continued his transformation back to normal. After taking advantage of the amenities offered, he walked into the den with a towel wrapped around his waist.

"Thank you. I'm feeling better. I could use some more food, though. Anything will do."

Martha went back to the kitchen and returned with crackers and cheese, and she and Sue each had a beer with him. Food and two beers later, Antonio was feeling fully recovered.

"I don't have my wallet or phone. I had them on the beach, but don't know what happened to them. If I can borrow your phone, I'll call my friend Baldo. Hopefully, he has my stuff and can bring them here and some clothes and I'll be leaving."

"Yes, sorry I don't have any men's clothes here. I'll get my phone for you. You must be eager to get your wallet and telephone."

Martha handed Antonio her phone. She sat at the kitchen table beside him as he placed his call. When Baldo didn't answer the call, Antonio shook his head in disappointment and left him a message.

"I'm sure he'll call you," comforted Martha as she accepted her phone back from Antonio. "Now that you've had something to eat, I'd like to talk about what happens next. Let's step outside. Sue, we'll be back in a bit."

"Yes, I have a lot of questions," Antonio responded sternly.

With food in his stomach, he felt more in control, ready to assert himself with contempt for his captors. Recognizing the change in Antonio, Martha chose her words wisely.

"First, I want you to know Sue and I had nothing to do with your coming here to Anguilla. I received a call and was told you would be arriving. I'm trying to help you."

"Why you? Why did you get a call?"

"I don't know why me. The call came from a very powerful man. He didn't give me a choice. He just said it was going to happen. But he didn't do this to you, either. After it was done, he was contacted and asked to remove you from the island. You can be angry that he cooperated, but it was not his idea."

Antonio was silent, weighing the possibility of what she said to be true.

"I'm glad I could rescue you, give you some food and let you get cleaned up. You owe me nothing and I owe nothing to you. You are free to leave whenever you want. Perhaps your friend will come to your rescue with clothes and your personal belongings, and you can be on your way. Until then, if you wish, you can wait for him here."

"I don't know what to believe."

"I've done nothing but offer kindness. I've told you the truth, but you can believe whatever you want."

Antonio decided to play along.

"Okay, I believe you. Thank you. If you want to help me one last time, I'll be on my way. Get me some clothes and take me to the ferry back to St. Martin."

"I'll be happy to help you again. But before I do, now that I've made you comfortable and answered your questions, I'd like you to hear me out."

Martha offered him a trial opportunity to stay on at the horse farm as her employee. She needed help with the horses, and she would teach him all he needed to know. She shared that she would soon complete a purchase in St. Martin to re-establish the Bayside Riding Club Ranch. If he did a good job, when the deal closed, he could move back to St. Martin and continue his employment.

"In the old days, they offered nude horse rides on the beach. I don't know if that's still possible, but if it is, you look made for the job," she said, trying unsuccessfully to lighten the mood.

"I'll consider it."

"Good. You haven't mentioned contacting your employer, so I guess leaving him won't be a problem for you. Perhaps he even had a hand in sending you here."

Antonio had already begun to think that might be the case.

"While you're thinking it over, come with me. You can start your training now. We're going to have a great future together."

SEVENTY-FIVE

LEXY AND JASON arrived at Orient Beach early Sunday morning before their friends. At the designated meeting area, Lexy set her beach bag between two chairs, and they placed their towels on two others to save them for Lauren and Ben.

"Let's take a short walk while we wait," suggested Lexy, stepping down to the water's edge. They ambled along, the clear water washing over their feet, until they came to an area unmarked by chairs. They stopped, shared a hug, and looked out over the calm bay.

Lexy looked back to where they had set their towels and beach bag. All was quiet there as well.

"What a peaceful morning. Come on," Lexy urged, pulling Jason by the hand. "Let's sit here for a few minutes."

She stepped up onto the dry sand, undressed and set her clothes in a neat pile. Walking back to the water's edge, she eased down onto the moist sand, the water just touching her toes.

Jason watched as the serenity of the beach was reflected in her face.

"Aren't you going to join me?" she asked softly. "It's perfect."

Jason undressed, placed his clothes under Lexy's, and lowered himself beside her.

"Isn't this fantastic?" she cooed, wiggling her bottom deeper into the beach. "This is like Happy Bay, but maybe even better, if that's possible."

"It looks like you've discovered another happy place. You're right, this is amazing," agreed Jason.

Lexy leaned back, her hands cupped behind her head, her bracelets sliding down her arms, before resting her hands in the sand.

"I'll be right back."

Jason walked the short distance to their belongings and brought back two glasses of red wine. He set them, and the bottle, on the small beach table he positioned behind Lexy.

"You look beautiful this morning. We need to do this more often."

"You're right. I've got a new addiction; I'm going to be in no hurry to leave today."

They lounged silently, sipping the early morning wine, mesmerized by the slight breeze as the water gently lapped the shore. Their reverie was broken when they heard Lauren calling to them.

"Good morning," greeted Lauren, waving as she approached, with Ben trailing behind her. "It looks like you've found a great spot on the beach."

"Oh, good morning," responded Lexy. "We took a short walk, and I just couldn't pass up sitting her for a few minutes. We have some chairs reserved," she continued, getting to her feet.

She and Jason swept some of the excess sand off their bodies and stepped toward Lauren and Ben.

"Right this way," waved Lexy, her glass of red wine in hand, signaling the chairs where they had placed their belongings. She moved her beach bag and motioned for Lauren and Ben to sit. She and Jason relaxed on their towels in the adjacent chairs.

"Thanks for saving us chairs."

"Is this where you normally sit?"

"Yes, this is perfect."

Lauren and Ben spread out their towels and undressed before reclining in their chairs.

"What a great wedding yesterday. Ben and I had a blast. And I love that we're having a beach day together. That might not have happened if we hadn't seen you at the wedding."

"Yes, we had an amazing time yesterday. We loved everything about it. Truly a special day for Debi and Dean, and a super party for friends. The last couple of days have also been very special to me. And now Jason and I are on Orient Beach." Lexy reached her hand over to Jason and let her fingers trail down his arm. "I can't believe how comfortable I am being here."

About thirty minutes later Paul and Lisa arrived, and as they did, they heard a greeting from the water. Brad and Sylvie had swum ashore from Brad's boat to join the group, towing their belongings in a sealed plastic container. Ben and Jason rounded up more chairs for their growing group of friends.

After everyone settled into their chairs, Lisa talked about their recent outing to Happy Bay with Lexy and Jason.

"It was so funny. Danny at Happy Bay is very nice, but he misheard Lekha's name. What made it so funny was how he complimented her on her name being so beautiful. After he did that, none of us could bring ourselves to correct him," she laughed.

"But you know what," interjected Lekha. "I really like the name Lexy. I'm glad he misheard, because I've made that my nickname."

"I love it," agreed Lisa. "You'll be Lexy to me from now on."

"It's kind of symbolic too," added Jason. "Lekha has always been reserved, shy actually. But as Lexy, she's acting with confidence and is more care-free. Maybe Danny didn't mishear, maybe he decided Lexy is a more fitting name," he chuckled.

"Jason, I thought I misheard yesterday when you called her Lexy," added Lauren. "But Danny was right, it's a beautiful name. Lexy, I love your nickname. It's totally you."

They continued their conversations, enjoying the morning. Forty minutes later, another familiar voice called out from the water. The group looked out and saw the sailboat as it glided closer to shore before passing by. Debi and Dean stood onboard waving.

"Good morning," shouted Debi. "How is everybody this morning?"

"We're all great," Sylvie shouted back. "How are the honeymooners?"

"Fantastic," responded Debi. "So tell me, how many?"

"How many what?" asked Sylvie. "What are you talking about?"

"The Newlywed Pyramid game. I want to know if you won. How many times last night for you and Brad?"

Everyone in the group of sunbathers now understood her question and began laughing.

"I forgot about the competition. But it was a good night. Twice for us."

"Then we won the game yesterday, fair and square. You tied us, you didn't top us by one," Debi laughed. "And that's with strict counting. I'm not including anything after midnight," she laughed as their sailboat left the area. "Have a wonderful day," she called as their boat moved out of hearing range.

"Oh, we will," responded Lexy to the other sunbathers. "I love being part of such a fun group."

SEVENTY-SIX

LATE AFTERNOON ROLLED around and the group on Orient Beach was ending their day. Sylvie and Brad swam back to *Eclipse* leaving the six of them.

"It's been a fun day today, but Ben and I are going to be leaving soon."

"Yes, it's about time for Lisa and me too."

The four friends stood and began gathering their possessions. Lexy stopped and turned to Jason.

"Jason, I'd like to stay a little longer if that's okay with you."

"Sure," he replied, lifting himself out of his chair to say his goodbyes. "It's been a great beach day, thank you for welcoming us," he offered as his friends stood, beach bags in hand and ready to go.

"Yes, it's been super," agreed Ben. "Vesna's is normally closed on Sunday nights, but they're open tonight. We're planning to go there tonight if any of you would like to join us."

"We could do that. Lisa and I don't have any dinner plans. Jason and Lexy, what about you guys?"

"I'd like to, but I want to stay on the beach for as long as Jason will agree to stay here with me."

"We don't have any certain time we need to eat. Why don't you call us after you leave the beach, and we can pick a time that works for everybody," volunteered Ben.

"Then it's a date," exclaimed Lexy.

"We'll come by and pick you up," continued Ben. "You can drink as much as you'd like while you're celebrating. I'll drive."

Jason and Lexy looked at each other, liking their friend's Uber service suggestion.

"We're happy to accept your offer," answered Lexy. "I'll call you when we're leaving."

She and Jason gave their soon-to-be dinner mates hugs goodbye.

As their friends left the beach, Lexy wanted to take one last walk on the beach.

"Just a short one if you're willing. I want to go where we sat on the beach in the sand this morning."

Jason agreed and the two leisurely walked hand-in-hand down the beach.

"Jason, this has been an unforgettable week," began Lexy as they strolled in the shallow water. "I can't believe everything that's happened. I loved Happy Bay and spending the day on Orient today. They're now my two favorite beaches."

Lexy found the smooth spot in the sand where they sat earlier and fortunately, they had the area all to themselves.

"Let's sit here," she said.

Jason obliged, happy to do as she asked. It had been a long time since he had seen her this carefree.

"It's something special about just sitting in the sand. Jason, let's never get too old to play at the beach. Sitting here, I feel like I don't have a worry in the world."

Jason agreed with a simple smile as he watched Lexy joyously draw stick-figures in the sand.

"It's back to work tomorrow, but tonight, we go to dinner with friends. I'm glad the break from work isn't ending yet. Give me a few more minutes and I'll be ready to go, maybe not ready, but as ready as I'll ever be."

Lexy sat back serenely, staring out over the vast ocean and savoring her final minutes on Orient Beach.

SEVENTY-SEVEN

VESNA PERSONALLY GREETED each of the couples when they arrived. She had arranged for a prime table for six. Jason ordered two bottles of Domaine Fouassier Sancerre Red for the table.

"Cheers," toasted Jason. "Lexy and I are celebrating. Ben and Lauren, I'm not sure how much you know, but we've enjoyed spending a lot of time with Paul and Lisa recently. Through their generosity, we have unexpected excess cash. Dinner is on us tonight."

Jason raised his glass toward the others.

"To our great friends, may this meal be one of many together. Cheers."

"Cheers," the others echoed back, lifting their glasses, clinking them with each other.

The menu at Vesna's offered both French and Greek dining, and the group had plenty to choose from. The conversation remained spirited, and the wine flowed throughout the meal.

Vesna checked on them frequently, and when they were done with their entrees, Jason ordered more wine as they contemplated dessert.

After many glasses of wine, Lexy glanced down at her oversize bag, as she had done throughout the meal. She turned to Lauren sitting next to her.

"Lauren, I have something I'd like to show you and Ben sometime. Paul and Lisa have already seen it. In fact, they gave it to us. It's a very valuable Arawak artifact. I'm taking it to the museum soon for them to display it for a few months. I would like to have all of you over to our house for dinner and let you see our treasure before I loan it out to the museum."

"That would be great. We'd love to have dinner at your place," answered Lauren.

Vesna came over to take their dessert order, and when she left, the conversation flowed as freely as the alcohol.

Passion fruit rum was served after dessert. They sat, leisurely drinking multiple shots of the after-dinner drinks.

"Before we head home, I'm going to stop by the restroom," shared Lexy. "Does anybody else need to go?" she asked, looking in Lauren's direction.

"It's just through the wine door down a narrow hall. I'll go with you and show you," volunteered Lauren.

"Okay, thanks."

Lexy stood and waited for Lauren before walking down the short hall.

"Thanks, I think you could tell I wanted you to step away with me."

Lauren nodded and waited for her to continue.

Lexy was feeling almost giddy. It had been a memorable day and dinner, and she was especially relaxed from the copious amount of wine.

"I have a favor to ask."

"Sure, what can I do?"

Lexy pulled her off to the side and explained her favor.

Before going back to the table, Lexy caught Vesna's attention and handed her a credit card to pay for the meal. The bill was paid, and Lexy returned to the table just after Lauren. Lauren turned to Ben, signaling she was ready to leave. Jason also picked up on her signal since they rode with the couple.

When Vesna came to the table to check on them, Jason asked her to bring the bill.

"It's been taken care of," Vesna responded, nodding toward Lexy. "Stay and enjoy the passion fruit rum. I can bring you more. Flag me down when you're ready."

"Jason, whenever you and Lexy are ready, I'll take you home."

"I think we're ready. We have to work tomorrow and should be on our way."

The four stood to leave, and Paul and Lisa stood as well.

"There's a little more passionfruit rum. You guys don't need to leave yet. Stay and finish the rum," coaxed Lauren. "We'll catch up soon."

Ben, Lauren, Lexy and Jason said their goodbyes and hugged Vesna on their way out. Paul and Lisa obligingly sat back to enjoy the remaining passionfruit rum.

Outside, the four stood beside Ben's rental car, waiting to leave. Lexy turned to Jason, grabbing his hands.

"Jason, you love me, and you'll do me a favor, no questions asked, no matter how crazy it is, right?" implored Lexy.

"Uhm, yes," he replied, wondering what was coming.

Between the cars parked on the road, Lexy began slipping out of her dress.

"What are you doing?" exclaimed Jason incredulously.

"Exactly what you're going to do. Hurry up, we don't have all night."

Jason stood watching as Lexy completed undressing and did a quick spin for him.

"What are you waiting for? I'll help you," she said, reaching over to pull his shirt over his head.

"But why?"

He took hold of her arms, stopping her.

"Because I want you to. It's going to be fun. Just do it, for me."

"This is crazy. You're crazy," spouted Jason. "For you, but let's make this quick," he said, shirt in hands while sliding down his trousers.

Lauren stood laughing at the sight.

"Ben, unlock the car so your crazy friends can get in before somebody sees us, or worse, we get arrested," pleaded Jason.

"Oh no," responded Lexy. "Here, Lauren, you take our clothes and my bag. Just leave me this one thing," she said, pulling out the draw bag from the larger bag.

Lauren took everything from Lexy, laughing with her good friend.

"Ben, it's time for us to go. Get in, I'll explain on the way to our house."

Ben looked at Jason, who stood in horror in the minimal cover between two cars.

"Sorry my friend, but both of the ladies insist. You guys have a great rest of your evening," he said, hopping in the car.

Still not sure he should leave his friends, he pulled away as Lauren laughingly encouraged him.

Jason was torn between smiling and the terror of the incident being reported. How could they face their many customers when they heard what he and Lexy had done?

"Now what, genius?"

"Here, you hold the artifact. You can hold it in front of you," she giggled. "It's your turn to blush. Now we have to wait, hoping to get a ride."

They stood at the edge of the main road in Simpson Bay in front of Vesna Taverna.

"Hey look. Those guys are naked," they heard from several people walking along the road to their cars.

"Cool dude, you guys rock," was another comment.

Fifteen minutes after disrobing, Jason finally saw Paul and Lisa walking out of Vesna's.

"Lisa," called out Lexy in a hoarse whisper.

Lisa looked around.

"Lexy?"

"Over here."

She stepped out from between cars and made herself visible.

"We need help. Can we get a ride with you?"

Lisa howled. "I love it. We're parked just down the road. We'll bring the car to you. Try to stay out of sight!"

Paul and Lisa pulled up a minute later and Jason and Lexy hopped in. Lexy waived the Arawak artifact in the air.

"Have you ever had such a good time that you just had to do it again? But with the roles reversed? Driver, if you will, take us to Ben and Lauren's house. The celebrating continues. They should have the hot tub warm by now."

Made in the USA
Middletown, DE
18 May 2022

65930974R00227